Anglican Religious Life

2014–2015

A Year Book of
Religious orders and communities in the Anglican Communion,
and tertiaries, oblates, associates and companions

Published by
Canterbury Press Norwich
a publishing imprint of The A & M Group Ltd *(a registered charity)*
108–114 Golden Lane, London EC1Y 0TG
www.canterburypress.co.uk

ARL 2014–2015 published August 2013

A catalogue record for this book is available from the British Library.

ISBN: 978 1 84825 464 0

Agents for Canterbury Press outside the UK:

Australia	Rainbow Book Agency	www.rainbowbooks.com.au
Canada	Novalis Books	www.novalis.ca
Europe (continental)	c/o marketing@hymnsam.co.uk	
Ireland	Columba Bookstores	www.columba.ie
New Zealand	Church Stores	christianbooksnz.com/churchstores
South Africa	Methodist Publishing House SA	http://methodist.org.za/work/publishing/methodist-publishing-house
USA	Westminster John Knox	www.wjkbooks.com
West Indies	c/o marketing@hymnsam.co.uk	

The Editorial committee of ARLYB and the publishers wish to thank
The Society of the Faith
for supporting the publication of this *Year Book.*

Drawings by Sister Mary Julian Gough CHC
The cover design is by Leigh Hurlock

The two photographs on the cover of Sisters at Malling Abbey (making jam and writing an icon) are courtesy of Thomas Paley Photography. Other images are of CSC sisters in the Solomons (top left), OHC brethren (bottom right), a group on the balcony at CHS New York (bottom left), SSF brothers in the Divine Compassion Province (three pictures), and (in the centre) guitar-playing at the Sisters of Jesus Way in the UK.

Contents

Foreword
by
Rt Revd Dominic Walker OGS, Bishop of Monmouth

One of the most popular icons adopted by churches in the West is Rublev's icon of the Holy Trinity which reflects the Old Testament account of the hospitality of Abraham. The icon depicts the three Persons of the Holy Trinity sitting around a table; the front of the table is open to welcome the worshipper into the very life of the Holy Trinity. The icon reflects the hospitality of God and the theme of hospitality runs throughout the Bible as being a sacred duty. It is therefore not surprising that hospitality features so much as part of the Religious Life and St Benedict told his monks to receive guests as Christ himself.

There is of course, the danger that nice religious people will just look after nice religious guests, but if monastic hospitality is to reflect the hospitality of Jesus then it needs to reach out to those on the edge. Wherever we look in the New Testament Jesus offers hospitality to those whom society spurns – the Samaritan woman at the well, Zaccheus stuck up his tree, a Prodigal Son, the poor, the blind, the lame and those with leprosy. Perhaps those on the edge today are the asylum seekers, mental health sufferers, family carers, single parents and victims of violence and abuse. St Benedict wrote of the care to be taken when receiving pilgrims and the poor because in them more particularly is Christ received. No wonder that today we use the term 'radical hospitality' to describe this ministry.

Hospitality however, is not just restricted to caring for guests; it is about developing a culture and mindset that not only welcomes strangers in the name of Christ but also welcomes new ideas and new ways of doing things. Hospitality is as much a matter of the mind as of the heart. Here I believe the Religious Life can teach the rest of the Church by example. So often new challenges and new ideas are resisted without any real consideration, but an hospitable heart and mind will be able to welcome new ideas, new ventures, new risks and recognise Christ presence in the life of the Spirit at work in our midst.

+ Dominic OGS

A Prayer for Vocations to the Religious Life

Setting a particular Sunday each year as a Day of Prayer for Vocations to the Religious Life was begun in 1992. This is currently the **Fourth Sunday after Easter**. All are also invited to pray each Friday for the life and work of the Religious communities in the Church, using the following prayer, written by a Little Brother of Francis, originally for communities in Australia and New Zealand.

Lord Jesus Christ
in your great love you draw all people to yourself:
and in your wisdom you call us to your service.
We pray at this time you will kindle in the hearts of men and women
the desire to follow you in the Religious life.
Give to those whom you call, grace to accept their vocation readily
and thankfully, to make the whole-hearted surrender
which you ask of them, and for love of you, to persevere to the end.
This we ask in your name. Amen.

A NOVENA OF PRAYER FOR RELIGIOUS LIFE

Day 1: 2 Thessalonians 1: 3
We give thanks for Religious communities throughout the world.

Day 2: Romans 14: 7–9
We give thanks for members in our communities who have died.

Day 3: Acts 15: 36–40
We pray for those who have left our communities.

Day 4: Ephesians 4: 1–6
We give thanks for our own vocations.

Day 5: 1 Thessalonians 5: 12–14
We pray for our leaders and for all who make decisions.

Day 6: Titus 2: 7–9
We pray for novice guardians and all who teach in our way of life.

Day 7: 1 Corinthians 12: 27–31
We pray that we will be faithful to our vows.

Day 8: Acts 2: 44–47
We pray for all who seek to know and to do your will and that men and women will be led to join our communities.

Day 9: 2 Corinthians 4: 16–18
We recognize that the future is in God's hands. We pray that the Holy Spirit will help and support us as we live in the Light of Christ.

1 Community of All Hallows *in the UK*
All Saints Sisters of the Poor *in the UK*
Society of the Precious Blood *in southern Africa & the UK*
2 Community of the Holy Spirit *in the USA*
Holy Spirit Sisters (Alsike kloster) *in Sweden*
Community of St Mary *in Malawi, the Philippines & the USA*
3 Community of the Resurrection *in the UK*
Community of the Resurrection of Our Lord *in South Africa*
4 Community of Saint Francis & Society of Saint Francis *throughout the world*
The Third Order SSF *throughout the world*
Little Brothers of Francis *in Australia*
Society of the Franciscan Servants of Jesus & Mary *in the UK*
5 Community of the Servants of the Will of God *in the UK*
Community of the Sisters of the Church *in Australia, Canada, Solomon Islands & UK*
6 Brotherhood of St Gregory and Sisterhood of St Gregory *in the USA and elsewhere*
Christa Sevika Sangha *in Bangladesh*
Church Mission Society *throughout the world*
7 Community of Jesus' Compassion *in South Africa*
Community of the Holy Name *in Lesotho, South Africa, Swaziland & the UK*
8 Society of the Servants of Jesus Christ *in Madagascar*
Order of Julian of Norwich *in the USA*
Society of Our Lady of the Isles *in the UK*
9 Community of St Denys *in the UK*
Society of the Sacred Advent *in Australia*
10 Community of St Laurence *in the UK*
Chita che Zita Rinoyera (Holy Name Community) *in Zimbabwe; and* Chita che Zvipo Zve Moto (Community of the Gifts of the Holy Fire) *in Zimbabwe*
11 Order of St Benedict *in independent Abbeys and Priories throughout the world*
Benedictine Community of Christ the King *in Australia*
Benedictine Community of the Holy Cross *in the UK*
Benedictine Community of Our Lady and St John *in the UK*
12 Community of the Holy Transfiguration *in Zimbabwe*
Community of the Transfiguration *in the Dominican Republic & the USA*
Oratory of the Good Shepherd *in Australia, north America, southern Africa & the UK*
13 Community of the Glorious Ascension *in the UK*
Brotherhood of the Ascended Christ *in India*
Sisters of Jesus' Way *in the UK*
14 Community of the Servants of the Cross *in the UK*
Order of the Holy Cross *in Canada, South Africa & the USA*
Society of the Holy Cross *in Korea*
Society of the Sacred Cross *in the UK*
15 Community of St Mary the Virgin *in the UK*
Society of Our Lady St Mary *in Canada*
16 Community of the Companions of Jesus the Good Shepherd *in the UK*
Community of the Good Shepherd *in Malaysia*

in the Church, and today we pray especially for:

17 Melanesian Brotherhood *throughout the Pacific region*
Community of the Sisters of Melanesia *in the Solomon Islands*
18 Companions of St Luke – OSB *in the USA*
Company of Mission Priests *in the UK*
Society of St Luke *in the UK*
19 Order of the Holy Paraclete *in Ghana, Swaziland & the UK*
Order of the Community of the Paraclete *in the USA*
Community of the Holy Name *in Australia*
20 Society of St Margaret *in Haiti, Sri Lanka, the UK & the USA*
Community of Nazareth *in Japan*
21 Community of St Clare *in the UK*
Little Sisters of St Clare *in the USA*
Order of St Helena *in the USA*
22 Community of the Sacred Passion *in the UK*
Community of St Mary of Nazareth and Calvary *in Tanzania & Zambia*
23 Community of Celebration *in the UK & the USA*
Community of St John the Evangelist *in the Republic of Ireland*
Order of the Teachers of the Children of God *in the USA*
24 Community of St John Baptist *in the UK & the USA*
Worker Brothers & Sisters of the Holy Spirit *in Australia, Canada, Haiti & USA*
25 Community of St Paul *in Mozambique*
Society of St Paul *in the USA*
Sisterhood of the Holy Nativity *in the USA*
26 Order of St Anne *in the USA*
Community of the Sisters of the Love of God *in the UK*
Church Army *in the UK*
27 Community of St John the Divine *in the UK*
Sisterhood of St John the Divine *in Canada*
Society of St John the Divine *in South Africa*
Brothers of St John the Evangelist *in the USA*
Society of St John the Evangelist *in north America & the UK*
Sisters of Charity *in the UK*
28 Society of the Sacred Mission *in Australia, Lesotho, South Africa & the UK*
Sisters of the Incarnation *in Australia*
Sisters of Jesus *in the UK*
29 Community of St Michael & All Angels *in South Africa*
Community of St Peter (Woking) *in the UK*
Community of St Peter, Horbury *in the UK*
Society of the Sisters of Bethany *in the UK*
30 Community of St Andrew *in the UK*
Community of the Sacred Name *in Fiji, New Zealand & Tonga*
31 Congregation of the Sisters of the Visitation of Our Lady *in Papua New Guinea*
Community of the Blessed Lady Mary *in Zimbabwe*
Community of St Aidan & St Hilda *in the UK*
Sisterhood of St Mary *in Bangladesh*

The Society of the Faith (Incorporated)

Registered charity number 232821

Sponsor of *Anglican Religious Life*

is an Anglican charity founded in 1905 by the Revd Canon John Douglas and his brother, the Revd Charles Douglas. It became a company limited by guarantee in 1926 and moved into its present home, Faith House, Westminster, in 1935. For many years it was well known as a publisher of theology and church music through its subsidiary, the Faith Press, and as a designer and manufacturer of church furnishings through Faith Craft.

Today, The Society of the Faith pursues its objects in a number of imaginative ways. As well as using Faith House proactively and as a base for the distinguished ecclesiastical firm of Watts and Company Ltd, it sponsors publications, holds an annual lecture, grant-aids theological study and makes its fine board room available as a meeting place for associated organisations.

Enquiries should be made to

The Secretary
The Society of the Faith (Incorporated)
Faith House
7 Tufton Street
London SW1P 3QB

News of Anglican Religious Life

Archbishop Rowan being presented with an icon by Abbot Stuart OSB from Mucknell Abbey at the October 2012 meeting at Lambeth Palace to publicise the Anglican Religious Communities Development Trust.

Oldest Anglican Religious

Early in 2012 a record was broken as Sister Constance SSJD in Canada reached her 108th birthday, celebrating her 109th on 2 February 2013. In the fifth edition of this *Year Book*, we had noted the death on 10 October 2004 of Mother Lilian CSW, who was six days short of her 108th birthday. She was then the oldest Anglican Religious known to the editors – now that lifespan has been surpassed by Sister Constance. On 21 December 2011, Sister Constance also reached another milestone in celebrating 75 years in life profession.

Born in 1904 in Baltimore, Maryland, where her grandfather was the founder and editor of a newspaper called *The Afro-American* and her father was the principal of an elementary school for fifty years, Constance graduated from the University of Pennsylvania in 1928 with a degree in Education. After teaching for some years, she began to explore a Religious vocation. However, because of segregation, she was prevented from joining the All Saints Sisters of the Poor in Baltimore, the Community she loved. Instead, she moved to Canada in 1933 to test her vocation in the Sisterhood of St John the Divine. After her Life Profession in 1936, she taught once more, rising to be Principal of a diocesan school. In 1958, she became the Sister-in-Charge of a Church Home for the Aged where she worked until 1972, after which she pioneered a ministry of pastoral visitation to shut-ins, nursing homes and Homes for Seniors. Nothing could stop Sister Constance from her pastoral visiting – not even a fresh snowfall. She studied at the University of Michigan and received her MA in Adult Education and a Certificate in Gerontology at the age of 73. Sister Constance has continued working with the elderly into the 21st century, far older than the 'elderly' she has been visiting.

For her work and for her advocacy on behalf of the older generation, she has received many awards – from the diocese, the city of Toronto, the state of Ontario, and at national level, and honorary degrees from several universities. In 2009, she received a personally-signed letter of congratulations from US President Barack Obama. Her autobiography, *Other Little Ships*, was published in 1997.

For a Religious life full of inspiring service, the *Year Book* editors salute Sister Constance!

Sri Lankan celebration

In the summer of 2012, the Sisters of St Margaret marked 125 years since Sisters first went to support the Church of Ceylon (as it was then) in 1887. Sister Raphael Mary from the community in England joined them for their celebrations in Sri Lanka and writes:

It was a privilege and pleasure to spend a month with our Sisters in Sri Lanka. Only 10% of the Sri Lankan population is Christian and of those 10% are Anglican. Yet the presence of the small group of SSM Sisters is so much appreciated and the 125th celebrations were enjoyed by many, including lovely tributes from those who had been brought up in the SSM children's home.

There were three lovely services of thanksgiving with singing and dancing and full involvement of many grateful old girls from St John's Children's Home, Bishop's College, and the residents from our home for the elderly in Colombo, Shanti Nivasa. The main Sunday Eucharist was held in St Michael's Church with a combined congregation from the local area in Colombo where the Sisters live and are involved in local projects. The service was in English, Sinhala and Tamil, with the hymns sung in all three languages at the same time!

It was all a good example of how people live enjoying the support of their families and neighbours in this lovely country with greater peace prevailing than for many years.

Lavinia House

Sister Sheila CAH writes:

The Community of All Hallows' on-site guest-house was in need of expansion and development. It re-opened in October 2012 after a summer in which, temporarily, architect, builders and allied trades and professions, joined the wider CAH family to transform All Hallows House, giving it a poustinia space, two extra bedrooms and an office. It has been a joy to welcome guests back to share our life in this renewed setting. A new name was chosen: Lavinia House- after our foundress – and we feel sure she would have approved. Fuller details on our website – or see our entry in the Directory pages (p. 31) to be in touch.

All Saints on the move... but not far!

Sister Frances Dominica ASSP writes:

Like so many other communities we have come to realise that the Victorian building in which we have lived for a number of years is extravagant in terms of energy – all kinds of energy! We are very fortunate that we have more appropriate accommodation within our own grounds here in East Oxford. Several sisters will live in one building while others will have their own front door. We will recite the three-fold daily Office and celebrate the Eucharist and we will also have greater opportunity to take part in parish worship. Some meals will be shared but we do want to enable one another to have greater freedom for ministry.

We resonate with Sandra Schneiders' description of "Ministerial Religious Life" and all that goes with it. Too often we have modelled ourselves on the Monastic Life and have not therefore been true to our charism, to serve Christ in the poor. Oxford may be best known as the City of Dreaming Spires but East Oxford with its wide diversity of ethnicity and faith is also the scene of homelessness, addiction, crime and loneliness. God has planted us in rich soil!

Visitors to Malling

Abbess Mary David OSB writes:

On 9 June 2012, the Archbishop of Canterbury, the Most Revd Rowan Williams, and Cardinal Kurt Koch of the Pontifical Council for Christian Unity came to the Abbey for a two and a half hour visit. The Cardinal, a Swiss-German academic, whose expertise is in the theology of the Swiss Reformation, had expressed a desire to know more about the Anglican Church. A four-day programme had been arranged to include: the place of Cathedrals in our church life; a visit with ordinands and a visit to Holy Trinity, Brompton and its Alpha Course ministry. We at Malling Abbey were to represent the Religious life in the Anglican tradition with which the Cardinal was unfamiliar. After informal talks with various sisters about aspects of our Benedictine life we had a formal discussion to explore the similarities and difference in the exercise of authority by the church in regard to Religious communities. Our guests joined us for Sext before departing for Canterbury. We hope we fulfilled our role with modesty and some panache!

Archbishop Rowan, Abbess Mary David and Cardinal Koch at Malling Abbey.

Encouraging Religious Life in Asia

The Society of the Holy Cross in Korea are assisting in training and nurturing novices in Myanmar, Malaysia and Hong Kong for opening a Religious community in each Province in the future. Two girls from Myanmar (Burma) were admitted as postulants of the Holy Cross on 14 September 2012. They were clothed as novices during Evensong on Christmas Eve 2012. They will live with SHC until they make their profession. They learned the Korean language for a year at the Anglican University in Seoul and manage well for normal daily communication. It will take 2–3 years in the novitiate and 3–4 years for junior and senior profession. Two more girls will come to test their vocation to the Religious Life in May. Novice OiLan from CGS in Malaysia will come in May for six months' training. Sister Margaret CGS in Malaysia has been very helpful for this formation project. A team of five women and two priests from Hong Kong Province has been to explore Religious community life with SHC for a few days in February 2011 and they keep in touch with our community.

ARC into the future

A meeting was held on 16 May 2012 at Mary Sumner House, Westminster, to look at the future of ARC (Anglican Religious Communities) in the UK. For some years, attendance at conferences has been dropping and the traditional communities are becoming smaller – yet at the same time new forms of Religious community are emerging. The meeting was attended by 31 members, representing 19 communities. Sister Hilda Mary CSC gave a background history from the 1964 meeting in Oxford and the 1967 Working Party, through the 1974 York Conference, the first time a large number of Religious had gathered together, to the formation of the Communities Consultative Council in 1975 and the change to Anglican Religious Communities in 2000. This was followed by looking at what ARC does now. Three possible future scenarios were then presented and the meeting split into larger groups to consider them: closing ARC; continuing with minor changes; or making radical changes.

The meeting was overwhelmingly in favour of radical change, enlarging the membership to include Acknowledged, and possibly other, communities, holding a large conference every 4 or 5 years, being more pro-active about publicity and vocation work and using social media. As a result, there will be a large conference in 2015 with members of newer communities being invited to attend, following which there will be a revision of structures and membership. There was obvious enthusiasm for ARC to continue and for ARC to change. Interesting times lie ahead!

ARCDT

The Anglican Religious Communities Development Trust was re-launched in October 2012 at a meeting at Lambeth Palace, addressed by Archbishop Rowan. Many communities, both traditional and new, were represented, and several gave presentations on their current work and needs. Archbishop Rowan was presented with an icon to mark his impending retirement and thanks were expressed for all his encouragement and support for the Religious life over many years.

ARCDT was founded in 2006 to provide funding support for communities' projects. As yet its resources are small, but it hopes to grow, as its work becomes better known. It looks to support Religious life throughout the Anglican Communion. Grants from the Trust this year include awards to: CSP in Mozambique for critical repairs to the convent roof; CZM in Zimbabwe to help establish a house in Harare for both ministry and care for the senior sisters; CSJD in Birmingham, UK, to re-furbish an old bakery for outreach to their neighbours in one of the most deprived areas of the city; MOOT as they continue to use their new expression of community to offer hospitality and outreach to the marginalised through their cafe project at St Mary Alder, London. Their catechesis project has already born fruit in several baptisms at Easter 2013.

Anyone wishing to support the work of ARCDT (and receive a regular newsletter) should contact Brother Damian SSF: damianssf@franciscans.org.uk.

Articles

An interior view of the new CSJB chapel at Harriet Monsell House, Cuddesdon, UK.

Vocations to Religious life come in many guises and to people at different ages and times in their lives. Exploring that call demands courage and patience and an appreciation of the different forms the commitment may take. In the articles in this section, Religious from various communities with a wide variety of witness and life-style share their experience and the form commitment in their community takes.

Journey
by Sister Rosemary SLG

It's really too soon for me to try and write about my 'vocational journey'. It's true I've been on this road for as long as I can remember, but forty years in monastic life is barely a beginning. I'm still discovering what it is really all about, and, in a word, it is astonishing. My childhood sense of astonishment at the extraordinariness of being alive is the root of it – it still overwhelms me. Indeed my earliest word for that was 'it', and 'itishness' meant the mood of ache and longing brought on by beauty or solitariness. We went to church on Sundays so I learned at some point to identify this intense and precious realization with 'God', and found in worship a channel to release and enlarge it. I remember a moment at the back of the cowshed at home during one Easter holidays when I said Yes to God quite specifically and consciously. I was about nine or ten.

The expectation of my parents and at school was for a girl to have fun, get married as soon and as happily as she could, and have wonderful children. All I learned about monastic life was in connection with the dissolution of the monasteries. Before I left school I visited a Careers Advice Bureau who recommended that I become a window dresser, because I enjoyed art and design and especially life classes (so perhaps I should do something with people). Despite this advice I did my best to opt for God and chose to train to teach divinity. This gave me the chance to study in and beyond the Christian tradition: in my fourth year of study for a B.Ed I immersed myself in texts relating to the via negativa and was nourished especially by *The Cloud of Unknowing*, the *Bhagavadgita* and contact with the local Buddhist society. Contemplative life was drawing me, and I realized that it wasn't just going to happen by itself, I had to do something about it.

I went to my college chaplain who twisted his dog collar and wondered if he might be able to put me in contact with an abbot in France whom he used to know. I wrote to Church House who sent me information about the Church Army. Eventually in desperation I responded to a Roman Catholic advertisement which read, 'Do you think you have A VOCATION?' Yes, I thought I had, but I was Church of England and didn't want to become a Roman Catholic. Nevertheless, the Vocation Sisters invited me to visit and sent me a package of leaflets which contained one about Fairacres. I warmed to what it said about a Carmelite ethos and mention of the writings of St John of the Cross. But I wasn't ready, yet, to investigate further. However, I rejoiced to learn that there are nuns in the Church of England and I admitted, at least to myself, that I had fallen in love with God and, astonishingly, some time in the future I'd enter a convent.

The future came sooner than I expected. I had a challenging and exciting teaching post with students who were not much younger than myself, and I relished being in central London, but somehow it was just dust and ashes compared to the pull of religious life. When I read the typescript of a talk by Mother Mary Clare SLG, I recognized in her someone who knew what 'it' was, who understood the ache and longing and stood at the gate of a whole life based on that reality. I took the plunge and visited Fairacres for a weekend, and things went on from there.

The biggest test was meeting the fierce and heart-broken opposition of my mother – how could I abandon her? I was her only child and my father had died only a few years previously. It was very hard for both of us, and only when she died in 1983 was I able to understand a little more clearly the pain of bereavement that I put her through. Sister Jane SLG said that if it was right for me it would be right for her too, but that it would take time. I began to learn how a vocation is not only – or primarily – for oneself, and if it's real it's discipleship and a way of the cross.

Eventually, still in my early twenties, I came, and was astonished. For about the first twenty years I'd even wake up each morning and think, 'this is extraordinary! What am I doing here?' In the struggle to arrive, I'd hardly thought beyond being admitted as a postulant, I'd thought of it as crossing a threshold into the beatific vision, so part of my immediate astonishment was how ordinary life went on. There was a bright red blanket on my bed, there was breakfast the next morning. I'd looked forward to getting to know fellow novices and resolved that in community I would conquer my natural shyness, but relationships develop differently in silence and besides, almost everyone was twice my age. So I was lonely. And there was the Night Office at 2 a.m., so I was tired. And my prayer life dried up. For some the novitiate is a spring time of fresh insights and discoveries, for me there was the discovery of how much I was a child of the 1960s, formed by *Honest to God* and with a propensity for scepticism and ironic humour. At least though it was humour, and that helped. Looking back on the tears, the homesickness, and how often I fell asleep during prayer time, I don't regret those formative years. I was thrown back on God and I was learning to bear the side of vocation that is so much more God's work than ours.

Scraps of wisdom from earlier tougher generations comforted me then, and still do: 'plead to him as the parched ground pleads' (Father Congreve SSJE); 'measure thy life by loss instead of gain' (Eleanor Hamilton King); from the *Ancrene Riwle* 'sit ye stone still at the feet of God', and from W. H. Auden, 'in the deserts of the heart, let the healing fountain start'.

And now? I am astonished at what the community has become, and how my expectations have changed over the years. I have witnessed many deaths, many new arrivals and various community projects; I have had to do a lot of growing up. There are fewer Sisters now, and we are older. It is hard, but salutary, to witness again and again the realities of aging, sickness and death, and astonishing to witness the daily miracle of community lived by such a diverse collection of people, and persevering. My initial longing and desire are undiminished and that, paradoxically, is a hunger which sustains me. I have both curiosity and detachment about the future. For me at the moment vocation is mostly about learning to see God in the ordinary and everyday, seeing through immediate complexities and difficulties, and something which our Rule describes like this: 'As the intercessor waits upon God to be taught of God both of the wonder of himself and of his will for the world, so she will see that world in the light of God and, with compassion, will hold its suffering and lack of purpose to his love for healing and restoration.'

CSC Solomon Islands

by Sister Phyllis CSC

Mother Emily founded the Community of the Sisters of the Church to establish a Religious community that was committed to the mission of the Church. This led her to send sisters to other countries to share in God's mission there. When the Community was asked in the late 1960s by the then Bishop of Melanesia, The Right Revd John Chisholm, to consider extending the ministry of the Community into the Solomon Islands, the Sisters considered it in the call of their Founder. After prayer and reflection the Community agreed. The three pioneering Sisters chosen were: Sister Beryl from the UK; Sister Frances from Australia, and Sister Helen Jane from Canada. Their journey was into the unknown and the unpredictable but with a belief and trust that God was there. They arrived in Honiara on Christmas Eve 1969. The Sisters knew their ministry was to the women and children, working with the SSF Brothers who ministered to the men. Their mission was working with the parish rector, with youth, teaching in Sunday schools and schools, visiting hospital and prison, with women and girls and with an open door to those in need.

In our society, Religious life is 'foreign'. Women are expected to stay at home, get married and have children. It was not intended therefore to have women from Melanesia join the Community. Nevertheless, several local women asked to become sisters. The Community needed to give thought and prayer as to what the future ministry in the Solomons might be, and it was eventually decided to begin a place where young women could test their vocations to the Religious life. In 1973 the CSC novitiate was opened at Tetete ni Kolivuti.

Today the number of Sisters has increased and the mission of CSC in the Solomon Islands has spread throughout all the dioceses. The first house was built in the diocese of Malaita, the most densely populated island in the country, and Sisters were sent to do mission work in that part of the Solomon Islands. As the number of Sisters increased, we opened more houses in the dioceses of Hanuato'o, Temotu and Isabel. CSC has established a total of seven community houses in the Anglican Church of Melanesia. A new area of mission is being planned for a house in the diocese of

Vanuatu for a small group of Sisters. Overall, there are fifty-three Sisters with eight novices, five postulants and six aspirants in training.

CSC's main mission is involvement with the people where the house is situated and also travelling to more rural places and villages. We teach in Sunday schools, youth programmes, Bible study; we visit old people, prisoners, and the sick in hospitals; we are involved in counselling, healing prayer and take services. When the Sisters travel to other places it is usually on foot, walking many miles up the hills, down the valleys and through jungles. Sometimes we need to cross rivers when the bridges are washed away by flooding. At times it takes a whole day to walk and by the time we arrive at the place we are already tired and worn out. We usually stay with the people in one village for a week and then move on to another village. This way the Sisters get to know the people and the people get to know the Sisters, and we build good relationships with the rural people, whatever their denomination. It sometimes takes months to complete a mission in a certain parish.

The women joining CSC are mostly in their twenties. Culturally, these women are ready to be given away, often in arranged marriages, and would fetch a good bride price. Often they are not ready for marriage and they would like to continue schooling but with lack of money for school fees for them as girls (as priority is given to boys), life in the village is their only option. Joining CSC provides an opportunity for continuing education, living a single consecrated life in community in which they are equipped with spiritual and vocational tools for their journey in life. Naturally, some who come to the Community to test their vocation leave, but they leave with more skills for life and an awareness that they are not being called to the Religious life in CSC. This contributes to the overall education in the Solomons Islands.

Another very important mission that CSC plays is their leading role in the Christian Care Centre. It is a safe shelter for the survivors of violence against women, child sexual abuse and rape. During the ethnic tension in the Solomon Islands in 1998 – 2002, women, young girls and children fled to the CSC Patteson House in Honiara. They fled away from their homes because of the abuse caused by men and boys who became militants and their perpetrators. So began the CSC vision for the need to establish a Christian Care Centre (CCC). This was officially opened in May 2005. It is run by members of the four Religious Orders and supported by volunteers, with four CSC Sisters and four Melanesian Sisters as the full-time staff. Sister Doreen CSC is the co-ordinator.

CCC works closely with other stakeholders towards the elimination of violence against women in the country. Some of the stakeholders include the Police, Ministry of Women, Children and Family Affairs, Social Welfare and the Solicitor's office. Women are provided with beds, food, clothing and get transported to the medical centres for medical checks and delivery of babies. Pastoral counselling is one of the main services provided to the survivors of domestic violence against women. On average three women with three children call at the Christian Care Centre on a weekly basis. The work is very challenging and the Sisters continue to provide this mission

Research in 2009 under the Family Health and Safety Study by the Secretariat of the South Pacific Community showed that out of every five females, three have experienced some forms of abuse in their life. It is therefore a very important mission that Sisters are providing at the Centre. There is also a male advocacy group to help in the work with the men.

Recently an earthquake and tsunami destroyed parts of Temotu Province. The Sisters who work and live in the area continue to assist with distribution of aid and support of those affected during this time of disaster. The Provincial in the Solomon Islands, Sister Phyllis, visited soon after to meet and support those who have been affected by the earthquake including the Sisters who reside in the area. The after shock waves still continue in the area.

At the last General Synod of the Province of Melanesia a resolution was passed to assist the people of Melanesia to consider the ordination of women in the Church of Melanesia. It is recognised that the Sisters and the members of the other Religious Communities are the ones who travel most around the islands visiting the people, meeting with them in their parish communities and they have been entrusted with the work of information and education on this issue. Mother Emily was aware that education was primary if people were going to live informed lives. The Sisters are being called by their Church to fulfil this function and it gives their call to mission another important aspect.

It is my hope that CSC in Melanesia will continue to grow and work effectively with the Sisters of Melanesia, the Franciscan Brothers and the Melanesian Brothers to provide the mission services towards God's people.

CSC Sisters dancing

Contemporary Religious Life in the Brotherhood of St. Gregory
by Brother Ronald Augustine Fox BSG

Long before "new monasticism" became fashionable, Brother Richard Thomas Biernacki, founder and Minister General of the Brotherhood of St. Gregory, had plans for an intentionally dispersed community. In the early days of the community, he envisioned a community of like-minded church musicians. Through the years this has evolved into a community of brothers – lay and ordained – serving the church as they follow Christ through living out a common Rule of Life.

In a recent vocations report to the Brotherhood's Council, I wrote, "The attraction to the Gregorian life is a mixture of several things. First and foremost, there is God's call. For me, that call isn't hearing a voice in my head, or any sort of distinct mystic vision. Rather, it's an awareness of myself and knowledge that there was something missing in my life/lifestyle. In my search for what that missing piece is/ was/will be, I discovered the Brotherhood of St. Gregory and felt at home; I felt that right there was where I was supposed to be."

Through the years, I have received many inquiries from people who perceived a vocation to Religious life. Many of those inquiries were put aside when the first questions asked were such things as "Does your community wear a habit?" or "How soon can I wear the habit?" But for people who wrote of already doing their best to pray the Daily Office, or to do specific ministries in or on behalf of a parish, more of a sense of call was seen.

For many people, and certainly for me, serving at the altar fostered a sense of vocation. My initial thoughts were toward the diaconate. That all changed in 1980, when I met a now former member of the Order of the Holy Cross. That brother, who remains a friend today, told me there were other ways of answering a call besides ordination.

Although the community for me happens to be the Brotherhood of St. Gregory, and I encourage people to explore our way of life, there are other paths to Religious life in the Episcopal Church and Anglican Communion. I urge people to look at various communities, knowing full well that ours is not the only path to follow. It is a path, and certainly the path for me.

It is always a good idea to give traditional community life some thought, or a try, even if it is for a few days or a week. Many traditional communities have specific times set aside where one can visit and "try out" Religious life. Observing firsthand how people live and pray together can give one a really good idea if this way of life might be the way to answer the call.

Our Rule of Life contains the Evangelical Councils of Poverty, Chastity and Obedience. They are spelled out thus:

A brother makes the vow of poverty by dedicating a major portion of the fruit of his labor to the Church and to the Brotherhood.

A brother makes the vow of chastity as follows: Chastity is the decision to live with all in love, with respect for each person's integrity. It is not a denial of one's sexuality and capacity for love, but a dedication of the whole self to God: free from indecency or offensiveness and restrained from all excess, in order to be free to love others without trying to possess or control.

A brother makes the vow of obedience to Jesus Christ as his only Lord and Savior, to the discipline of the Episcopal Church, the provisions of the Rule of the Brotherhood, and to the Minister General and other pastoral officials as appropriate.

When people first contact us about the community, they are often surprised when we talk about the Vow of Poverty. This is a very simple, accurate description: The Episcopal Church expects its members to tithe – we consider it a major part of the Vow of Poverty. Before someone is eligible to become a novice, he must be at the level of the tithe – which we view as a minimum of five per cent to the community and five per cent to the parish – of one's adjusted gross income. Stewardship and the concept of thankful tithing are central to our view of living a well-balanced Christian lifestyle.

The Brotherhood of St. Gregory remains in the forefront not only with contemporary Religious life but living that life in an honest way. Unlike many communities, we didn't and still don't shy away from the fact that we have gay brothers in the community, many of whom have partners. We also have heterosexual brothers who are married, with children. Our vow of Chastity involves much more than the sexual aspect, but we expect fidelity among all of our brothers, wherever they may find themselves along the broad spectrum of God's gift of sexuality.

For many Religious, whether the community is traditional or contemporary, the third vow of obedience can be the hardest to undertake. The common understanding of Holy Obedience is the submission of oneself to authority. Religious obedience is the act of acceptance to be governed by someone whom he/she believes that in obeying, he/she is following the will of God. The main purpose is direction in the ways of perfection according to the purpose and constitution of the order. Obedience comes from the Latin words *ob* and *audire* which mean "to hear." Before I entered the community, the question of women's ordination had become an issue in the Episcopal Church. It later expanded when we consecrated our first female bishop. Since our Rule specifically notes that we conform to the "discipline of the Episcopal Church," we were expected to accept women priests and bishops. Some left the community because of this.

Each summer, our community, which now numbers 49 members, gathers at Mt. Alvernia, a Franciscan retreat house in Wappingers Falls, New York. Our Annual Convocation and Chapter are mandatory for all members, regardless of their geographical location. It is a week filled with community prayer, daily Holy Eucharist, a retreat, fellowship and much laughter and sharing of stories.

For many, the end of the week means a return to a city or town where the brother may be the only Gregorian around. The first time this occurs can be a shock to many.

Being with the community for the week is such a joy, that when the brother returns to regular day-to-day activities, it can be cause for disorientation. For me, knowing that when I am praying Morning Prayer, or any of the Daily Offices, I know that others are doing the same, or already have, or about to. And that sense of palpable community is one that has to be lived to be understood, but is quite powerful and real.

Taken together, I could never trade life as a brother in the Brotherhood of St. Gregory for the lifestyle I knew before. For someone who senses a call, the first thing to do is to visit our website at www.gregorians.org or write to us at vocations@ gregorians.org.

From Society to Community
by Mark Berry of CMS

'Jesus presents us with a dream (embodied in the group image "Kingdom of God") that is irreducibly communal, familial and social. It is not just a dream of more and better individual Christians standing like isolated statues in a museum. It is a dream of a community vibrant with life, pulsating with forgiveness, loud with celebration, fruitful in mission... a substantial city whose streets bustle with life, whose buildings echo with praise, a city aglow with the glory of community.'
(Brian McLaren)

Constance Padwick once famously called the group who became the roots of what we now know as the Church Mission Society, "The Brethren of the Teapot". The now famous Teapot had been a gift to the The Eclectic Society, a group of Anglican clergymen and laymen, including John Venn Snr, who began to meet together in 1783 to discuss the question: "What methods can we use most effectively to promote the knowledge of the Gospel among the heathen?" The Tea Pot was presented to the group by John Bacon the famous sculptor. It was at one of these gatherings on the 12th April 1799 that CMS was born. The new society was supported by a group of activist evangelical Christians who we now know as "The Clapham Sect" but who in their own day were labeled "The Saints" by those who wanted to damn them with sarcasm. Despite dismissal from both secular and Church leaders together they worked to abolish the slave trade, to fight for the rights of oppressed people at home including that of education and to launch out on dangerous seas to unknown lands to share Jesus with the world. Sharing together this dream to see Jesus shared and lives changed, and a good cup to tea, they inspired a mission movement to which the Church Mission Society owes its birth.

It has always been important for People in Mission with CMS to be able to share their learning and Mission stories as well as their prayer needs and struggles. But in recent years our understanding of Mission has changed. We no longer see Mission as from the "West to the rest", today we see the whole world as "the Mission field" and recognize that all of us are included in the Great Commission of Matthew Chapter 28. We live in a world that is changing, where many of the countries to which CMS was instrumental in taking the Gospel now have a stronger Church than we do. At the same time CMS began a process of de-centralization and letting go of control. Each region of the World needed to be able to develop their own strategy and structure to best serve the region in the light of what God is doing where they are. This journey has led to CMS becoming an acknowledged community in the Church of England and then to begin working together to find a spirituality which underpins our values and vision.

But why the move from a society to a community? John V. Taylor, CMS General Secretary from 1963 to 1973, said: *Taking the Bible as a whole we can find no conception of man as an individual existing in and for himself, nor is its attention focused upon the individual's relation to God. The Christian can never truly say 'I am man', only 'I am in Man'; he exists not in his identity but in his involvement.*

For CMS, the change to becoming a global community of Mission means that we recognize the need for all people to be living a mission lifestyle both globally and locally. We knew we had to widen and deepen what was already in many ways a community for Mission Partners to be open and welcome to all. Mission is something we are all called to participate, to be involved in. For some this means crossing the world and for others crossing the street, for some it means working where we are for justice and mercy, for others it means praying faithfully, but we do it all in the name of Jesus and with the purpose of sharing Jesus and seeing lives changed. What enables us to support and resource each other is the acknowledgment that we need and learn from the whole community. So CMS is growing into a community of Mission or Mission order, where we welcome all who share our passion for mission and who want to share with and learn from others. A community fosters shared values, practices and spirituality which grow from the lives of its members. So the move has been from Organisation to Community (mission spirituality as a shared understanding of the greater Jesus), from Missionaries to Missional (evangelistic mission that is local/contextual & global/transcultural) and from Partnership to Networking (reciprocal interchange of mission within a globalised Christianity). Fundamentally this means that we have moved from being simply an organization, which facilitates the sending of Missionaries to other parts of the world, to being the soil from which Global and local mission can grow. In many ways this move has been because of the changing nature of the world we live in, but it is also recognition of our roots as a community pursuing God's call to mission.

The CMS community is not focused on control but is centered on Jesus and spread out in the mission of the Holy Spirit. It is made up of members who make a voluntary commitment to the Community's mission spirituality: its purpose, vision and mission, and to the values by which it interprets the Church's mission, i.e. as pioneering, relational, evangelistic, and faithful. This commitment is expressed in a mission lifestyle shaped by the Membership Promises and focused in mission service, by which the love of Jesus is shared for the transformation of our world.

The seven promises of the CMS community are:

We promise to participate in the life and mission of both the local and the CMS Community, to live a mission lifestyle in whatever and wherever it may lead

We promise be part of God's transforming of individuals, communities and societies. To be hope-bringers and peace-makers, sharing Jesus with others.

We promise to listen to how God is calling us and to be willing to take up the challenge. To play our part in local and Global mission.

We promise to shape each day of our lives in the way of Jesus, witnessing to his love in everything we are, say and do.

Inspiration for daily life: We promise to spend time in regular prayer, Bible reading, study, reflection and mutual encouragement.

We promise to work to see our community life shaped by the global ministry of Jesus and by sharing in the mission of both the local and worldwide church.

We promise to regularly review the 'rhythms of life' of both the local and CMS community. To be open to learning from and sharing with others.

The community is open to all who share this vocation to a mission lifestyle and are willing to make these promises and to share their learning and struggles. We now have community members exploring their calling by crossing the continents and by crossing their streets, as individuals and as local missional communities, in traditional settings and as pioneers. We still enable Mission Partners to cross cultures, we provide short term opportunities for people to step out of their comfort zones and reflect on their own calling, we now also train Pioneer ministers and connect new mission projects and communities through our "rooted + connected" scheme. It is this diversity and spread which makes community at times difficult but also makes it rich as we learn together what God is doing in Mission, here where we are and all over the Globe.

Mark Berry is the co-author of A New Monastic Handbook, *Canterbury Press, 2013.*

On the road to being a friar

by Brother Vaughan SSF

In July 2012, at the age of fifty-two, I was admitted as a professed brother of the First Order of the Society of St Francis. I had joined the noviciate in 2009, prior to which I had been in business, earning more money than I deserved, doing work I enjoyed, with a nice cottage in the country. What on earth, you might ask, made me decide to become an Anglican Religious?

Without faith

Through to my early teenage years, I attended various non-conformist and evangelical churches. By fifteen, I became disillusioned with the Church as I understood it. It seemed increasingly irrelevant. I associated the Church with neither spirituality nor social justice. It never occurred to me that there might be ways to God that I had yet to discover. By sixteen, I was a self-declared atheist.

From my early teens, I had possessed a strong desire to start my own business. So, at seventeen, I formed a sort of workers co-operative. But with no business experience and little discipline, the business failed after three turbulent years. Having reached an all-time low, I found a job working in sales for a computer maintenance company. I was good at this job and, as a result, was later given the chance to get into computer programming, and went on to develop business applications for companies ranging from Sony to the Department of Trade and Industry. I enjoyed all this work tremendously.

In 1988, I was offered the opportunity to move away from the lucrative but rather isolated work of software development. I joined a start-up business working within the area of direct marketing, which was at that time going through a revolution; I was lucky enough to be in at the beginning of it. As I rose up the company ladder, my focus moved to people management and marketing planning. I was eventually made a company director and later I was also appointed to the European Board. After sixteen years however, I realised it was time to move on. I wanted to get back to the directness and honesty of a small business. So in 1999, I quit and co-founded another company, providing electronic medicines information via the internet. It did well. Yet I had matured and in hindsight I now recognise there was a deep sense in me of searching for something more. In my personal life, I had married but then divorced. Neither achievement in business nor the attempt to find fulfilment in a relationship had succeeded in satisfying that search.

Finding faith

One afternoon, strolling along in London after a business meeting, I arrived at Westminster Abbey. A verger asked if I was 'there for evensong?' I nodded and was admitted. This was my first ever evensong and the sense of peace and beauty stunned me. As a direct result, I became what you might call a 'closet church-goer'. As well as the Abbey, I started attending Guildford Cathedral and the London church of St Martin's-in-the-Fields. At Guildford I was introduced to Canon Maureen Palmer who became my spiritual director and confessor. Study and praying the daily Office became very important. The cathedral community had an intelligent, questioning and inspiring approach and in 2002 I was baptised and confirmed there. I became very involved in the life of the cathedral and trained as a pastoral assistant. As a result of the insight gained on the course, and as a further step in faith, I began therapy with a psychologist which was very liberating.

A desire to deepen my commitment to Christ further sparked a conversation with my spiritual director about the possibility of the Religious life. This was comparatively early after my conversion and so I was very sensibly told to leave it for a few years. Much later, Canon Maureen suggested I might consider living under a rule of life as part of a dispersed community. This sounded a good route forward so I searched around and discovered the Third Order of the Society of St Francis. The Third Order are ordinary people, both lay and ordained, who live in the world, have partnerships, jobs and families but live to a Franciscan rule of life and meet regularly as a community. I hoped that joining the Third Order in 2007 might remove the itch to become a traditional celibate Religious. I knew very little about St Francis or St Clare – or indeed about the Religious life – but as I studied under the guidance of Mary Hillard (my wonderful Third Order novice guardian), I found a strong inspiration in their lives. My faith journey was also freeing my heart and mind to become open to the issues of human rights and social justice and as my knowledge of the 'active' Religious life deepened, I began to feel a strong call to follow Christ's way as a friar.

Living in faith as a Brother

So I spoke with the then novice guardian of the First Order Brothers and he confirmed that at the age of forty-seven I was a bit over the usual age limit for admission – and as a divorced man I would also need special permission. However, these issues did not automatically preclude me applying, and, after a further meeting, I was granted permission to test my vocation. It took me a year to sort out my affairs – not to mention making provision for my parents who had decided to relocate to a new home nearer to my sister. I also recognised the need to prepare properly myself before entering into community, so I decided to walk the pilgrimage route to Santiago de Compostella in northern Spain.

At a service of compline at Hilfield Friary in January 2009, I was finally admitted as a postulant of the brothers of the Society of St Francis, being clothed as a novice the next May. The following years as a novice were some of the most rewarding, frustrating and difficult years of my life. I knew at the beginning it was going to be hard and I was not disappointed. But as time, experience and prayer worked away within me, and the hard work of many of the senior brothers managed to penetrate my stubborn heart and mind, by God's grace I grew in my calling. So I found myself three and a half years later making my profession!

At the time of writing, I am living in the East End of London, sharing, supporting and being supported by our community there, which includes many destitute people, including mothers and children. It is a thin place full of the reality of life, good and bad, sad and joyful, justice and injustice side by side. Yet for me, a day hardly passes without sensing the presence of the Holy Spirit and I thank God he finally led me here to find a way to serve. And this way makes sense not just of my life as a friar but also uses the experience I had in my previous life. With hindsight, I can also see that without the time as a novice, particularly in relation to learning to make time for prayer, I would have burned out by now. Our lives here as brothers are transformed and made complete by the people who we help and who in turn help us.

Single Consecrated Life
by Bishop Dominic Walker OGS

God is still calling people to live the consecrated life in ways that may appear new, but nevertheless draw upon the ancient monastic tradition. I believe that there are real signs of renewal both within our traditional communities and also in the less familiar but growing phenomena of 'new monasticism' and the Single Consecrated Life.

I have had the privilege of chairing the sub-group of the Advisory Council that has been nurturing vocations to the Single Consecrated Life in England, Wales and beyond. Vatican II re-introduced two ancient forms of consecration through the Order of Consecrated Virgins and the Order of Hermits. More recently an Order of Widows has developed. Sister Wendy Beckett, the art critic, is perhaps one of the better-known consecrated virgins.

The Single Consecrated Life seeks to embrace men and women, lay and ordained, who feel called to consecrate their lives to God by taking a vow of consecrated celibacy and to live it in the place where they live. Some will have an active apostolate and others will live a more contemplative and even eremitical life. After a period of testing, the vow is received by the bishop and candidates are normally given a cross and a ring as a sign of their consecration. The bishop appoints a 'guardian of the vow' to provide pastoral oversight and the consecration is registered with the Advisory Council.

The number of vocations to the Single Consecrated Life has been growing steadily and there is now a Network of members who support one another in formation and prayer. They have a magazine *The Grapevine* and also a website:

www.singleconsecratedlife-anglican.org.uk

and members are invited to meet together twice a year. The Advisory Council has approved a Rite of Consecration which can be adapted to reflect the life style and spiritual life of the person being consecrated.

The Single Consecrated Life has been described as the earliest form of consecrated life and it finds its roots in the Church of the second century. Tertullian equated such a vocation with marriage. Since then it has been expressed in various ways by people like St Catherine of Sienna, a Dominican tertiary, by the English anchorite tradition and the early Beguine Movement. Like the traditional Religious life, its image of espousal is still reflected in the giving of a ring at consecration.

The Advisory Council has now handed over the work of the sub group to the Single Consecrated Life Network with the Revd Dr Sue Hartley, SCL as its Co-ordinating Dean. It retains its link with the Advisory Council through one of its members serving as the Episcopal Adviser. It has been a joy to encourage people in exploring the Single Consecrated Life and to witness its growth and thanks must be given to the Sisters of St John the Divine in Birmingham who have helped to bring this work of the Spirit to re-birth.

The directory entry for SCL can be found on page 141.

Directory of traditional celibate Religious Orders and Communities

Children arriving at the OHC school in Grahamstown, South Africa

Section 1

Religious communities in this section are those whose members take the traditional vows, including celibacy. For many, these are the 'evangelical counsels' of chastity, poverty and obedience. In the Benedictine tradition, the three vows are stability, obedience and conversion of life, celibacy being an integral part of the third vow.

These celibate communities may be involved in apostolic works or be primarily enclosed and contemplative. They may wear traditional habits or contemporary dress. However, their members all take the traditional Religious vows. In the Episcopal Church of the USA, these communities are referred to in the canons as 'Religious Orders'.

There are at least 1,872 celibate Religious in the Anglican Communion, (815 men and 1,057 women). There are no statistics currently available for some orders (so they are not included here) and therefore these figures are a minimum number.

The approximate regional totals are:

Region	Total	Breakdown
Africa:	321	(Men 38, Women 283)
Asia:	74	(Men 16, Women 58)
Australasia & Pacific:	774	(Men 558, Women 216)
Europe:	453	(Men 114, Women 339)
North & South America & Caribbean:	250	(Men 89, Women 161)

International telephoning

Telephone numbers in this directory are mainly listed as used within the country concerned. To use them internationally, first dial the international code (usually 00) followed by the country code (see list below).

Australia	+ 61	India	+ 91	Solomon Islands	+ 677
Bangladesh	+ 880	Republic of Ireland	+ 353	South Africa	+ 27
Brazil	+ 55	Japan	+ 81	Sri Lanka	+ 94
Canada	+ 1	Korea (South)	+ 82	Spain	+ 34
Fiji	+ 679	Lesotho	+ 266	Swaziland	+ 268
France	+ 33	Malaysia	+ 60	Tanzania	+ 255
Ghana	+ 233	New Zealand	+ 64	UK	+ 44
Haiti	+ 509	PNG	+ 675	USA	+ 1

Society of All Saints Sisters of the Poor

ASSP

Founded 1851

All Saints Convent
St Mary's Road
Oxford
OX4 1RU
UK
Tel: 01865 249127

Email:
leaderassp
@socallss.co.uk

Website:
www.asspoxford.org

Mattins 6.30 am

Eucharist
9.00 am or 12 noon

Vespers 5.30 pm

Compline 8.00 pm

Variations on Sun, Sat, & major festivals

Office book
Own Office book, based on Anglican Office Book 1980

God calls us to be channels of his love to those who are in need because of age, health or social circumstances, whatever way we believe the Holy Spirit is leading us.

The heart of our Community life is the worship of God in the daily Office and the Eucharist. We set aside time for prayer and spiritual reading. We share some meals, make time for each other and join in day-to-day decision-making. We consider vocation to be on-going and look for God in new situations.

We live in the same grounds as St John's Home, which cares for frail, elderly people, and Helen and Douglas House where respite and end-of-life care for children and young people with life-shortening conditions are offered. Across the road, the Porch Steppin' Stones is a day centre for homeless or vulnerably-housed people. These all have separate management but Sisters are involved in a variety of ways.

Our guest house gives a warm welcome to individuals or groups needing retreat or spiritual refreshment. Sisters also offer Spiritual Direction and the ordained Sister ministers in Oxford parishes and chaplaincies.

Sister Jean Raphael ASSP
(Community Leader, assumed office 18 October 2010)
Sister Frances Dominica ASSP
(Assistant Community Leader)

Sister Margaret
Sister Helen Mary
Sister Ann Frances
Sister Margaret Anne *(priest)*
Sister Jane

Obituaries
5 Sep 2012 Sr Jean Margaret, aged 82, professed 55 years
26 May 2013 Sr Mary Julian, aged 88, professed 52 years

Companions
Those who want to commit support for the community and, where possible, practical help may be invited to become Companions.

Community Publication
New Venture, published annually in November. Order from the Society of All Saints.

Community Wares
All Saints Embroiderers make, repair and remount vestments, frontals etc. Suellen Pedley, Tel: 01367 710680

Bishop Visitor: Rt Revd Bill Ind

Guest and Retreat Facilities
Brownlow House, our guest house with six en-suite rooms, including one double and one twin. Self-catering facilities are available.
Email: guestsister@socallss.co.uk

Other Addresses

St John's Home (for elderly people), St Mary's Road, Oxford OX4 1QE, UK Tel: 01865 247725 Fax: 01865 247920
Email: admin@st_johns_home.org Website: www.stjohnshome.org.

Helen and Douglas House, 14a Magdalen Road, Oxford OX4 1RW, UK
Tel: 01865 794749 Fax: 01865 202702
Email: admin@helenanddouglas.org.uk
Website: www.helenanddouglas.org.uk
Registered Charity No: 1085951

The Porch Steppin' Stone Centre, 139 Magdalen Road, Oxford OX4 1RL, UK Tel: 01865 728545
Email: info@theporch.fsbusiness.co.uk
Website: www.theporch.org.uk
Registered Charity No: 1089612

Community History & Books
Peter Mayhew, *All Saints: Birth & Growth of a Community,* ASSP, Oxford, 1987.

Kay Syrad, *A Breath of Heaven: All Saints Convalescent Hospital,* Rosewell, St Leonard's on Sea, 2002.

Sister Frances Dominica ASSP, *Just My Reflection: Helping families to do things their own way when their child dies,* Darton, Longman & Todd, London, 2nd ed 2007. Available from Helen & Douglas House, £6.50.

Behind the big red door: the story of Helen House, Golden Cup, Oxford, 2006, £6.00.

Registered Charity: No. 228383

All Saints Convent
PO Box 3127
Catonsville
MD 21228-0127
USA

Tel: 410 747 4104
Fax: 410 747 3321

Three All Saints Sisters went to Baltimore, Maryland, and the community house they began became an independent house in 1890.

In September 2009, the majority of the members of this American community of All Saints Sisters were received into the Roman Catholic Church.

Whilst still living at the Convent in Catonsville with the rest of the community, one sister remains in the Anglican Communion.

Sister Virginia of All Saints *(sometime Mother)*

Website: www.asspconvent.org

Brotherhood of the Ascended Christ

BAC

Founded 1877

Brotherhood House
7 Court Lane
(Rustmji Sehgal Marg)
Delhi 110054
INDIA
Tel: 11 2396 8515
or 11 2393 1432
Fax: 11 2398 1025

Email:
delhibrotherhood@gmail.com

Website: http://delhibrotherhood.org

Morning Worship & Eucharist 7.00 am

Forenoon Prayer (Terce) 10.00 am

Midday Prayer (Sext) 12.45 pm

Afternoon Prayer (None) 3.50 pm

Evening Worship 7.30 pm

Night Prayer (Compline) 8.30 pm

Today, the Brotherhood has one bishop, three presbyters, two deacons who belong to the Church of North India. Since the earliest days, the Brotherhood has had a concern for serving the poor and underprivileged. In 1973, the Delhi Brotherhood Society was set up to organise social development projects in the poorer parts of Delhi. The work and social outreach of the Brotherhood is with and not for the poor of Delhi. The Brotherhood has initiated programmes of community health, education, vocational training and programmes for street and working children.

COLLIN THEODORE BAC *(Senior Member)*

Monodeep Daniel
Solomon George
Raju George
Jaikumar
Dinesh Singh

Probationers: 2

Obituaries

30 Apr 2013 Ian Weathrall, aged 91, professed 60 years, Head 1970–88, 2004–13

Associates and Companions

There are 23 Presbyter Associates and 8 Lay Companions who follow a simple Rule of Life adapted to their individual conditions.

Community Publication

Annual Newsletter and Report (free of charge).

Community History

Constance M Millington, *"Whether we be many or few": A History of the Cambridge/Delhi Brotherhood,* Asian Trading Corporation, Bangalore, 1999.

Available from the Brotherhood House.

Guest and Retreat Facilities

The Brotherhood House at Court Lane has a large garden and well-stocked library. It is used as a centre for retreats, quiet days and conferences. The small Guest Wing receives visitors from all over the world. There are four rooms. Both men and women are welcome.

Most convenient time to telephone:

7.30 am – 8.30 am, 4 pm – 5 pm (Indian Standard Time)

Office Book: The Church of North India Book of Worship & Lesser Hours & Night Prayer (BAC)

Bishop Visitor: Most Revd Dr P P Marandih

Blog: http://delhibrotherhood.blogspot.in

Facebook: http://facebook.com/delhibrotherhood

Chama cha Mariamu Mtakatifu (Community of St Mary of Nazareth & Calvary)

CMM

Founded 1946

The Convent
Kilimani
PO Box 502
Masasi, Mtwara
TANZANIA
Tel (mobile):
0784 236656 or
0756 988635
(Mother)

Email:
masasi_cmmsisters@yahoo.com

Morning Prayer 5.30 am

Mass 6.30 am

Midday Prayer 12.30 pm

Evening Prayer 3.00 pm

Compline 8.30 pm

The Community was founded in 1946 by the Community of the Sacred Passion (CSP). Bishop Frank Weston is the Grandfather Founder of CMM, while Bishop William Vincent Lucas is the Father Founder of CMM. Both were Universities' Missionaries to Central Africa. The CMM Sisters are trying their best to keep the aims of the founders: to serve God, His Church and His people.

There are eleven Houses in Tanzania and one in Zambia.

SISTER GLORIA PRISCA CMM
(Mother Superior, assumed office 22 May 2004)
SISTER HELEN CMM (*Sister Superior*)
SISTER MARTHA BRIJITA CMM
(*Sister Superior, Northern Zone*)
SISTER MAGDALENE CMM
(Sister-in-charge, Mother House)

Sister Rehema
Sister Cesilia
Sister Ethel Mary
Sister Neema
Sister Esther
Sister Christine
Sister Tabitha
Sister Eunice Mary
Sister Joy
Sister Franciska
Sister Anjela
Sister Anna
Sister Prisca
Sister Nesta
Sister Bertha
Sister Aneth
Sister Mary
Sister Agatha
Sister Lucy
Sister Berita
Sister Mercy
Sister Lyidia
Sister Stella
Sister Agnes Margreth
Sister Merina Felistas
Sister Jane
Sister Rabeca
Sister Dorothy
Sister Perpetua
Sister Anjelina
Sister Julia Rehema
Sister Joyceline Florence
Sister Jane Rose
Sister Anna Beatrice
Sister Mariamu Upendo
Sister Josephine Joyce
Sister Skolastika Mercy
Sister Mary Prisca
Sister Paulina Anna
Sister Janet Margaret
Sister Theckla Elizabeth
Sister Janeth Elizabeth
Sister Edna Joan
Sister Josephine Brijita
Sister Dainess Charity
Sister Agnes Edna
Sister Jane Felistas
Sister Asnath Isabela
Sister Ethy Nyambeku
Sister Vumilia Imelda
Sister Anna Mariamu
Sister Deborah Skolastika
Sister Foibe Edina
Sister Veronica Modesta
Sister Harriet Helena
Sister Hongera Mariamu
Sister Lulu Lois
Sister Martha Anjelina
Sister Lucy Lois
Sister Penina Skolastika

Sister Anet Oliver
Sister Rhoda Rachel
Sister Judith Natalia
Sister Harriet
Sister Victoria Judith
Sister Deborah Dorothy
Sister Nesta Sophia
Sister Hongera Elizabeth
Sister Bernadine Jane
Sister Phillipa Sapelo
Sister Antonia Thereza
Sister Violet Monica
Sister Beata
Sister Hope
Sister Erica Mary
Sister Rose Monica
Sister Mariamu Elizabeth
Sister Ema Agatha
Sister Joyce Agnes
Sister Merina Maria
Sister Veronica
Sister Aida
Sister Juliana
Sister Merina Happy
Sister Rehema

Novices: 10 *Postulants:* 7

Community Wares
Vestments, altar breads, agriculture products, cattle products, crafts, candles & poultry.

Office Book:
Swahili Zanzibar Prayer Book & The Daily Office SSF

Bishop Visitor:
Rt Revd Patrick P Mwachiko, Bishop of Masasi

Other addresses

P.O. Box 116
Newala, Mtwara Region
TANZANIA

P.O Box 162
Mtwara
TANZANIA
Tel: 023 2333587

P.O. Box 45
Tanga Region TANZANIA
Tel: 027 2643245

P.O. Box 195
Korogwe, Tanga Region
TANZANIA
Tel: 027 2640643

The Convent
P.O. Kwa Mkono
Handeni, Tanga Region
TANZANIA

P.O. Box 25068
Dar-es-Salaam TANZANIA
Tel: 022 2863797

P.O Box 150
Njombe TANZANIA
Tel: 026 2782753

P.O. Box 6
Liuli
Mbing Ruvuma Region
TANZANIA

Sayuni Msima
P.O. Box 150
Njombe
TANZANIA
Tel: 026 2782753

Fiwila Mission
P.O. Box 840112
Mkushi
ZAMBIA

Mtandi
Private Bag
Masasi
Mtwara Region
TANZANIA
Tel: 023 2510016

Chita Che Zita Rinoyera (Holy Name Community)

CZR

Founded 1935

St Augustine's Mission
PO Penhalonga
Mutare
Zimbabwe
Tel: Penhalonga 22217

Bishop Visitor:
Rt Revd Julius Makoni

Our Community was started by Father Baker of the CR Fathers at Penhalonga, with Mother Isabella as the founder. The CZR Sisters were helped by CR Sisters, and later by OHP Sisters. When they left, Sister Isabella was elected Mother. Today the CZR Sisters work at the clinic and at the primary and secondary schools. Some do visiting and help teach the catechism. We make wafers for several dioceses, including Harare. Some of the Sisters look after the church, seeing to cleaning and mending of the church linen. We have an orphanage that cares for thirty children, with an age range of eighteen months to eighteen years.

In 1982, half the Sisters and the novices left CZR and created another community at Bonda. Six months later, some of those Sisters in turn went to found Religious Life at Harare. So CZR has been the forerunner of other communities in Zimbabwe. Please pray that God may bless us.

Mother Betty CZR
(Reverend Mother, assumed office 2007)

Sister Stella Mary
Sister Anna Maria
Sister Hilda Raphael
Sister Felicity
Sister Elizabeth
Sister Emilia
Sister Annamore
Sister Sibongile

Community Wares: We sell chickens, eggs, milk, cattle (two or three a year) and wafers.

Community of the Blessed Lady Mary

CBLM

Founded 1982

The Sisters care for orphans on St John's Mission, Chikwaka, and do parish work there and in Masvingo.

Mother Sylvia CBLM
(Reverend Mother)

Sister Dorothy
Sister Anna
Sister Faustina
Sister Praxedes

Address: Shearly Cripps Children's Home, PO Box 121 Juru, Zimbabwe

Bishop Visitor: Rt Revd Chad Gandiya

Chita che Zvipo Zve Moto

(Community of the Gifts of the Holy Fire)

CZM

Founded 1977

Convent of Chita che Zvipo Zve Moto
PO Box 138
Gokwe South
ZIMBABWE
Telefax: 263 059 2566

House Prayer
5.00 am

Mattins followed by meditation 5.45 am

Holy Communion
6.00 am

Midday prayers
12 noon

Evensong followed by meditation 5.00 pm

Compline 8.30 pm

Office Book
BCP & CZM Office Book 2002

Bishop Visitor
Rt Revd Ishmael Mukuwanda, Bishop of Central Zimbabwe

The Community is a mixed community of nuns and friars, founded by the Revd Canon Lazarus Tashaya Muyambi in 1977. On a visit to St Augustine's Mission, Penhalonga, he was attracted by the life of the CR fathers and the CZR sisters. With the inspiration of the Spirit of the Lord, he believed it was of great value to start a Religious community. The first three sisters were attached to St Augustine's for three months. The first convent was officially opened in 1979 and the initial work was caring for orphans at St Agnes Children's Home.

In January 2000, Canon Muyambi stepped down from leadership, believing the Community was mature enough to elect its own leaders, which it did in March 2000. The Community have a Rule, Constitution and are governed by a Chapter. They take vows of Love, Compassion and Spiritual Poverty. The Community is progressing well with young people joining every year.

SISTER PHOEBE CZM *(Archsister in charge)*
FRIAR JOSHUA CZM *(Archfriar)*
(both assumed office December 2006)

Sister Gladys A
Sister Eugenia
Sister Elizabeth
Sister Eustina
Sister Lydia
Sister Anna Kudzai
Sister Vongai Patricia
Sister Gladys B
Sister Teresah
Sister Alice
Sister Tendai A
Sister Itai
Sister Juliet
Sister Tirivatsva
Sister Lilian
Sister Cynthia
Sister Precious
Sister Joyline
Sister Vongai
Friar Tapiwa Costa
Sister Violet
Sister Blessing
Sister Bonita
Sister Tendai B

Novices: 3 *Postulants:* 1

Other addresses in Zimbabwe:

St Patrick's Mission Branch House, Bag 9030, Gweru

St James Nyamaohlovu
Bulawayo P. Bag, Matebeleland

No 9 Coltman Close, Mt. Pleasant, Harare

Community Wares

Sewing church vestments, school uniforms, wedding gowns; knitting jerseys; garden produce; poultry keeping.

Christa Sevika Sangha
(Handmaids of Christ)
CSS
Founded 1970

Jobarpar
Barisal Division
Uz Agailjhara 8240
BANGLADESH

Oxford Mission,
Bogra Road
PO Box 21
Barisal 8200
BANGLADESH
Tel: 0431 54481

Morning Prayer

Holy Communion

Midday Prayer

Quiet Prayer together

Evening Prayer

Compline

Office Book
Church of Bangladesh BCP & Community Office Book
(all Offices are in Bengali)

The Community was founded in 1970 and was under the care of the Sisterhood of the Epiphany until 1986, when its own Constitution was passed and Sister Susila SE was elected as Superior. The Sevikas supervise girls' hostels and a play-centre for small children. They also help in St Gabriel's School and supervise St Mary's Asroi (Home) at Barisal. The Community also produces for sale a wide variety of goods and produce.

SISTER JHARNA CSS
(Sister superior, assumed office June 2011)
SISTER RUTH CSS *(House Sister, Jobarpar)*

Sister Sobha	Sister Kalyani
Sister Agnes	Sister Shefali
Sister Dorothy	Sister Shalomi
Sister Margaret	Sister Shikha

Obituaries
15 May 11 Mother Susila, aged 86, professed 55 years, Mother Foundress 1970

Fellowship of the Epiphany
The Oxford Mission Fellowship of the Epiphany was founded in 1921 for friends of the Mission in India, Bangladesh, the British Isles and elsewhere.
There is also a Prayer Fellowship group.

Community Wares
Vestments, children's clothes, embroidery work, wine, wafers, candles. Farm produce: milk, poultry, fish. Land produce: rice, fruit, coconuts & vegetables.

Community Publication
The Oxford Mission News, twice a year. Write to Oxford Mission, PO Box 86, Romsey, Hampshire SO51 8YD.
Tel: 01794 515004 Annual subscription: £4.00.

Community History
Brethren of the Epiphany, *A Hundred Years in Bengal,* ISPCK, Delhi, 1979
Mother Susila CSS, *A Well Watered Garden,* (editor: M Pickering), Oxford Mission, Romsey, 2000 available from O. M. address above, £5 including p & p.

Guest and Retreat Facilities
Two rooms for men outside the Community campus. One house (three beds) for women. Donations received.

Bishop Visitor: Most Revd Paul S Sarker, Bishop of Dhaka

Community of All Hallows

CAH

Founded 1855

All Hallows Convent
Belsey Bridge Road
Ditchingham
Bungay, Suffolk
NR35 2DT
UK
Tel: 01986 892749 (office) Mon-Fri

01986 895749 (Sisters)

Fax: 01986 895838

Email: allhallowsconvent@btinternet.com

Website
www.all-hallows.org

Lauds 7.30 am

Eucharist
8.00 am (9.30 am Sat, 10.00 am Sun)

Sext 12.15 pm

Evening Prayer
5.30 pm

Compline 8.00 pm

We are a group of women with diverse personalities and gifts called together in a common commitment to prayer and active work under the patronage of the Saints. Central to our life are the daily Eucharist and the Divine Office, combined with time for personal prayer, meditation and spiritual reading. Together they draw us deeper into the desire to "serve Christ in one another and love as He loves us". This overflows into our active works – particularly in our ministry of hospitality, expressed mainly through our Guest Houses, Spiritual Direction, and leading Retreats for individuals and small groups. It also includes some pastoral ministry at our All Hallows Hospital and Nursing Home, which were founded and developed by us, but now form a separate Charity. In addition there is a large Conference Centre and a Day Nursery within our grounds. Our former convent building opposite is now home to an Emmaus community for the homeless.

The ministry of hospitality and prayer continues to flourish at our house in Rouen Road, Norwich, which is closely linked with the adjacent Julian Shrine and Centre.

All enquiries about the life and work of CAH should be directed in the first place to the leaders at the Convent.

SISTER ELIZABETH CAH & SISTER SHEILA CAH
(Joint Leaders, assumed office 7 July 2010)
[election due June 2013]
SISTER PAMELA CAH (*Assistant Leader*)

Sister Violet
Sister Jean
Sister Margaret
Sister Edith Margaret
Sister Rachel

Obituaries
12 Jul 2011 Sister Winifred, aged 91, professed 56 years

Companions, Oblates, Associates and Contact Members
COMPANIONS, OBLATES, ASSOCIATES and CONTACT MEMBERS offer themselves to God within the community context in a varying degree of 'hands-on' commitment. Apply to the Convent for details.

Community Publication
A newsletter is circulated yearly at All Saints tide. To be included on the mailing list, please write to All Hallows Convent at the address above.

Other addresses and telephone numbers

Lavinia House (address as All Hallows Convent above)
Tel: 01986 892840

All Hallows House, St Julian's Alley, Rouen Road, Norwich NR1 1QT, UK Tel: 01603 624738

Community Wares
A wide selection of photography cards, as well as some others.

Community History and books
Sister Violet CAH, *All Hallows, Ditchingham,* Becket Publications, Oxford, 1983.

Mother Mary CAH, *Memories*, privately published 1998.
(A collection of memories and reflections primarily intended for friends and associates but available to all.)

Sister Winifred Mary CAH, *The Men in my Life*, privately published 2009.
(reminiscences of prison chaplaincy)

Sister Violet CAH, *A Book of Poems,* privately published 2011.

Guest and Retreat Facilities
Suitable for individuals, couples or small groups. Other details available on request.
Enquiries about staying at our guest houses should be addressed to Barbara Pascali, Lavinia House (address as above) or to The Guest Sister (Norwich address as above).

Most convenient time to telephone:
9.00 am – 12 noon; 2.15 pm – 4.30 pm; 7.00 pm – 7.45 pm (any day)

Bishop Visitor: Rt Revd Graham James, Bishop of Norwich

Office Book: Daily Prayer (for the most part)

Registered charity:
No 230143

Benedictine Community of Christ the King

CCK

Founded 1993

344 Taminick Gap Road
South Wangaratta
Victoria 3678
AUSTRALIA
Tel/Fax:
61 3 57257343
Email: cck94@bigpond.com

Monastic Mattins & Prayer Time 4.30 am

Terce 7.40 am

Eucharist 8.00 am

Sext 12 noon

None 1.15 pm

Vespers & Prayer Time 5.00 pm

Compline 7.15 pm

Office Book
The Divine Office is based on the Sarum Rite, using AAPB for the Psalms. Whenever the Office is sung, it is in Plainsong using BCP Psalms.

The Community of Christ the King is a Traditional Anglican Benedictine order, enclosed and contemplative. Its members endeavour to glorify God in a life of prayer under the threefold vow of Stability, Conversion of Life and Obedience. They follow a rhythm of life centred on the worship of God in the Daily Eucharist and sevenfold Office. The convent, on a 37 hectare property, provides agistment for Dorpor sheep. It is surrounded by attractive flower gardens, a citrus orchard and a kitchen garden. The fruit and vegetables ensure a certain amount of self-sufficiency, and afford the opportunity and privilege of manual labour, essential to the contemplative life. Hospitality aimed at helping visitors deepen their spiritual lives through prayer is a feature of the life. The property, with its extensive views, bush walks and seclusion, is ideally suited to relaxation, quiet reflection and retreat. We hold silent retreats and hope to develop this outreach.

MOTHER RITA MARY CCK
(*Revd Mother, assumed office 31 July 1997*)
SISTER PATIENCE CCK (*Assistant*)

Oblates: An Order of Benedictine Oblates has been established, open to women and men, clerical and lay.

Community Publication
The Community publishes a letter twice a year, sent free of charge to all interested in CCK (approximately 300 copies).

Community History
Dr Lesley Preston, *Called to Pray: Short History of the Community of Christ the King*, Benedictine Press, Camperdown, VIC., Australia, 2009. Available from Dr E. M. Crowther, 31 Hazlewood Close, Kidderminster, Worcs., DY11 6LW (for the price of the postage).

Guest and Retreat Facilities
We cater for those who want to deepen their life in Christ. There is a guest house which can accommodate three people (women or men): a self-contained cottage. There is no charge. A flat is attached to the chapel. A large fellowship room provides for parish quiet days and study groups. The original farmhouse is also available.

Most convenient time to telephone:
10 am – 12 noon, 2 pm – 4 pm, 6.45 pm – 7.40 pm.

Visitor: Father Bernard McGrath OSB

Community of the Companions of Jesus the Good Shepherd

CJGS

Founded 1920

Harriet Monsell House
Ripon College
Cuddesdon
Oxfordshire
OX44 9EX
UK
Tel: 01865 877103
Email: cjgs@csjb.org.uk

Morning Prayer 7.30 am

Tierce 9.00 am (9.30 am in term)

Eucharist 9.15 am (after Morning Prayer in term)

Midday Office 12.30 pm

Evening Prayer 5.00 pm

Compline 8.30 pm

(all subject to variation in term time)

When the Community was founded, the first Sisters were all teachers living alone or in small groups but coming together during the school holidays. In 1943, West Ogwell House in South Devon became the Mother House and the more usual form of conventual life was established as well. The work of Christian education has always been of primary concern to the Community, whether in England or overseas, although not all the Sisters have been teachers.

In 1996, the Community moved to Windsor to live and work alongside the Community of St John Baptist, while retaining its own ethos. The Community aims 'to express in service for others, Christ's loving care for his flock.' At present, this service includes involvement in lay and ordained local ministry training; offering companionship to those seeking to grow in the spiritual life through spiritual direction and quiet days; and especially the befriending of the elderly, lonely, deaf and those in need.

In 2012, the Community moved with CSJB to Ripon College, Cuddesdon.

MOTHER ANN VERENA CJGS
(Mother Superior, assumed office 20 March 1996)
SISTER FLORENCE CJGS (*Assistant Superior*)
Sister Kathleen Frideswide

Associates
Associates of the Community are members of the Fellowship of St Augustine. They follow a rule of life drawn up with the help of one of the Sisters. They give support to the Community through their prayer, interest and alms, and are remembered in prayer by the Community. They and the Community say the 'Common Devotion' daily. They are truly our extended family.

Community Publication
CJGS News. Contact the Mother Superior.

Office Book: Common Worship with additions from the old CSJB Office.

Bishop Visitor: Rt Revd Dominic Walker OGS, Bishop of Monmouth

Registered Charity: No. 270317

Community of the Glorious Ascension

CGA

Founded 1960

The Priory
Lamacraft Farm
Start Point
Kingsbridge
Devon TQ7 2NG
UK

Tel & Fax:
01548 511474

Email:
ascensioncga@fsmail.net

The Community seeks to live a common-life centred upon daily work, prayer and worship. The corporate pattern of the monastic life is at the heart of our life together; which aims to be informal and inclusive both in worship and hospitality. From its beginning, CGA has had a vibrant sense of mission which we try to maintain through our friendship with those who stay or visit, and also through involvement with people in the local area.

BROTHERS

BROTHER SIMON CGA
(Prior, assumed office 20 May 1993)
Brother David
Brother John

SISTERS

SISTER JEAN CGA (*Prioress*)
Revd Sister Cécile

Community Publication
CGA Newsletter, published annually. Write to the Prior.

Guest and Retreat Facilities
The priory in Devon offers accommodation for retreats or holiday in self-catering cottages. A purpose-built barn enables us to offer hospitality to local groups and churches on a daily basis.

Bishop Visitor: Rt Revd Edward Holland

Registered Charity: No. 254524

Community of the Good Shepherd

CGS

Founded 1978

Christ Church Likas
PO Box 519
88856 Likas
Sabah
MALAYSIA

Tel: 088 383211

Residential address:
MQ8, Jalan Teluk Likas
Kota Kinabalu
88400 Likas
Sabah
MALAYSIA

Email:
sacgs8@gmail.com

Morning Prayer
6.30 am

Evening Prayer
4.30 pm

Compline
8.00 pm

Holy Communion
8.00 am
(1st & 3rd Thu of month)

The CGS Sisters in Malaysia were formerly a part of the Community of the Companions of Jesus the Good Shepherd in the UK *(see separate entry)*. They became an autonomous community in 1978. Their Rule is based on that of St Augustine and their ministry is mainly parish work.

In October 2000, the Sisters moved to Kota Kinabalu, the capital of Sabah, and have settled in at Likas, just opposite to Christ Church. Since January 2013, our Bishop Vun has appointed Canon Chak Sen Jen, the Dean of All Saints' Cathedral to be our new chaplain. The Diocesan project of building a new Community House has been completed, and occupied in November 2007. It has a spacious ground in front with cool breezes from Likas Bay beyond. There are rooms for visitors and enquirers to Religious Life.

In Kota Kinabalu, the Community, with the help of the associates, see the need to supply wafers to the Diocese and to gather the associates to pray for the Diocese.

SISTER MARGARET LIN-DIN CGS
(Sister-in-charge, assumed office 1978)

Novices: 1
Postulants: 1

Associates
In Kota Kinabalu, some committed Christian women from the three Anglican Churches join in fellowship with the Community and have become associate members. They follow a simple rule of life to support the Community through prayer and to share in the life and work of the Community. Whenever they can, they come to join the annual retreat.

Community Wares
Stoles and wafers
(to supply the Sabah diocese at present).

Office Book
ASB and the Service Book of the Province of the Anglican Church in S E Asia.

Bishop Visitor
Rt Revd Albert Vun Cheong Fui, Bishop of Sabah

Benedictine Community of the Holy Cross, Costock

CHC

Founded 1857

Holy Cross Convent
Highfields
Nottingham Road
Costock
LE12 6XE
UK
Tel: 01509 852761
Email: sisters@ holycrosschc.org.uk

Website: www. holycrosschc.org.uk

(SOUTHWELL DIOCESE)

Matins 6.15 am

Lauds 7.30 am

Terce 9.15 am

Mass 9.30 am (subject to change)

Sext 12.15 am (subject to change)

None 1.30 pm

Vespers 4.30 pm (4.00 pm Thu)

Compline 8.00 pm

Office Book: CHC Office

The Community of the Holy Cross was founded in 1857 by Elizabeth Neale (sister of John Mason Neale, the hymnographer), at the invitation of Father Charles Fuge Lowder. The foundation was intended for Mission work in Father Lowder's parish of London Docks, but succeeding generations felt that the Community was being called to a life of greater withdrawal, and in the twentieth century the Benedictine Office, and later the *Rule of St Benedict*, were adopted.

The Community aims to achieve the Benedictine balance of prayer, study and work. All the work, whether manual, artistic or intellectual, is done within the Enclosure. The daily celebrations of the Eucharist and the Divine Office are the centre and inspiration of all activity.

Apart from worship, prayer and intercession, and the work of maintaining the house, garden and grounds, the Community's works are: the publications and greetings cards described below; providing retreats and quiet days; and dealing with a large postal apostolate.

SISTER MARY LUKE WISE CHC
(Mother Superior, elected 8 November 1991)
SISTER MARY JULIAN GOUGH CHC *(Assistant Superior)*
Sister Mary Michael Titherington
Sister Mary Bernadette Priddin
Sister Mary Joseph Thorpe
Sister Mary Cuthbert Aldridge
Sister Mary Hannah Kwark
Sister Mary Catherine Smith

Oblates and Associates: The Community has women and men Oblates who are attached to it in a union of mutual prayers. Each has a rule of life adapted to her particular circumstances. Oblates are not Religious but they seek to live their life in the world according to the spirit of the *Rule of St Benedict*. Associates have a much simpler rule.

Community Wares: A great variety of prayer and greeting cards are available for sale. Some are produced by the sisters and others are from a number of different sources.

Community Publications: A Newsletter published in the Spring. Available free from the Publications Secretary. A wide range of short publications is available on the website.

Bishop Visitor: Most Revd Dr David Hope

Registered Charity: No 223807

Community History

Alan Russell, *The Community of the Holy Cross Haywards Heath 1857–1957: A Short History of its Life and Work*, 1957.

A leaflet: A short history of the Community of the Holy Cross.
Available from the Publications Secretary.

Guest and Retreat Facilities

There is limited accommodation for residential, private retreats. The Community also provides for Quiet Days for individuals or groups up to 16. The Guest House is closed at Christmas.

Community of the Holy Name

CHN

Founded 1888

Community House
40 Cavanagh Street
Cheltenham
Victoria 3192
AUSTRALIA
Tel: 03 9583 2087
Fax: 03 9585 2932

Email: chnmelb@bigpond.com

Website: www.chn.org.au

Eucharist times vary

Mattins 9.00 am

Midday Office 12.45 pm

Vespers 5.30 pm

Compline 7.30 pm

The Community of the Holy Name was founded in 1888 within the Diocese of Melbourne by Emma Caroline Silcock (Sister Esther). The work of the Community was initially amongst the poor and disadvantaged in the slum areas of inner-city Melbourne. Over the years, the Sisters have sought to maintain a balance between a ministry to those in need and a commitment to the Divine Office, personal prayer and a daily Eucharist.

For many years, CHN was involved in institutions, such as children's homes and a Mission house. There were many and varied types of outreach. The Holy Name Girls' High School was established in Papua New Guinea, and the indigenous Community of the Visitation of Our Lady fostered there.

Today, Sisters are engaged in parish work in ordained and lay capacities, and in a variety of other ministries, including hospital chaplaincies, both general and psychiatric, spiritual companionship and leading of Quiet Days and retreats. The offering of hospitality to people seeking spiritual refreshment or a place away from their normal strains and stresses has become an important part of the life and ministry, especially at St Julian's, the new Retreat and Spirituality Centre.

Other Australian Addresses

St Julian's Retreat and Spirituality Centre,
33 Lorna Street, Cheltenham, VIC 3192
68 Pickett Street, Footscray, VIC 3011
2/7 James Street, Brighton, VIC 3186
8/7 James Street, Brighton, VIC 3186

Office Book

CHN adaptation of the Anglican Office Book.

Community Wares

Cards are sold at the Community House.

SISTER CAROL CHN
(Mother Superior, assumed office 12 April 2011)

Council members: SISTERS ELIZABETH GWEN, MARGOT, PAMELA & VALMAI

Sister Andrea	Sister Francine	Sister Maree	Sister Philippa
Sister Avrill	Sister Hilary	Sister Margaret Anne *(priest)*	Sister Ruth
Sister Betty	Sister Jean	Sister Margot *(priest)*	Sister Sheila *(priest)*
Sister Elizabeth Gwen	Sister Josephine Margaret	Sister Pamela	Sister Sheila Anne
Sister Felicity	Sister Lyn	Sister Penelope	Sister Shirley
			Sister Valmai

Obituaries

25 Nov 2011 Sister Winifred Muriel, aged 91, professed 67 years

Oblates and Associates

The Order of **Oblates** is for women and men who desire to lead lives of prayer and dedication in close association with the Community. The Oblates have a personal Rule of Life based on the Evangelical Counsels of Poverty, Chastity and Obedience and renew their dedication annually.

The **Associates and Priest Associates** support and pray for the Community. Each of these Groups meet regularly at the Community's House for fellowship and spiritual input. Priest Associates offer the Eucharist with special intention for the Community and seek to promote the Religious Life.

Guest and Retreat Facilities

Day groups of up to twenty-five people are welcome in the Prayer Group and Gathering Space. There is accommodation for six residential guests at the Community House and a Sister is available for help and guidance if requested. St Julian's Retreat and Spirituality Centre accommodates ten guests in affordable and comfortable surroundings. A self-contained hermitage in the grounds available for private retreats.

Most convenient time for guests to telephone: 10am – 12.30 pm, 2pm – 5pm

Community Publication: An Associates Letter is published four times a year. Write to Sister Avrill, the Associates Sister, for a subscription, which is by donation.

Community History

Sister Elizabeth CHN, *Esther, Mother Foundress*, Melbourne, 1948.

Lynn Strahan, *Out of the Silence*, OUP, Melbourne, 1988.

Bishop Visitor: Most Revd Dr Philip Freier, Archbishop of Melbourne

Warden: Rt Revd Garry Weatherill

Sisters Carol & Elizabeth Gwen either side of a photograph of the Mother Foundress of CHN, Sister Esther.

Community of the Holy Name (UK Province)

CHN

Founded 1865

Convent of the Holy Name
Morley Road
Oakwood
Derby
DE21 4QZ
UK

Tel: 01332 671716
Fax: 01332 669712

Email: bursarsoffice @tiscali.co.uk

Website: www.chnderby.org

Bishop Visitor
Rt Revd John Inge, Bishop of Worcester

The Sisters combine the life of prayer with service to others in their evangelistic and pastoral outreach and by maintaining their houses as centres of prayer where they can be available to others. They run a small guest house in Derby. In our houses, and from the Convent in Derby, the Sisters are involved in parish work, hospital visiting, retreat-giving and work among the wider community, and with those who come for spiritual guidance.

The members of the Fellowship of the Holy Name are an extension of its life and witness in the world.

We encourage those who wish to live alongside for a period of time.

SISTER PAULINE MARGARET CHN
(Provincial Superior, assumed office 23 January 2013)
SISTER EDITH MARGARET CHN *(Assistant Superior)*

Sister Judith
Sister Ruth
Sister Marjorie Jean
Sister Barbara
Sister Joy
Sister Brenda
Sister Verena
Sister Jean Mary
Sister Lilias
Sister Theresa Margaret
Sister Mary Patricia
Sister Lisbeth
Sister Vivienne Joy
Sister Charity
Sister Elizabeth Clare
Sister Diana
Sister Carol
Sister Monica Jane
Sister Pippa
Sister Rosemary
Sister Irene
Sister Lynfa
Sister Elaine Mary
Sister Julie Elizabeth
Sister Linda Frances
Sister Catherine

Postulants: 1

Obituaries
27 Aug 2012 Sr Constance, aged 85, professed 51 years

Fellowship of the Holy Name
The Fellowship is comprised of ecumenically-minded Christians who feel called to share with the Community in their life of prayer and service.
Members have a personal Rule of Life, which they have drawn up in consultation with a particular Sister. This will keep in contact and help with a regular review. This rule includes daily private prayer, regular prayer and worship with the local Christian community, as well as time and space for their own well-being and creativity.

Each rule varies with the individual. A six-month probation living the rule is required before formal admission to the Fellowship. This usually takes place at the Convent in the context of the Eucharist. There are regional meetings for members living in the same area, and the Community distributes newsletters throughout the year and encourages members to contribute articles for the Community magazine.

Prime
7.45 am

Eucharist
8.00 am
(12.20 pm Tue & Thu)

Mattins
9.15 am
(8.45 am Tue & Thu)

Midday Office
12.45 pm
(12.05 pm Tue & Thu)

Vespers
5.00 pm

Compline
9.15 pm
(8.45 pm Sat)

Other Addresses

St John's Rectory, St John's Road, Longsight, Manchester M13 0WJ

64 Allexton Gardens, Welland Estate, Peterborough PE1 4UW Tel: 01733 352077

Community History

History of the Community of the Holy Name, 1865 to 1950, published by CHN, 1950.

Una C. Hannam, *Portrait of a Community,* printed by the Church Army Press, 1972.

Community Publication

Community magazine – contact the editor.
Set of four leaflets:
- Community of the Holy Name;
- Fellowship of the Holy Name;
- Living Alongside;
- Facilities.

Office Book
Daily Office CHN

Community Wares

Various cards.

Booklet of Stations of the Cross, from original paintings by Sister Theresa Margaret CHN, with biblical texts. Can be ordered from the Convent: £5.00 each, or for orders of ten or more £4.50 each. Icons are also available.

Sister Pauline Margaret CHN, *Jesus Prayer*, £3.50.
Can be ordered from the Convent or SLG Press.

Sister Verena CHN, *A Simplified Life*, Canterbury Press, Norwich. Available at convent £10.

Most convenient time to telephone:
10.00 am – 12.30 pm
2.00 pm – 5.00 pm
5.30 pm – 9.00 pm

Guest and Retreat Facilities

There are opportunities for individuals to make a private retreat at the guest house, and Sisters would be prepared to give help and guidance if requested. Six single rooms, one double – see our website.

Registered Charity:
No. 250256

Community of the Holy Name (Lesotho Province)

CHN

Founded 1865 (in UK)
1962 (in Lesotho)

Convent of the Holy Name
PO Box 22
Ficksburg 9730
SOUTH AFRICA
Tel: 22400249
Email: cohona @datacom.co.ls

Website: www.chnderby.org

Morning Prayer
6.30 am
(6.45 am Sun)

Terce
7.45 am (Sun only)

Eucharist
7.00 am (8.00 am Sun; 12 noon Wed)

Midday Office
12.15 pm (12.30 pm Sun, 11.45 am Wed)

Evening Prayer 5 pm

Compline 8.15 pm

Office Book
South African Prayer Book, supplemented by CHN Office Book

The Basotho Community of St Mary at the Cross was founded in Leribe, Lesotho, in 1923, under CSM&AA, Bloemfontein. In 1959, CHN Sisters were invited to take over this work and started at Leribe in 1962. They had invited the Sisters of S. Mary at the Cross to become members of CHN and the full amalgamation of the two communities was completed in 1964. As a multi-racial community, the witness against racism at a time when apartheid was in the ascendant in South Africa was an important strand of the Community's vocation. In succeeding years, the Sisters have continued the evangelistic and pastoral work which is also an important part of the CHN vocation. Sisters are involved in children's work, prison visiting, as well as other outreach in both Lesotho and South Africa. There is a church sewing room and wafer room. The Sisters in Leribe run a hostel for secondary school students. Some Sisters are 'Volunteers of Love' for families where there is HIV/AIDS. This work is enabled and strengthened by the daily round of prayer, both corporate and private, which is at the heart of the Community's Rule. A daily Eucharist at the centre of this life of prayer is the aim. There is a small guest house.

SISTER JULIA CHN
(*Provincial Superior, assumed office April 2007*)
SISTER MPOLOKENG CHN *(Assistant Superior)*

Sister Calista
Sister Alphonsina
Sister Hilda Tsepiso
Sister Maria
Sister Lucia
Sister Angelina
Sister Mary Selina
Sister Josetta
Sister Gertrude
Sister Ryneth
Sister Lineo
Sister Exinia Tsoakae
Sister Leboheng
Sister Malineo
Sister Malefu
Sister Molehobeng
Sister Mookho
Sister Maseeng

Novices: 2 *Postulants:* 2

Other houses: Please contact the main house.

Community Wares: Church sewing (including cassocks, albs, stoles); communion wafers; Mothers Union uniforms; mohair and woven goods from the Leribe Craft Centre and the disabled workshop, started by the Community.

Bishop Visitor: Rt Revd Adam Taaso

Community of the Holy Name

(Zulu Province)

CHN

Founded 1865 (in UK)
1969 (in Zululand)

Convent of the Holy Name
Pt. Bag 806
Melmoth 3835
Zululand
SOUTH AFRICA
Tel: 3545 02892
Fax: 3545 07564

Email:
chnsisters@telkomsa.net

Website:
www.chnderby.org

Terce 6.30 am

Eucharist
6.30 am (Wed & Fri)
6.45 am (Tue & Thu)
4.30 pm (Mon)

Mattins 8.30 am

Midday Office
12.30 pm

Evening Prayer
4.00 pm (Mon & Wed)
5.00 pm (Tue & Thu)
4.30 pm (Fri)

Compline 7.45 pm

The Community of the Holy Name in Zululand was founded by three Zulu Sisters who began their Religious life with the Community in Leribe. All three Provinces of CHN have the same Rule of life, but there are differences of customary and constitutions to fit in with cultural differences. The daily life of the Community centres around the daily Office, and the Eucharist whenever the presence of a priest makes this possible.

The Sisters are involved extensively in mission, pastoral and evangelistic work. The Zulu Sisters have evangelistic gifts which are used in parishes throughout the diocese at the invitation of parish priests. Several Sisters have trained as teachers or nurses. They work in schools or hospitals, where possible within reach of one of the Community houses. Their salaries, and the handicrafts on sale at the Convent at Kwa Magwaza, help to keep the Community solvent.

MOTHER NOKUBONGWA CHN
(*Provincial Superior, assumed office February 2008*)
SISTER BENZILE CHN (*Assistant Superior*)

Sister Claudia
Sister Olpha
Sister Nesta Gugu
Sister Nokuthula Victoria
Sister Sibongile
Sister Zodwa
Sister Mantombi
Sister Bonakele
Sister Nonhlahla
Sister Jabu
Sister Thulisiwe
Sister Thembelihle
Sister Sebenzile
Sister Samkelisiwe
Sister Thandazile
Sister Thandiwe
Sister Nondumiso
Sister Thokozile
Sister Duduzile
Sister Patricia
Sister Phindile
Sister Nqobile
Sister Sibekezelo
Sister Xolisile
Sister Philisiwe
Sister Ntsoaki
Sister Nomathemba
Sister Thandukwazi
Sister Zamandla
Sister Bongile
Sister Sindisiwe
Sister Maureen
Sister Neliswa
Sister Hlengiwe
Sister Nkosikhoma
Sister Thembekile
Sister Sezeka
Sister Thandeka

Novices: 1

Obituaries

May 2012 Sister Gertrude Jabulisiwe, aged 82, professed 55 years

Office Book: Offices are mainly in Zulu, based on the South African Prayer Book & the CHN Office Book.

Community Wares: Vestments, cassocks, albs and other forms of dressmaking.

Other Houses

Usuthu Mission, PO Box 8, Luyengo, SWAZILAND
PO Box 175, Nongoma 3950, SOUTH AFRICA
St Benedict House, PO Box 27, Rosettenville 2130, SOUTH AFRICA

Bishop Visitor: Rt Revd Dino Gabriel, Bishop of Zululand

Community of the Holy Spirit

CHS

Founded 1952

454 Convent Ave
New York
NY 10031-3618
USA
Tel: 212 666 8249
Fax: 801 655 8249

Email: chssisters @chssisters.org

Website
www.chssisters.org

The daily schedule varies with the seasons. Please call ahead for current schedule. Monday is a Sabbath in each house of the Community, during which there is no corporate worship.

Each person is given an invitation to follow Christ. The Sisters of our monastic community respond to that invitation by an intentional living out of the vows of poverty, chastity, and obedience within the structure of a modified Augustinian Rule. Through the vow of poverty, we profess our trusting dependence upon God by embracing voluntary simplicity and responsible stewardship of creation. Through chastity, we profess the sanctity of all creation as the primary revelation of God. Through obedience, we profess our desire to be dependent on God's direction and to live and minister in ways that respect all creation, both now and for generations to come. Compassionate, respectful love is God's gift to life. Prayer and the worship of God are the lifeblood and heart of our Community and the source of inspiration for all that we undertake. Through our prayer, worship, and creative talents we encourage others to seek God. Through our ministries of hospitality, retreat work, spiritual direction, and education through simple, sustainable, spiritual living, we seek to grow in love and communion with all whose lives touch us and are touched by us. We also provide spiritual support for women and men who wish to be linked with our Community as Associates. By adopting a personal rule of life, they extend the Community's ministry through prayer, worship and service.

Other Address

The Melrose Convent – Bluestone Farm and Living Arts Center, 118 Federal Hill Road, Brewster, NY 10509-5307, USA
Tel: 845 363 1971 Fax: 888 404 7169
Email: Melroseconvent@chssisters.org

Office Book: CHS Office book

Sister Heléna Marie CHS, Sister Faith Margaret CHS,
Sister Catherine Grace CHS
(Community Council, assumed office June 2001)

Sister Élise
Sister Mary Christabel
Sister Mary Elizabeth
Sister Jerolynn Mary
Sister Emmanuel
Sister Maria Felicitas
Sister Leslie
Sister Claire Joy
Sister Carol Bernice
Resident Companions:
Jody Ballew
Revd Matthew Wright

Obituaries
28 May 2010 Sister Dominica, aged 79, professed 34 years

Associates
From the Community's early days, Christian women and men have sought an active association with the Sisters, wishing to live out their baptismal commitments by means of a rule of life.

The Community provides four rules: Fellowship, St Augustine, Confraternity and Priest Associate. Each consists of prayer, reading, self-denial and stewardship. Each provides an opportunity for growth toward God and daily renewal of life in Christ. Each calls for a commitment to pray daily for the Sisters and all others in their life, worship and ministry, using the collect for Pentecost and the Lord's Prayer.

In consultation with the Sister for Associates, they may formulate their own rule if the ones provided cannot be fulfilled as they stand, or if they need to be expanded. As far as is possible Associates support the Community through gifts of time, talents and financial resources. There is an annual fee of $75, if possible.

Community Wares: [From Bluestone Farm]:
Food items as available; crafts.

Community Publication: Monthly electronic newsletter.
Please send email address to inquiries@chssisters.org.

Community History: The Revd Mother Ruth CHS, *"In Wisdom Thou Hast Made Them"*, Adams, Bannister, Cox, New York, 1986

Guest and Retreat Facilities
The Longhouse at Melrose; seven rooms, total capacity eight. Closed irregularly; call in advance to make reservations.
Visit www.chssisters.org for further information.
Tel: 845 278 9777 ex 30 Email: BFLACreservations@chssisters.org

Most convenient time to telephone:
Generally, phones are staffed irregularly between 9.00 am and 5.00 pm EST Tuesday through Saturday, though you may leave a message at any time.

Bishop Visitor
Rt Revd Marc H. Andrus, Bishop of California

Community of the Holy Transfiguration

CHT

Founded 1982

St David's Bonda Mission
P Bag T 7904
Mutare
ZIMBABWE

The Community started in 1982 with 8 members who broke away from the Community of the Holy Name (Chita Che Zita Rinoyera). The Community is stationed at St David's Bonda Mission and it is an open community. We assist the Church in evangelistic work and other ministerial duties. Some members are employed by the diocese as priests and some as Evangelists. We run an orphanage with a maximum number of thirty young children. As of now, the age-group is going beyond this age range because of the HIV/AIDS pandemic. We are also a self-reliant community through land tilling and poultry. There is now another house at St Francis Mission, Sherugwi, in the diocese of Masvingo.

SISTER MILDAH CHT
(Mother, assumed office 2006)

Sister Merina
Sister Violet
Sister Dorothy
Sister Felicity
Sister Letwin
Evangelist Friar Henry

at Sherugwi:
Sister Winnie *(superior)*
Sister Gloria
Sister Francesca
Sister Lucy
Sister Gloria Mary
Rev Friar Fungayi Leonard

Community of Jesus' Compassion

CJC

Founded 1993

PO Box 153
New Hanover
3230
SOUTH AFRICA
Tel: 072 625 3039
(Mother's mobile)

Founded in the Diocese of Natal by a sister from the Community of the Holy Name in Zululand, CJC have been based in Newcastle and Ixopo. However, the sisters have now settled at New Hanover, which is half an hour's drive from the cathedral city of Pietermaritzburg. The main work of the sisters is evangelising in the local parish and children's ministry. The Sisters care for around thirty-five children, which is demanding, but good progress is being made.

On the 19th December 1998, the first professions within the community were received. The Community's formal recognition by the Church of the Province of South Africa followed in 2000 with the first life professions. In 2006, Sister Thandi became the first nun in the diocese to be ordained to the stipendiary ministry, and she now serves in a parish in Durban. Her priesting followed in June 2007.

Community Wares
Girdles, Prayer Book and Bible covers, vegetables.

Bishop Visitor: Rt Revd Rubin Phillip, Bishop of Natal

Morning Prayer, followed by Terce
5.30 am

Midday Prayer
12.30 pm

Evening Prayer
4.30 pm

Compline
8.15 pm

MOTHER LONDIWE CJC
(*Mother Superior, assumed office 8 January 2000*)
SISTER THANDI CJC (*Assistant Superior)*

Sister Yeki	Sister Mbali
Sister Ntombi	Sister Thelma
Sister Zandile	Sister Ayanda
Sister Nontokozo	Sister Makhosazana
Sister Thokozile	Sister Sibongile
Sister Nqobile	*Postulants:* 1
Sister Nonhlanhla	

Office Book: Anglican Prayer Book 1989 of the CPSA Midday Office book & Celebrating Night Prayer

---

Community of Nazareth CN

Founded 1936

4-22-30 Mure
Mitaka
Tokyo 181-0002
JAPAN
Tel: 0422 48 4560
Fax: 0422 48 4601

Morning Prayer
6.25 am

Eucharist 7.00 am

Terce 8.15 am

Sext 12 noon

None after lunch

Evening Prayer
5.00 pm

Night Prayer 8.15 pm

Under the guidance of the Sisters of the Community of the Epiphany (England), the Community of Nazareth was born and has grown. The Community is dedicated to the Incarnate Lord Jesus Christ, especially in devotion to the hidden life which he lived in Nazareth.

In addition to the Holy Eucharist, which is the centre and focus of our community life, the Sisters recite a sixfold Divine Office. We run a Retreat house and make wafers.

We welcome enquirers and aspirants.

SISTER NOBU CN
(*Reverend Mother, assumed office 2012*)
SISTER MIYOSHI CN (*Assistant Mother)*

Sister Yachiyo	Sister Asako	
Sister Kayoko	Sister Setsuko	*Novices: 1*
Sister Chizuko	Sister Junko	*Postulants: 1*

Obituaries
25 Dec 2012 Sister Yukie, aged 94, professed 50 years

Associates: Clergy and laity may be associates.

Other Address
81 Shima Bukuro, Naka Gusuku Son, Naka Gami Gun, Okinawa Ken 901-2301, JAPAN

Community Wares: Wafers.

Guest and Retreat Facilities: There are some rooms for meditation and retreat, but not tourists. Please contact us to ask further details about staying.

Office Book: BCP of Nippon Seiko Kai Office Book

Bishop Visitor: Rt Revd Yoshimichi Ohata, Bp of Tokyo

Benedictine Community of Our Lady & Saint John

Alton Abbey OSB

Founded 1884

Alton Abbey
Abbey Road
Beech, Alton
Hampshire
GU34 4AP
UK
Tel: 01420 562145
& 01460 563575
Email: abbot@altonabbey.org.uk
or
guestmaster@altonabbey.org.uk

Morning Prayer
6.30 am

Conventual Mass
9.00 am (10 am Sun)

Midday Office
12.00 noon

Evening Prayer 5 pm

Night Prayer
8.30 pm (7.30 pm Sun)

The monks follow the Rule with its balance of prayer, work and study, supported by the vows of stability, conversion of life and obedience. A wide ministry of hospitality is offered, and visitors are welcome at the daily Mass and Divine Office. The purpose built monastery is built around two cloister garths; the Abbey Church dates from the beginning of the twentieth century. Set in extensive grounds, with contrast between areas that are cultivated and others that are a haven for wildlife, the Abbey is situated about four miles from Alton.

RT REVD DOM WILLIAM HUGHES OSB
(Abbot, assumed office 5 November 2010)
VERY REVD DOM ANDREW JOHNSON OSB *(Prior)*

Rt Revd Dom Giles Hill OSB *(Abbot emeritus)*
Revd Dom Nicholas Seymour OSB
Dom Anselm Shobrook OSB
Rt Revd Dom Timothy Bavin OSB
Brother John Towson OSB (*Guest Master)*

Novices: 1

Oblates
For details of the Oblates of St Benedict, please contact the Oblate Master.
For details of the Companions of Our Lady and Saint John, please contact the Master of the Companions.

Community Wares
Altar bread and incense: contact Alton Abbey Supplies Ltd. Tel: 01420 565977

Guest and Retreat Facilities
Guest house facilities for up to eighteen persons, for both group and individual retreats. There is a programme of retreats each year, available from the Guestmaster.
No smoking in the house.

Most convenient time to telephone: 4.00 pm – 4.30 pm.

Office Book: Alton Abbey Office Book

Website: www.altonabbey.org.uk

Bishop Visitor: awaiting appointment

Registered Charity: No. 229216

Community of the Resurrection

CR

Founded 1892

House of the Resurrection
Mirfield
West Yorkshire
WF14 0BN
UK
Tel: 01924 494318
Fax: 01924 490489
Email: community @mirfield.org.uk

Website: www. mirfieldcommunity. org.uk

Mattins
6.45 am (7.30 am Sun)

Midday Office
12.00 noon

Mass 12.15 pm
On festivals on week days, the time of Mass may change.

Evensong 6.00 pm

Compline 9.15 pm

Office Book
CR Office

Registered Charity
No. 232670

The Community consists of priests and laymen living a life of worship, work and study within the monastic life. They undertake a wide range of pastoral ministry including retreats, teaching and counselling.

George Guiver CR
(assumed office 29 December 2002)
Oswin Gartside CR *(Prior)*

Roy France
Vincent Girling
Eric Simmons
Aidan Mayoss
Robert Mercer
Simon Holden
Crispin Harrison
Antony Grant
Nicolas Stebbing
John Gribben
Peter Allan
Philip Nichols
Thomas Seville
Steven Haws
Dennis Berk
Jacob Pallett

Obituaries
9 Dec 2012 Andrew Norton, aged 89, professed 27 years
16 Jan 2013 Timothy Stanton, aged 95, professed 62 years
12 Jun 2013 Dominic Whitnall, aged 98, professed 65 years

Oblates, Companions & Associates

Oblates, clergy and lay, are those who desire to make a special and permanent offering of themselves to God in association with the Community of the Resurrection.

Companions seek to live the baptismal vocation of all Christians through a commitment to each community to which they belong and also to the Community of the Resurrection; a commitment to Eucharistic worship, corporate and private prayer and the use of the sacrament of reconciliation; a commitment of time, talents and money. Those who wish to be Companions keep their commitments for at least a year before being admitted, and thereafter, with all Companions, renew their commitment each year. All Companions have a spiritual director or soul friend with whom their commitments are discussed and who undertakes to support them on their journey.

Associates have a less demanding relationship with the Community for whatever reason, but do have an obligation of prayer and worship. For more information contact the Chaplain to the Companions at Mirfield.

Community History: Alan Wilkinson, *The Community of the Resurrection: A centenary history,* SCM Press, London, 1992.

Bishop Visitor: Rt Revd Graham James, Bishop of Norwich

Community Publication: *CR Quarterly*. Write to the Editor. Many subscribe to this who are not Oblates, Companions or Associates. The minimum annual subscription is £15.00.

Community Wares: Postcards of the buildings, theological and spiritual books, leaflets on prayer, CDs of Community's music, clothes with logo: apply to Mirfield Publications at the House of the Resurrection. Purchases available online through the website.

Guest and Retreat Facilities

Retreats are listed on the website.

House of the Resurrection

Twenty-four single rooms, two double rooms, nine en-suite rooms, one small flat.

Most convenient time to telephone: 9.00 am – 12 noon, 2.00 pm – 6.00 pm

Mirfield Centre

The Centre offers a meeting place at the College for about fifty people. Small residential conferences are possible in the summer vacation. Day and evening events are arranged throughout the year to stimulate Christian life and witness.

The Mirfield Centre (College of the Resurrection), Mirfield, West Yorks WF14 0BW, UK Tel: 01924 481920 Fax: 01924 418921
Email: centre@mirfield.org.uk

College of the Resurrection

The College, founded in 1902 and run by its own independent Council, trains men and women and also provides opportunities for others to study for degrees.

Acting Principal: Fr Peter Allan CR

College of the Resurrection, Mirfield, West Yorkshire WF14 0BW, UK
Tel: 01924 481900 Email: registrar@mirfield.org.uk

Community of the Resurrection of Our Lord CR

Founded 1884

St Peter's, PO Box
Grahamstown 6140
South Africa
Tel & Fax:
046 622 4210

This Community was founded in 1884 by Bishop Allan Becher Webb and Cecile Isherwood to undertake pastoral and educational work in Grahamstown. These two types of work, and later Social Welfare work, have predominated throughout the Community's history. The regular life of monastic Offices and personal prayer and intercession has always been maintained in all houses, wherever situated. Grahamstown is now the only centre where the Community life continues. The Sisters are involved in various ministries: at the Cathedral and other churches as needed; in the Raphael Centre for people suffering from HIV/Aids etc; in visiting at Old Age Homes and the hospital; soup kitchens; and needlework/banners. In April 2012, the Community opened an orphanage, named Ikhay Lethu, in our old convent. At present, it has two sisters and a brother, aged 1–6.

Email:
mother_zelma
@geenet.co.za

MOTHER ZELMA CR *(priest)*
(Mother Superior, assumed office 24 November 2005)
SISTER KEKELETSO CR *(Assistant Superior)*
Sister Dorianne
Sister Carol *(priest)*

Novices: 2

Morning Office
7.00 am

Eucharist 7.30 am (or 7.00 am at the Cathedral

Midday Office
12.30 pm

Evening Office
5.30 pm

Compline 7.30 pm

Greater Silence: 9 pm

Office Book
Anglican Prayer Book 1989, CPSA; Traditional Midday Office & Compline

Community Wares
Cards, banners, girdles, stoles and altar linens etc, corporals and purificators.

Bishop Visitor
Rt Revd Eric Pike

Oblates and Associates

OBLATES OF THE RISEN CHRIST live under a Rule drawn up for each individual according to circumstances, on their observance of which they must report monthly to the Oblate Sister.

ASSOCIATES undertake a simple Rule, including regular prayer for the Community. Priest Associates undertake to give an address or preach on Religious Vocation at least once a year.

FRIENDS are interested in the Community and pray for it, and keep in touch with it.

There is a Fellowship Meeting twice a year, after Easter and near the Foundress's birthday on 14 November.

Also there is a Festival gathering of UK Associates at St Peter's Bourne, Whetstone, north London, on the Saturday nearest to St Peter's Day, 29 June, each year, at which two Sisters from South Africa are always present to preserve our links with the UK.

Community Publication: A Newsletter is sent out three times a year to all bishops and Religious communities of CPSA, and also to all the Oblates and Associates of the Community.

Guest and Retreat Facilities: Ten or more guests can be accommodated; though prior consultation is needed. The charge is negotiable. There is also a guest flatlet for two.

Community History and Books

A pictorial record of the Community's history, with commentary, was published in its centenary year, 1984. It was a collaborative work.

A Sister of the Community (compiler), *Mother Cecile in South Africa 1883–1906: Foundress of the Community of the Resurrection of Our Lord,* SPCK, London, 1930.

A Sister of the Community, *The Story of a Vocation: A Brief Memoir of Mother Florence, Second Superior of the Community of the Resurrection of Our Lord,* The Church Book Shop, Grahamstown, no date.

Guy Butler, *The Prophetic Nun*, Random House, 2000. (Life and art works, with colour illustrations, of Sisters Margaret and Pauline CR, and Sister Dorothy Raphael CSMV.) This is a coffee-table type book available in South Africa and the UK.

Community of the Sacred Name

CSN

Founded 1893

300 Tuam Street
Christchurch 8011
NEW ZEALAND
Tel: 03 366 8245
Email: comsacnm @xtra.co.nz

Morning Prayer
7.15 am

Mass 8.00 am (Thu & Fri)

Midday Office
12 noon

Vespers 5.15 pm

Compline 7.00 pm

Office Book
A New Zealand Prayer Book
He Karakia Mihinare o Aotearoa

Community Wares
Embroidery, cards, vestments.

Bishops Visitor
Rt Revd Victoria Matthews
Rt Revd Winston Halapua

The Community of the Sacred Name was founded in Christchurch in 1893 by Sister Edith (Deaconess). She was released from the Community of St Andrew in London to establish an indigenous community to respond to the needs of the colonial Church. A wide variety of teaching, childcare and parish work has been undertaken over the years. Today there are five houses. Since 1966, the Sisters have run a large children's home in Fiji and now also run St Mary's girls' hostel at Labasa, Vanua Levu. Three Sisters have returned to Christchurch and are currently living in the retreat house, which was part of the Barbadoes Street property. Four Sisters are based in Ashburton where we do ecclesiastical embroidery. Underpinning all the work is a life of worship.

MOTHER KELENI CSN
(Mother Superior, assumed office 9 November 2006)
SISTER KALOLAINE CSN *(Assistant)*

Sister Annette	Sister Mele	Sister Alena
Sister Brigid	Sister Litia	Sister Fehoko
Sister Lu'isa	Sister Judith	Sister Vutulongo
Sister Anne	Sister Miria	Sister Sandra

Oblates and Associates
The Community has Oblates, men and women called by God to live the contemplative life in the world.
We also have Companions, Associates, Friends of St Christopher's. For women or men, priests or lay people.

Community History
Ruth Fry, *The Community of the Sacred Name – a Centennial History,* 1993; copies available from Revd Mother.

Guest and Retreat Facilities
8 bedrooms for retreats or guests. Contact (03) 366 8245
Most convenient time to telephone: 9.15 am – 5.15 pm

Community Publication
Community *Newsletter*, published at Easter, Holy Name and Christmas. Write to the Reverend Mother.

Other addresses

53 Morris Road, RD2, Ashburton 7772, NEW ZEALAND Tel: 9030 307 1121

St Christopher's Home, PO Box 8232, Nakasi, Suva, FIJI Tel: 679 341 0458

St Mary's Hostel, PO Box 4121, Labasa, FIJI

PO Box 1824, Nuku'alofa, TONGA Tel: 27998

Community of the Sacred Passion

CSP

Founded 1911

Convent of the Sacred Passion
22 Buckingham Road
Shoreham-by-Sea
West Sussex
BN43 5UB
UK
Tel: 01273 453807
Email: communitysp@yahoo.co.uk

Morning Prayer
7.10 am

Prayer before noon
8.05 am

Mass 9.30 am
(Mon, Thu, Fri)

Midday Office
12.10 pm

Evening Prayer
6.00 pm

Compline 7.30 pm

The Community was founded to serve Africa by a life of prayer and missionary work, bringing to Africans a knowledge of God's love. After the Church in Tanzania gained independence, and the Community of St Mary of Nazareth and Calvary (CMM), which they nurtured, became self-governing, CSP withdrew from Tanzania and now offers support from England. Much of the help is channelled through CMM to whom they offer encouragement, advice and financial support. The Sisters also collect money for some of the work that they founded, including the Polio Hostel at Kwa Mkono, caring for disabled children, and building work at the Nursing School at Muheza to cater for extra student nurses and modern equipment. At Shoreham, the Sisters offer hospitality for small day events and meetings. They are involved in guidance of individuals and have various contacts in the local community. The Sister who lives in Clapham is involved with the World Community for Christian Meditation and has contacts with people of various faiths. Prayer remains the foundation of the life of the Community.

MOTHER PHILIPPA CSP
(Revd Mother, assumed office 30 August 1999)
SISTER JACQUELINE CSP *(Deputy Superior)*

Sister Dorothy
Sister Gillian Mary
Sister Rhoda
Sister Angela
Sister Lucia

Obituaries

9 Jun 11 Sr Etheldreda, aged 86, professed 60 years
16 Jul 11 Sr Joan Thérèse, aged 92, professed 50 years
3 Nov 12 Sr Mary Kathleen, aged 88, professed 42 years
17 Nov 12 Sr Thelma Mary, aged 90, professed 56 years

Oblates: Men and women who feel called to associate themselves with the aims of the community, by prayer and service, and by a life under a Rule. Their own Rule of Life will vary according to their particular circumstances. Oblates are helped and advised by the Oblates' Sister.

Associates: Men and women who share in the work of the community by prayer, almsgiving and service of some kind. They pray regularly for the community.

Priest Associates: Pray regularly for the community and offer Mass for it three times a year, of which one is Passion Sunday (the Sunday before Palm Sunday).

Friends: Pray regularly for the community and help it in any way they can.

Other Address:
725 Wandsworth Road
London SW8 3JF
UK

Bishop Visitor
Rt Revd Ian Brackley
Bishop of Dorking

Registered charity No:
800080

All those connected with the community are prayed for daily by the Sisters and remembered by name on their birthdays. They receive the four-monthly intercession paper, and newsletter.

Guest and Retreat Facilities
One room with self-catering facilities. Donations. Women only for overnight stay.

Most convenient time to telephone: 4 pm – 7.30 pm.

Community History
Sister Mary Stella CSP, *She Won't Say 'No': The History of the Community of the Sacred Passion*, 1984
Margaret Gooch, *Zanzibar to Shoreham in 100 years,* Paul Davies, Great Yarmouth, 2011 – obtainable from the Convent, £11, cheques payable to Community of the Sacred Passion.

Community of St Andrew CSA

Founded 1861

Correspondence address:
Revd Mother Lillian, CSA
40 Homecross House
21 Fishers Lane
Chiswick
W4 1YA

Tel: 020 8747 0001

Email:
lillianmorris959@btinternet.com

In the mid 19th century Elizabeth Ferard felt called to restore the diaconate of women. After training for several months with Lutheran deaconesses at Kaiserswerth and with the Anglican Sisters of Mercy at Ditchingham (CAH), she was authorized by the Bishop of London, A. C. Tait, to begin an Institute to train women as Deaconesses which started on St Andrew's Day, 1861. The Bishop commissioned Elizabeth as the first Deaconess of the Church of England on 18 July 1862. The Bishop laid hands on the head of each person to be made Deaconess, give her his blessing and she would be admitted to the Community of the London Diocesan Deaconess Institution. From about 1887 the Community evolved into a Religious Community known as the Deaconess Community of St Andrew; thus the dual vocation of life commitment in community and ordained ministry in the Church. The fundamental ministry is the offering of prayer and worship, evangelism, pastoral work and hospitality, now mainly through retirement ministries. In 2011 we celebrated our 150th anniversary as a Community. Because the restoration of the Deaconess Order began with us, in 2012 we co-sponsored the celebration of the 150th anniversary of the Deaconess Order of the Church of England at Lambeth Palace at which the Archbishop presided and a former deaconess, the Revd Ann Gurney, preached.

REVD MOTHER LILLIAN CSA *(deacon)*
(Mother Superior, 1982–94, 2000–)
Revd Sister Donella *(deacon)*
resident at 40 Homecross House, 21 Fishers Lane, Chiswick, W4 1YA
Tel: 020 8747 0001

Revd Sister Patricia *(deacon)*
resident at: St Mary's Convent & Nursing Home, Burlington Lane, Chiswick, London W4 2QE Tel: 020 8742 8434

Sister Pamela *(deaconess)*
resident at: 17 War Memorial Place, Harpsden Way, Henley on Thames, Oxon RG9 1EP Tel: 01491 572224

Revd Dr Sister Teresa *(priest)*
resident at: St Andrew's House, 16 Tavistock Crescent, London W11 1AP
Tel: 020 7221 4604 Email: teresajoan@btinternet.com

Associates
Our Associates are part of our extended Community family. They may be men, women, clergy or lay, and follow a simple Rule of Life, which includes praying for the Sisters and their work. The Sisters pray for the Associates every day.

Community Publications
St Andrew's Newsletter. Write to Sister Teresa.

Community History
Sister Joanna [Baldwin], Dss. CSA, "The Deaconess Community of St Andrew", *Journal of Ecclesiastical History*, Vol. XII, No.2, October 1961, 16pp.
Henrietta Blackmore, editor, *The Beginnings of Women's Ministry: The Revival of the Deaconess in the 19th-Century Church of England*, Boydell & Brewer, Woodbridge, 2007, ISBN 978-843-308-6.
Sister Teresa [Joan White], CSA, *The (Deaconess) Community of St Andrew, 1861–2011,* St Andrew's House, 2012, reprinted 2013, 225 pp. plus photos. £13.60 plus postage (£2.60 in UK). Please enquire to sisterteresa@btinternet.com.
Sister Edna Mary [Skinner], Dss.CSA, *The Religious Life*, Penguin, Harmondsworth, 1968.

Office Book: Common Worship – Daily Prayer

Bishop Visitor: Rt Revd & Rt Hon Richard Chartres, Bishop of London

Registered Charity: No 244321

CSA Crib now used at Homecross House

Community of St Clare OSC

Founded 1950

St Mary's Convent
178 Wroslyn Road
Freeland
Witney
OX29 8AJ
UK
Tel: 01993 881225
Fax: 01993 882434

Email: community @oscfreeland.co.uk

Morning Prayer
7.30 am

Eucharist
8.30 am

Midday Prayer
12.30 pm

Evening Prayer
5.30 pm

Night Prayer
8.00 pm

Office Book
The Daily Office SSF

The Community of St Clare is part of the Society of St Francis. We are a group of women who live together needing each other's help to give our whole lives to the worship of God. Our service to the world is by our prayer, in which we are united with all people everywhere. We have a guest house so that others may join in our worship, and share the quiet and beauty with which we are surrounded. We try to provide for our own needs by growing much of our own food, and by our work of printing, wafer baking, writing and various crafts. This also helps us to have something material to share with those in greater need.

Sister Damien Davies OSC
(Abbess, elected 13 May 2013)
Sister Paula Fordham OSC *(Assistant)*

Sister Alison Francis Hamilton
Sister Kathleen Marie Staggs
Sister Mary Kathleen Kearns
Sister Mary Margaret Broomfield
Sister Susan Elisabeth Leslie

Community Wares
Printing, cards, crafts, altar breads.

Guest and Retreat Facilities
Men, women and children are welcome at the guest house. It is not a 'silent house' but people can make private retreats if they wish. Eleven rooms (some twin-bedded). Donations, no fixed charge. Closed for two weeks mid-May and two weeks mid-September, and 16 Dec–8 Jan. Please write to the Guest Sister at the Convent address.

Most convenient time to telephone:
6.00 pm – 7.00 pm – on Convent telephone: 01993 881225

Address of the Guest House (for guests arriving)
The Old Parsonage, 168 Wroslyn Road, Freeland, Witney OX29 8AQ, UK Tel: 01993 881227

Community History
Petà Dunstan, *This Poor Sort,* DLT, London 1997, pp157–167

Bishop Protector
Rt Revd Michael Perham, Bishop of Gloucester

Community of St Francis

CSF

Founded 1905

Minister General
Email:
ministergeneralcsf@franciscans.org.uk

UK Houses:

St Francis House
113 Gillott Road
Birmingham
B16 0ET
Tel: 0121 454 8302
Email:
birminghamcsf@franciscans.org.uk

St Matthew's House
25 Kamloops Crescent
Leicester LE1 2HX
Tel: 0116 253 9158
Email:
leicestercsf@franciscans.org.uk

San Damiano
38 Drury Street
Metheringham
Lincs LN4 3EZ
Tel: 01526 321115
Email:
metheringhamcsf@franciscans.org.uk

As Franciscan sisters, an autonomous part of the Society of St Francis, our primary vocation is to live the gospel in the places to which we are called. The context is our life in community, under vows. Our wide range of backgrounds, abilities and gifts contributes to many ways of expressing the three elements of prayer, study and work. Prayer together and alone, with the Eucharist being central, is the heart of each house and each sister's life. Six sisters, including one in the American Province, are priests; and three live the solitary life. Study nurtures our spiritual life and enables and enriches our ministries. Work encompasses practical domestic tasks and a wide range of ministries: currently these include hospitality, spiritual direction, prison chaplaincy, administration, teaching computer skills, supporting people with various disabilities, parish work and missions, preaching, leading quiet days and retreats, writing, being a presence in poor urban areas, and work with deaf blind people. Some of this work is salaried, much is voluntary. Each new sister brings her unique gifts, thus enriching our shared life. Now in our second century, we are excited by the challenge of living the Franciscan life in today's world.

HELEN JULIAN CSF
(Minister General, assumed office February 2012)

EUROPEAN PROVINCE

SUE CSF
(Minister Provincial, assumed office February 2012)

Angela Helen
Beverley
Chris
Christine James
Elizabeth
Gina
Gwenfryd Mary
Hilary
Jannafer
Jenny Tee
Judith Ann
Liz
Maureen
Nan
Patricia Clare
Phyllis
Sue
Teresa

Sisters resident in Korea:
Frances
Jemma

Office Book: Daily Office SSF

Website: www.franciscans.org.uk

Bishop Protector
Rt Revd Michael Perham, Bishop of Gloucester

Registered Charity: No. 286615

The Vicarage
11 St Mary's Road
Plaistow
London E13 9AE
Tel: 020 8552 4019
Email: stmaryscssf@franciscans.org.uk

St Alphege Clergy House
Pocock Street
Southwark
London SE1 0BJ
Tel: 020 7928 8912
Email: southwarkcsf@franciscans.org.uk

Minister Provincial:
Email: ministercsf@franciscans.org.uk
Tel: 020 7928 7121

Box 1003
Gumi Post Office
Gumi
Gyeongbukdo
730-600
REPUBLIC OF KOREA
Tel: (054) 451 2317
Email: csfkorea@gmail.com

St Francis House
3743 Cesar Chavez Street
San Francisco
CA 94110
USA
Tel: 415 824 0288
Fax: 415 826 7569

Email: csfsfo@aol.com

Website: www.communitystfrancis.org

Companions & Third Order

Companions are individual Christians who wish to associate themselves with the Society through prayer, friendship and in seeking to live the spirit of the Gospel in the way of St Francis. For more information about becoming a Companion contact the Secretary for Companions, Hilfield Friary, Dorchester, Dorset DT2 7BE, UK.

For the Third Order SSF, *see separate entry.*

Community Publication

franciscan, three times a year. Subscription: £8.00 per year. Write to the Editor of *franciscan*, The Friary of St Francis, Hilfield, Dorset DT2 7BE, UK.

Community History: Elizabeth CSF, *Corn of Wheat*, Becket Publications, Oxford, 1981.

Guest and Retreat Facilities

METHERINGHAM

In rural Lincolnshire on the edge of a peaceful village, the sisters welcome day visitors, either in the house or the comfortable hermitage in the garden. The house also has one room for a residential guest for retreat or quiet break. Two meeting rooms are available for groups of up to 8 and 24. The house is normally open to guests from Wednesday to Sunday. The sisters sometimes also welcome Working Guests who stay for a period sharing in the life and work.

SOUTHWARK

In central London the house welcomes day guests, and also has two rooms available for residential guests. Two meeting rooms accommodate groups of up to 8 and 20.

For more information please see the website, or contact the relevant house.

AMERICAN PROVINCE

The Sisters came to the United States in 1974, and for over thirty years we have engaged in many types of ministry, but with special concern for the poor, the marginalized, and the sick. We can be found in hospitals and nursing homes; among the homeless, immigrants, and people with AIDS; teaching student deacons and serving on diocesan commissions; providing spiritual direction and directing retreats in parishes. In all things we strive to be instruments of God's love.

PAMELA CLARE CSF
(Minister Provincial, assumed office June 2010)

Cecilia	Lynne	Ruth
Jean	Maggie	

Associates
Contact: Brother Derek SSF, Secretary for Associates, 2449 Sichel Street, Los Angeles, CA 90031-2315, USA. Email: broderekssf@yahoo.com

Community Wares: *CSF Office Book,* home retreat booklets, Franciscan prayer cards.

Community Publication
The Canticle. Contact St Francis House to subscribe – $5 for two years.

Community History
Pamela Clare CSF, 'The Early History of the First Order Brothers and Sisters of the Society of St Francis', *The Historiographer,* Vol L, No 4, (Fall 2012), The National Episcopal Historians and Archivists and The Historical Society of the Episcopal Church, Phoenx, AZ, USA.

Guest and Retreat Facilities: At the San Francisco house, there is a guest apartment, which has one bedroom (two beds) and a small kitchen. It has its own entrance. The suggested cost is $50 per night.

Most convenient time to telephone: 9.00 am – 5.00 pm, 7.45 pm – 9.00 pm.

Office Book: CSF Office Book

Bishop Protector: Rt Revd Nedi Rivera, Bishop of Eastern Oregon

---

Community of St John Baptist

(UK)

CSJB

Founded 1852

Harriet Monsell House
Ripon College
Cuddesdon
Oxfordshire
OX44 9EX
Tel: 01865 877100
(office)
01865 877102
(Community Room)

Email: csjbteam @csjb.co.uk

Founded by Harriet Monsell and Thomas Thelluson Carter to help women rejected by the rest of society, we are now a Community of women who seek to offer our gifts to God in various ways. These include parish and retreat work, spiritual direction, and ministry to the elderly. Two sisters are ordained to the priesthood: both work in local benefices as well as presiding regularly at the community Eucharist. Sisters are also involved in the ministry of spiritual accompaniment, retreat giving and are available to facilitate quiet days. We have close links with the sisters of our affiliated community at Mendham, New Jersey, USA *(see separate entry);* and we also have links with the Justice and Peace Movement.

Daily life centres on the Eucharist and the Divine Office, and we live under the threefold vows of poverty, chastity and obedience. Following the Rule of St Augustine, we are encouraged to grow into 'an ever-deepening commitment of love for God and for each other as we strive to show forth the attractiveness of Christ to the world'.

In 2012, we moved to Ripon College, Cuddesdon, where we hope to contribute to the life of the community and the spiritual development of the students.

Website: www.csjb.org.uk

Sister Ann Verena CJGS
(Leader, assumed office 2010)

Sister Doreen Aldred
Sister Jane Olive Stencil
Sister Monica Amy
Sister Elizabeth Jane Barrett
Sister Mary Stephen Britt
Sister Anne Proudley

Obituaries
22 May 12 Sister Edna Frances Wilson, aged 94, professed 50 years, Revd Mother 1978–92

Oblates & Associates
CSJB has women oblates. Men and women may become Associates or members of the Friends of Clewer – these answer to a call to prayer and service while remaining at home and work. This call includes a commitment to their own spiritual life development and to active church membership. Oblates, Associates and Friends support the sisters by prayer and in other ways, and are likewise supported by the Community, and are part of the extended family of CSJB.

Community Wares: Anglican prayer beads.

Community Publication
Associates' Letter, has been published three times a year, but this is now under review. Contact the magazine editor at csjbteam@csjb.org.uk for information.

Community History
Books by Valerie Bonham, all published by CSJB:
A Joyous Service: The Clewer Sisters and their Work (1989) – revised edition 2012.
A Place in Life: The House of Mercy 1849–1883 (1992),
The Sisters of the Raj: The Clewer Sisters in India (1997).

Guest and Retreat Facilities
Facilities vary according to the time of year and the needs of the student body. We hope to be able to offer some facilities in the future.

Most convenient time to telephone:
10 am – 11.45 am; 2.30 pm – 4.30 pm, 7 pm – 8 pm, Mon to Sat.

Morning Prayer
7.30 am

Tierce
9.00 am
(9.30am in term)

Eucharist
9.15 am
(after Morning Prayer in term)

Midday Office
12.30 pm

Evening Prayer
5.00 pm

Compline
8.30 pm

(all subject to variation in term time)

Office Book
Common Worship Daily Prayer, with our own plainsong hymns and antiphons

Bishop Visitor
Rt Revd
John Pritchard
Bishop of Oxford

Registered Charity:
No 236939

Community of St John Baptist

(USA)

CSJB

Founded 1852 (in UK)
1874 (in USA)

**PO Box 240 –
82 W. Main Street
Mendham, NJ
07945
USA
Tel: 973 543 4641
Fax: 973 543 0327
Email:
csjb@csjb.org**

Lauds
7.30 am

Eucharist
8.00 am

Terce
9.30 am

Noonday Office
12 noon

Vespers
5.45 pm

Compline
8.30 pm

Website
www.csjb.org

The Community of St John Baptist was founded in England in 1852. The spirit of the Community is to "prepare the way of the Lord and make straight in the desert a highway for our God." We follow the call of our patron through a life of worship, community, and service.

Our Community is made up of monastic women, who share life together under the traditional vows of poverty, chastity and obedience. Our life includes daily participation in the Eucharist and the Divine Office, prayer, and ministry to those in need. We also have married or single Oblates, who commit themselves to a Rule of life and service in the Church, and Associates, who make up the wider family of CSJB.

We live by an Augustinian Rule, which emphasizes community spirit. Those who live with us include Oblates and friends, as well as our pony, dog, and cat. Our Retreat House and guest wing are often full of persons seeking spiritual direction and sacred space. Our buildings are set in a beautiful wooded area. Our work includes spiritual direction, retreats, hospitality, youth ministry and ordained ministry (two sisters are priests). The Community participates in a mission in Africa, helps the homeless, and works in parishes.

SISTER ELEANOR FRANCIS CSJB
(Sister Superior, assumed office 14 December 2009)
SISTER BARBARA JEAN CSJB *(Novice Director)*

Sister Suzanne Elizabeth
Sister Laura Katharine
Sister Pamela
Sister Mary Lynne
Sister Margo Elizabeth
Sister Deborah Francis
Sister Linda Clare

Novices: 2

Obituaries

14 Jul 2013 Sister Lura Grace, aged 64, professed 8 years

Oblates & Associates

Oblates make promises which are renewed annually. The Rule of Life includes prayer, study, service, spiritual direction, retreats. Associates keep a simple Rule. Membership is ecumenical.

Address of other house

St Mary's Mission House, 145 W. 46th Street, New York, NY 10036, USA. Tel: 212 869 5830

Office Book
Our own book based upon the Book of Common Prayer of the Episcopal Church of the USA

Community Publication
Community Notes, Michaelmas, Christmas, Easter Newsletters.

Most convenient time for guests to telephone:
between 10 am and 4.45 pm

Bishop Visitor
Rt Revd Prince Singh, Bishop of Rochester

Community History & Books
J. Simpson & E. Story, *Stars in His Crown*, Ploughshare Press, Sea Bright, NJ, 1976.

Books by Valerie Bonham, all published by CSJB:
A Joyous Service: The Clewer Sisters & their Work (2nd ed 2012)
A Place in Life: The House of Mercy 1849-1883 (1992)
The Sisters of the Raj: The Clewer Sisters in India (1997)

P. Allan, M. Berry, D. Hiley, Pamela CSJB & E. Warrell, *An English Kyriale.*

Guest and Retreat Facilities

ST MARGUERITE'S RETREAT HOUSE
This has twenty-seven rooms. The address is the same as for the Convent but the telephone number is: 973 543 4582 There is one new room for a disabled person with disabled-access bathroom.

CONVENT GUEST WING
This has six rooms (for women only). The cost is $75.00 for an overnight stay with three meals. Closed Mon and Tue.

Community Wares
Tote bags, mugs, cards, jewelery, candles, ornaments, tapes, prayer beads.

Community of St John the Divine

CSJD

Founded 1848

For 37 years, CSJD has been in Birmingham, our House situated in an area amongst the worst 5% of poverty nationally, and with the highest child poverty in the city. Our Community witnesses to Religious life by being a praying presence amidst this highly diverse, deprived area. We seek to be a resource for all in the Diocese, ordained and lay, providing a space for physical and spiritual renewal to enable others to continue their ministries.

The past year has been busier than ever with 1300 people coming to the House: parish away-days, clergy training, local community meetings, spiritual accompaniment, pastoral care, reflexology. Some are convalescing after surgery, accident or injury; others are facing serious illness or have other needs. Sisters welcome all visitors to share in our life and worship, and develop personal ministries within and beyond that hospitality.

Developing our relations with our local multi-faith neighbours in Alum Rock has long been part of our vision. We have recently begun links with the Christian and

Muslim Women's Forum, participated in inter-faith events elsewhere in Birmingham, and hosted other meetings. Through the Near Neighbours Programme, we meet people of other Faiths, seek good relationships and explore and address local needs together. To create a safe meeting space for these events, we are refurbishing an annexe, encouraged by a grant from the Anglican Religious Communities Development Trust. We ask you to join us in praying that God will bless the new ministries which flow from this.

We are a small Community, with a group of enthusiastic Associates who share much of our life. An Alongsiders' Programme has been running for 10 years for those wishing to live with us for short periods of time. We are always delighted to hear from anyone interested in our work and witness.

SISTER CHRISTINE CSJD
& SISTER MARGARET ANGELA CSJD
(Leaders of the Community, assumed office April 2007)

Sister Teresa
Sister Elaine
Sister Ivy
Sister Shirley

Novices: 1

Associates
Associates are men and women from all walks of life who desire to have a close link with the life and work of the Community. They make a simple Commitment to God, to the Community and to one another. Together with the Sisters, they form a network of love, prayer and service. (Guidelines available.)

Alongsiders
Alongsiders come to the Community for varying lengths of time, usually six months to one year. The aim is to provide an opportunity of sharing in the worship and life of the Community, and could be useful for a sabbatical, a time of spiritual renewal, study, to respond to a specific need, or to allow time and space to consider the way ahead. (Guidelines available.)

Community History: The brochure written for the 150th anniversary contains a short history.

Guest and Retreat Facilities: Quiet Days for individuals and groups. Facilities for residential individual private retreats. Openness to be used as a resource.

Most convenient time to telephone:
9.00 am, 2.30 pm, 6.00 pm

St John's House
652 Alum Rock Road
Birmingham
B8 3NS
UK

Tel: 0121 327 4174

Email: csjdivine@btinternet.com

Website
www.csjd.org.uk

Office Book
Theb Daily Office SSF (new revised edition 2010)

Community Wares:
Various hand-crafted cards for different occasions.

Community Publication:
Annual Report

Bishop Visitor
Rt Revd David Urquhart, Bishop of Birmingham

Registered Charity
No. 210 254

Community of St John the Evangelist

CSJE

Founded 1912

St Mary's Home
Pembroke Park
Ballsbridge
Dublin 4
IRISH REPUBLIC
Tel: 668 3550

Meditation 6.50 am
Lauds 7.30 am
Terce 9.00 am
Mass 10.30 am (Fri)
Sext: 12 noon
None after dinner
Vespers 5.00 pm
Compline 7.45 pm

Founded in Dublin in 1912, CSJE was an attempt to establish Religious Life in the Church of Ireland, although it did not receive official recognition. The founder believed that a group of sisters living hidden lives of prayer and service would exercise a powerful influence. When he died in 1939, there were twenty-four professed sisters and six novices. From the 1930s, the Community had a branch house in Wales, which became the Mother House in 1967. In 1996, however, the Sisters returned to Dublin to the house originally taken over in 1959 from another small community. This present house was formerly a school and then a home for elderly ladies of the Church of Ireland. It is now a Registered Nursing and Residential Home under the care of the Community but run by lay people. The remaining Sisters of CSJE continue to live the Religious Life to the best of their ability and leave the future in the hands of God.

Sister Verity Anne
Sister Kathleen Brigid

Obituaries
19 Mar 2013 Sister Ann Dora, aged 104,
professed 71 years

Associates and Companions: Associates have a simple Rule, Companions a fuller and stricter Rule. Both groups are now much reduced in number.

Community History
A private booklet was produced for Associates in 1962.

Office Book: Hours of Prayer with the Revised Psalter.

Community of St Laurence

CSL

Founded 1874

Registered Charity:
No. 220282

The Community was founded in 1874. The Sisters cared for the 'Treasures' of the Church – those in need of love and care, including elderly ladies. In 2001 the Community moved to a new purpose-built convent in Southwell, adjacent to Sacrista Prebend Retreat House and the Cathedral. The Convent closed in 2012.

Sister Dorothea
Sister Margareta Mary

Associates
Associates pray regularly for the community, and include priests and lay people. We have over one hundred associates.

Bishop Visitor
Rt Revd Paul Butler, Bishop of Southwell & Nottingham

Community of St Mary

(Eastern Province)

CSM

Founded 1865

St Mary's Convent
242 Cloister Way
Greenwich
NY 12834-7922
USA

Tel: 518 692 3028
Fax: 518 692 3029

Email: compunun@ stmaryseast.org

Website
www. stmaryseast.org

Matins 6.30 am (7.30 am Sat & Sun)

Mass 7.00 am (8.00 am Sat & Sun)

Terce 9.30 am

Sext 12 noon

Vespers 5.30 pm

Compline 7.30 pm

The Sisters of St Mary live a vowed life in community, centered around the daily Eucharist and a five-fold Divine Office. Each sister has time daily for private prayer and study. Our way of life is a modern expression of traditional monastic practice including silent meals in common, plainchant in English for much of our corporate worship, a distinctive habit, and a measure of enclosure.

Our ministry is an outward expression of our vowed life of poverty, chastity and obedience. The specific nature of our work has changed over the years since Mother Harriet and our first sisters were asked to take charge of the House of Mercy in New York City in 1865. Being "mindful of the needs of others," as our table blessing says, we have been led in many ways to care for the lost, forgotten and underprivileged. Today our work is primarily hospitality, retreats, and exploration of outreach through the Internet. Sisters also go out from time to time to speak in parishes, lead quiet days and provide a praying community within the Diocese of Albany's Spiritual Life Center and the Diocese of Northern Malawi.

MOTHER MIRIAM CSM
(*Mother Superior, assumed office 31 August 1996*)
SISTER MARY JEAN CSM (*Assistant Superior*)

Sister Mary Angela
Sister Catherine Clare
Sister Mary Elizabeth
Sister Martha
Sister Monica
Sister Jane

Juniors:
Sister Silvia
Sister Mary Lucia

Novices: 2

Address of other house
Sisters of St Mary, St Mary's Convent, PO Box 20280, Luwinga, Mzuzu 2, MALAWI, South Central Africa

Community Publication: *St Mary's Messenger*. Contact the subscriptions editor. Cost to subscribers in the USA is $10, to those outside the USA $15.

Community History: Sister Mary Hilary CSM, *Ten Decades of Praise,* DeKoven, Racine, WI, 1965. (*out of print*). Video: *The Hidden Life,* heritage videos, 2002 (58 minutes)

Guest and Retreat Facilities
Accommodations for seven in the Convent Guest wing and a further 50 accommodations on first-come, first-serve basis at adjacent Spiritual Life Center, in Greenwich, NY.

Most convenient time to telephone: 10 am – 7 pm ET.

Office Book
The Monastic Diurnal Revised, (The Community of St Mary, New York, 1989): a modern English version of the *Monastic Diurnal* by Canon Winfred Douglas with supplemental texts based upon the American 1979 BCP. Copies are for sale.

Community Wares
Assorted illuminated greeting cards.

Bishop Visitor
Rt Revd William Love, Bishop of Albany

Associates
Associates of the Community of St Mary are Christian men and women who undertake a Rule of life under the direction of the Community, and share in the support and fellowship of the Sisters, and of one another, whilst living dedicated and disciplined lives in the world. Any baptized, practising Christian who feels called to share in the life and prayer of the Community of St Mary as part of our extended family is welcome to inquire about becoming an Associate. Each prospective Associate plans his or her own Rule with the advice of a Sister. An outline is provided covering one's share in the Eucharist and the Divine Office; a rule of private prayer; abstinence and fasting; and charity and witness. Individual vocations and circumstances vary so widely in today's world that a 'one size fits all' Rule is no longer appropriate. We do ask Associates to pray specifically for the Community, as we do for them, and, because the Divine Office is central to our way of life, to undertake some form of Daily Office. An Associate is also expected to keep in touch with us, and to seek to bring others to know the Community.

Community of St Mary

(Western Province)

CSM

Founded 1865

St John's -on-the-Lake
840 N Prospect Avenue #504,
Milwaukee
WI 53202
USA
Tel: 404 239 7908

Email: srletitia@ earthlink.net

The Western Province of the Community of St Mary as set apart as a separate branch of the community in 1904. We share a common Rule, but have separate administration. Our basic orientation is toward a life of prayer, corporate and personal, reaching out to the Church and the world according to the leading of the Holy Spirit. We live singly or in small groups, each sister using her gifts for ministry as she feels led with the support of the whole group.

Sister Letitia Prentice CSM
(*President, assumed office January 1992*)
Sister Mary Grace Rom CSM (*Vice President*)
Sister Mary Paula Bush

Obituaries
16 Jun 2013 Sister Dorcas Baker

Associates
Associates (both men and women) are part of the community family. They follow a Rule of Life and assist the sisters as they are able.

Bishop Visitor
Rt Revd Steven A. Miller, Bishop of Milwaukee

Community of St Mary (Southern Province)

CSM

Founded 1865

1100 St Mary's Lane
Sewanee
TN 37375
USA
Tel: 931 598 0046
Fax: 931 598 9519
Email:
stmsis@att.net

Morning Prayer & Holy Eucharist
7.00 am
(8.00 am Holy Eucharist Sat & Sun)

Noonday Prayer
12 noon
(12.30 pm Sun)

Evening Prayer
5.00 pm

Compline 7.00 pm
(not Sat & Sun)

Office Book
BCP of ECUSA plus Plainsong Psalter, Book of Canticles

Bishop Visitor
Rt Revd John Bauerschmidt, Diocese of Tennesee

The Community of St Mary began in New York in 1865. It was the first women's monastic community founded in the United States, and now has three provinces. The Southern Province has its mother house in Sewanee, Tennessee, and a branch house in the Mountain Province, Philippines. The primary focus of our life together is prayer and worship. The sisters gather four times a day for corporate prayer. We nourish ourselves spiritually through meditation, spiritual reading, Bible study and retreats. The sisters take the threefold vows of simplicity, chastity and obedience. We live in community and hold all things in common. We choose to live a simple life and endeavour to treat God's creation with care. Hospitality and mission are important components of our community's life.

Sister Lucy
Sister Elizabeth Grace
Sister Julian Hope
Sister Madeleine Mary
Sister Mary Martha
Sister Mary Zita
Sister Miriam
Sister Margaret
Sister Mary Hope
Sister Ines *(Philippines)*

Associates and Oblates
Associates are a fellowship of men and women who help CSM through friendship, prayer, support and by their dedicated lives in the world. Each associate writes his/her own rule of life, according to guidelines. We offer associates hospitality, retreats and spiritual companionship.

Oblates are a fellowship of men and women who pattern their lives on the monastic tradition of prayer and service. Oblates work closely with the sisters.

Other Address: St Mary the Virgin Church, St Mary's Convent, 2619 Sagada, Mountain Province, PHILIPPINES

Community wares: Photo cards, hand-painted note cards, rosaries (Anglican & Dominican).

Community publication: *The Messenger*

Community history: James Waring, *Saint Mary's, the Sewanee Sisters and their School,* Sewanee Trust, 2010

Guest and Retreat Facilities: St Dorothy's guest house. A one-bedroom unit with small kitchen and bath and a two-bedroom unit with kitchen and bath. All welcome. Contact CSM for the current fees.

Most convenient time to telephone
Mon-Sat, 9.30 am – 11.30 am, 2 pm – 5 pm

Community of St Mary the Virgin

CSMV

Founded 1848

St Mary's Convent
Challow Road,
Wantage
Oxfordshire
OX12 9DJ
UK
Tel: 01235 763141

Email:
sisterincharge
@csmv.co.uk

Website:
www.csmv.co.uk

Lauds 7.00 am

Terce 8.15 am

Eucharist 10.00 am
(9.30 am Sun & feasts)

Sext 12.30 pm

Vespers 5.00 pm

Compline 8.15 pm

Office Book
CSMV publication

Registered Charity:
No 240513

The Community of St Mary the Virgin was founded in 1848 by William John Butler, then Vicar of Wantage. In January 2013, 11 sisters left CSMV to join the Ordinariate of Our Lady of Walsingham and were received into full communion in the Roman Catholic Church. Those of us who remain as Anglicans in CSMV are grateful for the warm and generous support we have received since their departure.

As Sisters, we are called to respond to our vocation in the spirit of the Virgin Mary: "Behold, I am the handmaid of the Lord. Let it be to me according to your word." Our common life is centred in the worship of God through the Eucharist, the daily Office and in personal prayer. From this all else flows. For some, as at our Smethwick house in the West Midlands, in a multicultural area, it will be expressed in outgoing ministry in neighbourhood and parish, in offering people a quiet place for prayer and reflection and in pastoral care for the elderly. For others it may be expressed in spiritual direction, in retreat giving or in craft and art work. At the Convent, hospitality on the guest wing is the main focus of our ministry. The Community has had a share in the nurturing and training of a small indigenous community in Madagascar *(see entry for FMJK)*.

SISTER JEAN FRANCES CSMV
(Sister-in-charge, assumed office January 2013)
SISTER STELLA CSMV *(Deputy)*

Sister Cecily Clare
Sister Christiana
Sister Barbara Noreen
Sister Anne Julian
Sister Catherine Naomi
Sister Honor Margaret
Sister Helen Philippa
Sister Valeria
Sister Phoebe Margaret
Sister Mary Jennifer
Sister Christine Ann
Sister Bridget Mary
Sister Eileen
Sister Lorna
Sister Anna
Sister Trudy

Obituaries

5 Jul 2011 Sr Joan Elizabeth, aged 91, professed 63 years
8 Aug 2011 Sr Anne Mary, aged 103, professed 57 years
23 Jun 2012 Sr Yvonne Mary, aged 86, professed 62 years
4 Nov 2012 Sr Louise, aged 91, professed 61 years
20 Dec 2012 Sr Enid Mary, aged 96, professed 52 years
5 Jan 2013 Sr Francis Honor, aged 76, professed 32 years

Other Address: **366 High Street, Smethwick, B66 3PD, UK** **Tel: 0121 558 0094**

Oblates & Associates

Oblates: The Oblates of the Community respond to their vocation in the same spirit as Mary: "Behold, I am the handmaid of the Lord. Let it be to me according to your word." Oblates may be married or single, women or men, ordained or lay. Most are Anglicans, but members of other denominations are also welcome. There is a common Rule, based on Scripture and the Rule of St Augustine, and each Oblate also draws up a personal Rule of Life in consultation with the Oblates Councillors and the Oblate Liaison Sister. There is a two-year period of testing as a Novice Oblate; the Promise made at Oblation is renewed annually. In addition to a close personal link with the Community, Oblates meet in regional groups and support each other in prayer and fellowship.

Associates: Associates are men and women, ordained and lay, who wish to be united in prayer and fellowship with the Community, sharing in the spirit of Mary's 'Fiat' in their daily lives. Each Associate keeps a personal Rule of Life, undertakes regular prayer for the Community and makes an annual retreat. He or she is expected to keep in touch with the Associates' Steering Group in conjunction with the Associates' Liaison Sister. The Community sends out a quarterly letter with an intercession leaflet. Every two years an Associates' Day is held at the Convent. Associates are encouraged to meet in regional groups.

Guest and Retreat Facilities

St Mary's Convent Guest Wing

The Guest Wing is a still place, enabling space and refreshment for all who come. Everyone is welcome at the Eucharist and Daily Office in St Mary Magdalene's Chapel. St Mary's Chapel is available for private prayer. Facilities include a sitting room with a library, a dining room, informal quiet room, computer room and art room. For group retreats and group quiet days we offer a spacious room with its own kitchen attached. Those coming for individual quiet days are allocated a room, and are able to share in a meal in the guests' dining room if they so wish. The Guest Wing is closed from after lunch on Sunday until Monday morning each week. Rooms: 21 bedrooms, including 2 twin rooms, 1 bedroom with sitting room, 1 small flat with ensuite facilities, 1 re-furbished ground-floor bedroom with ensuite shower for the less able. Full Board cost: £54.00 per person, per night.

Most convenient time to telephone:

Contact the Guest Wing (01235 763141) 9.00 am – 7 pm, Mon to Sat. Answerphone outside these hours. Email: guestwing@csmv.co.uk

Community History: *A Hundred Years of Blessing*, SPCK, London, 1946.
Sister A. F. Norton, *A History of CSMV*, Parts I & II (1974 MA thesis) & Parts III & IV (1978 MPhil thesis), available for reading in the Convent library.

Community Wares

The Printing Press offers a variety of cards and plainchant music. Orders are not received for cards, which may be purchased at the Convent.
Books and a variety of other items are for sale in the Reception Area.

Bishop Visitor: Rt Revd John Pritchard, Bishop of Oxford

Community of St Michael & All Angels

CSM&AA

Founded 1874

Room 23
Serenicare,
51 General Hertzog Avenue,
Dan Pienaar,
Bloemfontein 9301,
SOUTH AFRICA
Tel: 051 436 7188

The Community of St Michael and All Angels was founded by the second Bishop of Bloemfontein, Allan Becher Webb, for pioneer work in his vast diocese, which included the Orange Free State, Basutoland, Griqualand West and into the Transvaal. The sisters were active in mission, nursing and education. Sister Henrietta Stockdale became the founder of professional nursing in South Africa. The South African Synod of Bishops has placed her on the *CPSA Calendar* for yearly commemoration on 6 October. In 1874, the sisters established St Michael's School for Girls in Bloemfontein, which still exists today as one of the leading schools in South Africa. Today, one sister remains.

Sister Joan Marsh CSM&AA

Community Histories

Margaret Leith, *One the Faith,* 1971 & Mary Brewster, *One the Earnest Looking Forward,* 1991.

Booklets by Sister Mary Ruth CSM&AA: *Dust & Diamonds* (on work in Kimberley); *Cave, Cows & Contemplation* (on thirty years of work at Modderpoort Mission); *Ma'Mohau, Mother of Mercy* (on Sister Enid CSM&AA); *Medals for St Michael's* (CSM&AA in Anglo-Boer War); *Uphill all the Way* (on work in Basutoland/Lesotho)

Obtainable from St Michael's School, PO Box 12110, Brandway 9324, SOUTH AFRICA.

Bishop Visitor: Rt Revd Dintoe Letloenyane

Warden: Rt Revd T S Stanage

Community of St Paul

CSP

Founded 1980

Maciene
MOZAMBIQUE

The Community was founded in 1980 in Maputo (Lebombo Province). The present house in Maciene was originally the branch house of the community and is where the sisters live today. They have been supported by CHN sisters from Zululand. The four sisters in life vows are all Portuguese-speaking.

Their present work includes a local ministry centred on the Cathedral, with hospitality offered through Bishop's House, support for the Sunday School and pastoral visiting.

Sister Cassilda
Sister Julieta
Sister Francina
Sister Persina

Community of St Peter

CSP

Founded 1861

St Peter's Convent c/o St Columba's House Maybury Hill Woking, Surrey GU22 8AB UK Tel: 01483 750739 (9.30am–5pm Mo–Th) Fax: 01483 766208 Email: reverendmother@ stpetersconvent. co.uk

Office Book: CCP

Community Publication: Associates' newsletter at Petertide and Xmas; a letter sent by Reverend Mother, spring and autumn.

Bishop Visitor: Rt Revd David Walker, Bishop of Dudley

Community History Elizabeth Cuthbert, *In St Peter's Shadow,* CSP, Woking, 1994

Registered Charity: No. 240675

The Community was founded by Benjamin Lancaster, a Governor of St George's Hospital, Hyde Park, London. He wished his poorer patients to have convalescent care before returning to their homes. The Sisters also nursed cholera and TB patients, and opened orphanages and homes for children and the elderly. They were asked to go to Korea in 1892. They have close links with the Society of the Holy Cross in Korea, which was founded by the Community *(see separate entry)*. Since the closure of their Nursing/Care Home, new work is undertaken outside the Community in the way of continued care, using Sisters' abilities, talents and qualifications. The Sisters live in houses located where they can carry out their various works and ministry. They recite their fourfold daily Office either together in their houses or individually.

REVD MOTHER LUCY CLARE CSP
(Mother Superior, assumed office 29 June 2005)
(Fosbrooke House, Apartment 33, 8 Clifton Drive, Lytham, Lancashire, FY8 5RQ)

Sisters Margaret Paul & Rosamond:
St Mary's Convent & Nursing Home, Burlington Lane, Chiswick, London W4 2QE

Sister Angela: 41 Sandy Lane, Woking, Surrey, GU22 8BA
Sister Georgina Ruth: Flat 1 Block 4,
Whitgift Alms Houses, North End, Croydon CR0 1UB

Associates and Companions

The associates' fellowship meets at St Columba's at Petertide. The associates support the community in prayer and with practical help, as they are able. They have a simple rule and attend the Eucharist in their own Church. Companions have a stricter rule and say the Daily Office.

Guest and Retreat Facilities

Chaplain & Programme Developor: Revd Gillaine Holland
St Columba's House (Retreat & Conference Centre)
Maybury Hill, Woking, Surrey GU22 8AE, UK
Tel: 01483 713006 or 07069 067116 Fax: 01483 740441
Website: www.stcolumbashouse.org.uk

22 en-suite single bedrooms (2 with disabled facilities), 5 twin bedrooms (4 ensuite). Programme of individual and group retreats. Conference centre for residential and day use, completely refurbished in 2009 for retreatants, parish groups etc. Outstanding liturgical space with a pastoral, and liturgical programme.

Most convenient time to telephone: 9.30 am – 5.00 pm.

Community of St Peter, Horbury CSPH

Founded 1858

St Peter's Convent
14 Spring End Road
Horbury
Wakefield
West Yorkshire
WF4 6DB
Tel: 01924-272181
Email: stpetersconvent @btconnect.com

The Community seeks to glorify God by a life of loving dedication to him, by worship and by serving him in others. A variety of pastoral work is undertaken including Quiet Days, spiritual direction and ministry to individuals in need. The spirit of the community is Benedictine and the recitation of the Divine Office central to the life.

Mother Robina CSPH
(Revd Mother, assumed office 14 Apr 1993)
Sister Elizabeth CSPH *(Assistant Superior)*

Sister Gwynneth Mary
Sister Mary Clare *(priest)*
Sister Phyllis
Sister Jean Clare

Sister Margaret Ann, 2 Main Street, Bossall, York YO2 7NT, UK Tel: 01904 468253

Oblates and Associates
The Community has both oblates and associates.

Community Publication: Annual newsletter at Petertide

Bishop Visitor: Rt Revd Stephen Platten, Bishop of Wakefield

Lauds 7.30 am
Mass 8.00 am
Midday Office 12.00 noon
Vespers 6.00 pm
Compline 7.15 pm

Community of the Servants of the Cross CSC

Founded 1877

resident at:
Rustington Hall
Station Road
Rustington
Littlehampton
West Sussex
BN16 3AY

The Community has an Augustinian Rule and for much of its history cared for elderly and infirm women. In 1997, because of decreasing numbers, the Convent at Lindfield (Sussex) was sold and the Mother House transferred to Chichester, where the former Theological College is now a retirement home. From there, the remaining sisters moved to St Katharine's House, Wantage, but have now moved back to Sussex, to live in a home near to their Warden. There are only two members of the Community left and both are over the age of 90.

Mother Angela CSC
(Mother Superior, assumed office October 1995)
Sister Jane

Bishop Visitor
Rt Revd Martin Warner, Lord Bishop of Chichester

Warden
Father John Lyon, The Vicarage, 33 Vicarage Lane, East Preston, Littlehampton, BN16 2SP Tel: 01903 783318

Community of the Servants of the Will of God

CSWG

Founded 1953

The Monastery of the Holy Trinity
Crawley Down
Crawley
West Sussex
RH10 4LH
UK

Tel: 01342 712074

Email:
(for guest bookings & enquiries)
brother.andrew@cswg.org.uk

Vigils 5.00 am

Lauds 7.00 am

Terce 9.30 am

Sext 12.00 noon

Vespers 6.30 pm

Mass
7.00 pm Mon – Fri
11.00 am Sat & Sun

This monastery is set in woodland. The Community of men and women lives a contemplative life, uniting silence, work and prayer in a simple life style based on the Rule of St Benedict. The Community is especially concerned with uniting the traditions of East and West, and has developed the Liturgy, Divine Office and use of the Jesus Prayer accordingly.

FATHER COLIN CSWG
(Father Superior, assumed office 3 April 2008)
FATHER PETER CSWG *(Prior)*

Brother Martin
Sister Mary Angela
Brother Christopher Mark
Brother John of the Cross
Brother Andrew

Novices: 1
Postulants: 1

Obituaries
17 Feb 2012 Father Brian, aged 85, professed 46 years

Associates
The associates keep a rule of life in the spirit of the monastery.

Community Publication
CSWG Journal: *Come to the Father*, issued Pentecost and All Saints. Write to the Monastery of the Holy Trinity.

Community History
Father Colin CSWG, *A History of the Community of the Servants of the Will of God,* 2002. Available from Crawley Down.

Guest and Retreat Facilities
Six individual guest rooms; meals in community refectory; Divine Office and Eucharist, all with modal chant; donations c.£20 per day.

Most convenient time to telephone: 9.30 am – 6.00 pm.

Community Wares
Mounted icon prints, Jesus Prayer ropes, candles and vigil lights, booklets on monastic and spiritual life.

Office Book
CSWG Divine Office and Liturgy

Bishop Visitor
Rt Revd John Hind

Community of the Sisters of the Church

CSC

Founded 1870

for the whole people of God

Worldwide Community Website: www. sistersofthechurch .org

ENGLAND
Registered Charity No. for CEA: 200240

CANADA
Registered Charity No. 130673262RR0001

AUSTRALIA
Tax Exempt – NPO

Founded by Emily Ayckbowm in 1870, the Community of the Sisters of the Church is an international body of lay and ordained women within the Anglican Communion. We are seeking to be faithful to the gospel values of Poverty, Chastity and Obedience, and to the traditions of Religious Life while exploring new ways of expressing them and of living community life and ministry today. By our worship, ministry and life in community, we desire to be channels of the reconciling love and acceptance of Christ, to acknowledge the dignity of every person, and to enable others to encounter the living God whom we seek.

The Community's patrons, St Michael and the Angels, point us to a life both of worship and active ministry, of mingled adoration and action. Our name, Sisters of the Church, reminds us that our particular dedication is to the mystery of the Church as the Body of Christ in the world.

The Eucharist and Divine Office (usually fourfold) are the heart of our Community life. Community houses provide different expressions of our life and ministry in inner city, suburban, coastal town and village setting.

LINDA MARY SHUTTLE CSC
(Mother Superior, assumed office July 2009)
Email: lindacsc@bigpond.com
29 Lika Drive, Kempsey, NSW 2440, AUSTRALIA

ENGLAND

SUSAN HIRD CSC
(*UK Provincial, assumed office September 2008*)
Email: susan@sistersofthechurch.org.uk
CATHERINE HEYBOURN CSC *(Assistant Provincial)*

Aileen Taylor
Anita Cook
Ann Mechtilde Baldwin
Annaliese Brogden
Dorothea Roden
Hilda Mary Baumberg
Jennifer Cook
Judith Gray
Margaret Sarah Linsley
Marguerite Gillham
Mary Josephine Thomas
Rosina Taylor
Ruth Morris
Ruth White
Scholastica Ferris
Sheila Julian Merryweather
Sue McCarten
Teresa Mary Wright
Veronica Vasethe
Vivien Atkinson

Obituaries
Beryl Hammond, aged 88, professed 63 years
Lydia Corby, aged 93, professed 69 years

Addresses in the UK

St Michael's Convent, 56 Ham Common, Richmond, Surrey TW10 7JH
Tel: 020 8940 8711 & 020 8948 2502 Fax: 020 8948 5525
Email for general enquiries: info@sistersofthechurch.org.uk

82 Ashley Road, Bristol BS6 5NT Tel: 01179 413268
Email: bristol@sistersofthe church.org.uk

St Gabriel's, 27A Dial Hill Road, Clevedon, N. Somerset BS21 7HL
Tel: 01275 544471 Email: clevedon@sistersofthe church.org.uk

10 Furness Road, West Harrow, Middlesex HA2 0RL
Tel: 020 8423 3780 Email: westharrow@sistersofthe church.org.uk

112 St Andrew's Road North, St Anne's-on-Sea, Lancashire FY8 2JQ
Tel & Fax: 01253 728016

Well Cottage, Upper Street, Kingsdown, near Deal, Kent CT14 8BH
Tel: 01304 361601 Email: wellcottage@sistersofthechurch.org.uk

Canada

Arrived in Canada 1890. Established as a separate Province 1965.

Margaret Hayward CSC
(Provincial, assumed office 26 September 2009)
Email: margaretcsc@sympatico.ca

Heather Broadwell	Michael Trott
Marguerite Mae Eamon	Rita Dugger

Obituaries

13 Dec 2012 Elizabeth Nicklin (Benedetta) aged 89, professed 66 years

Addresses in Canada

Sr Margaret Hayward CSC
(& the Community of the Sisters of the Church, c/o Sr Margaret)
Apt 1003 – 6 John St, Oakville, ON, L6K 3T1
Tel: 905 849 0225
General email: sistersofthechurch@sympatico.ca

Sr Michael Trott CSC, Apt 604 – 6 John St, Oakville, ON, L6K 3T1
Tel: 905 845 7186

Sr Marguerite Mae Eamon CSC, Unit 1110 – 1240 Marlborough Court, Oakville, ON, L6H 3K7 Tel: 905 842 5696

Sr Heather Broadwell CSC,
Unit 303 – 28 Duke St, Hamilton, ON, L8P 1X1 Tel: 289 396 6103

Australia

Arrived in Australia 1892. Established as a separate Province 1965.

Linda Mary Shuttle CSC
(*Provincial, assumed office November 1999*)
Email: lindacsc@bigpond.com

Audrey Floate
Elisa Helen Waterhouse
Fiona Cooper
Frances Murphy
Helen Jamieson
Rosamund Duncan

Addresses in Australia
Sisters of the Church, PO Box 1105, Glebe, NSW 2037
Email: cscaust@hotmail.com

Sisters of the Church, 29 Lika Drive, Kempsey, NSW 2440
Tel: 2 6562 2313 Fax: 2 6562 2314

PO Box M191, Missenden Road, NSW 2050 Tel: 2 9516 2407
Email: francescsc@bigpond.com

Unit 15/75, St John's Road, Glebe, NSW 2037

103/28-30 Jackson Street, Toorak, Victoria 3142 Tel: 3 9827 1658

PO Box 713, Melton, Victoria 3337 Tel: 3 9743 6028
Email: elisacsc@tpg.com.au

Solomon Islands

Arrived in Solomon Islands 1970. Established as a separate Province 2001.

Phyllis Sau CSC
(Provincial, assumed office 18 October 2010)
Email: phyllissauu@yahoo.co.uk
Emily Mary Ikai CSC *(Assistant Provincial)*
Email: emilymaryi@yahoo.com

Agnes Maeusia
Anna Caroline Vave
Anneth Kagoa
Annie Meke
Beglyn Tiri
Beverlyn Aosi
Caroline Havideni
Clarine Tekeatu
Daisy Gaoka
Doralyn Sulucia
Doreen Awaisi
Eleanor Ataki
Emmerlyn Teku
Enny Lobi
Evelyn Yaiyo
Faith Mary Maiva
Florence Toata
Jennifer Clare
Jennifer Imua
Jessica Maru
Joan Yape
Joanna Suunorua
Kathleen Kapei
Kristy Arofa
Lillian Mary Manedika
Lucia Sadias
Margrosa Funu
Marina Tuga
Marrion Kauholau
Martha Vale
Mary Gheraga
Mary Gladys Nunga
Mary Kami
Mary Leingala
May Peleba
Minnie Holago
Muriel Tisafa'a
Neverlyn Tohe
Patricia Kalali
Priscilla Iolani
Rachel Teku
Rebecca Margaret Sulupi
Rose Glenda Kimanitoro
Rose Houte'e
Rose Tengo
Rosina Kapa
Ruth Hope Sosoke
Shirley Hestead
Vivian Marie Von Amevuvlian

Novices: 8 *Postulants:* 7

Addresses in the Solomon Islands
Tetete ni Kolivuti, Box 510, Honiara

Patteson House, Box 510, Honiara Tel: 22413 & 27582

PO Box 7, Auki, Malaita Tel: 40423

St Gabriel's, c/o Hanuato'o Diocese, Kira Kira, Makira/Ulawa Province Fax: 677 50128 Mobile: 7553947

St Mary's, Luesalo, Diocese of Temotu, Santa Cruz Mobile phone: 7440081

St Scholastica's House, PO Box 510, Honiara

Sisters of the Church, Henderson, PO Box 510, Honiara

Associates
Associates are men and women who seek to live the Gospel values of Simplicity, Chastity and Obedience within their own circumstances. Each creates his/her own Rule of Life and has a Link Sister or Link House. They are united in spirit with CSC in its life of worship and service, fostering a mutually enriching bond.

Community History
A Valiant Victorian: The Life and Times of Mother Emily Ayckbowm 1836-1900 of the Community of the Sisters of the Church, Mowbray, London, 1964.

Ann M Baldwin CSC, *Now is the Time: a brief survey of the life and times of the Community of the Sisters of the Church,* CSC, 2005.

Community Publication: *Newsletter*, twice a year.
Information can be obtained from any house in the community and by email.

Community Wares
Books by Sister Sheila Julian Merryweather: *Colourful Prayer*; *Colourful Advent; Colourful Lent.* All published by Kevin Mayhew, Buxhall, Stowmarket.
Some houses sell crafts and cards. Vestments are made in the Solomon Islands.

Guest and Retreat Facilities
Hospitality is offered in most houses. Ham Common and Tetete ni Kolivuti have more accommodation for residential guests as well as day facilities. Programmes are offered at Ham Common: please apply for details. Please contact individual houses for other information.

Office Book used by the Community
The Office varies in the different Provinces. Various combinations of the Community's own Office book, the New Zealand psalter, the UK *Common Worship* and the most recent prayer books of Australia, Canada and Melanesia are used.

Bishops Visitor

UK	Rt Revd Chistopher Chessun, Bishop of Southwark
Australia	Rt Revd Barbara Darling, Bishop of Eastern Region, Melbourne
Canada	Rt Revd Michael Bird, Bishop of Niagara
Solomon Islands	*awaiting appointment*

Address of Affiliated Community
Community of the Love of God (*Orthodox Syrian*)
Nazareth, Kadampanad South 691553, Pathanamthitta District, Kerala, INDIA
Tel: 473 4822146

Community of the Sisters of the Love of God

SLG

Founded 1906

Convent of the Incarnation
Fairacres
Parker Street
Oxford
OX4 1TB
UK
Tel: 01865 721301
Fax: 01865 250798
Email:
sisters@slg.org.uk
Guest Sister:
guests@slg.org.uk

Website:
www.slg.org.uk

Matins
6.00 am (6.15 am Sun & Solemnities)

Terce & Mass
9.05 am (Sat no Mass)

Sext 12.15 pm

None
2.05 pm (3.05 pm Sun)

Vespers 5.30 pm

Compline 8.05 pm (7.35 pm in Winter)

A contemplative community with a strong monastic tradition founded in 1906, which seeks to witness to the priority of God and to respond to the love of God – God's love for us and our love for God. We believe that we are called to live a substantial degree of withdrawal, in order to give ourselves to a spiritual work of prayer which, beginning and ending in the praise and worship of God, is essential for the peace and well-being of the world. Through offering our lives to God within the Community, and through prayer and daily life together, we seek to deepen our relationship with Jesus Christ and one another. The Community has always drawn upon the spirituality of Carmel; life and prayer in silence and solitude is an important dimension in our vocation. The Community also draws from other traditions; therefore our Rule is not specifically Carmelite. Another important ingredient is an emphasis on the centrality of Divine Office and Eucharist together in choir, inspired partly by the Benedictine way of life.

SISTER MARGARET THERESA SLG
(Revd Mother, assumed office 24 June 2007)
SISTER CLARE LOUISE SLG (*Prioress)*

Sister Mary Magdalene
Sister Mary Margaret
Sister Benedicta
Sister Isabel
Sister Adrian
Sister Anne
Sister Jane Frances
Sister Mary Kathleen
Sister Edwina
Sister Barbara June
Sister Susan
Sister Edmée
Sister Christine
Sister Rosemary
Sister Helen Columba
Sister Catherine
Sister Julie
Sister Shirley Clare
Sister Avis Mary
Sister Alison
Sister Tessa
Sister Raphael
Sister Stephanie Thérèse
Sister Freda
Sister Judith *(Novice Guardian)*
Sister Eve
Sister Elizabeth
Sister Helen

Postulants: 1

Obituaries

3 Mar 2012 Sister Cynthia, aged 92, professed 36 years
8 Feb 2013 Sister Josephine, aged 88, professed 63 years

Oblates and associates

The Community includes Oblate Sisters, who are called to the contemplative life in the world rather than within the monastic enclosure. There are three other groups of associates: Priest Associates, Companions, and the Fellowship of the Love of God. Information about all these may be obtained from the Revd Mother at Fairacres.

Community Publication: *Fairacres Chronicle.*
Published twice a year by SLG Press (see under Community Wares).

Community Wares
SLG Press publishes the *Fairacres Chronicle* and a range of books and pamphlets on prayer and spirituality. Contact details:
The Editor, SLG Press, Convent of the Incarnation, Fairacres, Parker Street, Oxford OX4 1TB, UK
Tel: 01865 241874 Fax: 01865 241889
Best to telephone: Mon-Fri 10.00 am – 2.45 pm. A message can be left if there is no-one currently in the office.
Email: General matters: editor@slgpress.co.uk
Orders only: orders@slgpress.co.uk Website: www.slgpress.co.uk

Guest and Retreat Facilities
There is limited accommodation for private retreats, for both men and women, at Fairacres. Please write to or email the Guest Sister to make a booking.
Email: guests@slg.org.uk Tel (for guest sister): 01865 258152 (with voicemail)

Most convenient time to telephone:
10.30 am – 12 noon; 3.30 pm – 4.30 pm; 6.00 pm – 7.00 pm
Sunday and Friday afternoons, and Saturdays, are ordinarily covered by an answer phone, but messages are cleared after Vespers.

Office Book: SLG Office

Bishop Visitor: Rt Revd Michael Lewis, Bishop of Cyprus & the Gulf

Registered Charity: No. 261722
SLG Charitable Trust Ltd: registered in England 990049

Sister Mary Magdalene SLG on her 100th birthday.

Community of the Sisters of Melanesia

CSM

Founded 1980

KNT/Headquarter
Verana'aso
PO Box 19
Honiara
SOLOMON ISLANDS

First Office, Mattins & Mass 5.45 am

Morning Office
7.45 am

Mid-day Office & Intercession
11.55 am

Afternoon Office
1.30 pm

Evensong & Meditation 5.30 pm

Compline 8.45 pm

Office Book
CSM Office Book (adapted from MBH Office book)

The community of the Sisters of Melanesia is a sisterhood of women in Melanesia. It was founded by Nester Tiboe and three young women of Melanesia on 17 November 1980. Nester believed that a Religious community of women in Melanesia was needed for the work of evangelism and mission, similar to the work of the Melanesian Brotherhood, founded by Brother Ini Kopuria.

On 17 November 1980, the four young women made their promises of Poverty, Celibacy, and Obedience to serve in the community. The ceremony took place at St Hilda's Day at Bunana Island and officiated by the Most Reverend Norman Kitchener Palmer, the second Archbishop of the Province of Melanesia.

The community aims to offer young women in Melanesia an opportunity of training for ministry and mission, so that they may serve Christ in the church and society where they live. To provide pastoral care for women and teenage children and uphold the Christian principles of family life. To be in partnership with the Melanesian Brotherhood and other Religious communities by proclaiming the Gospel of Jesus Christ in urban and rural areas in the islands. To give God the honour and glory, and to extend His Kingdom in the world.

Professed. c. 50, Noviciate c. 40

Addresses of other houses in the Solomon Islands

Joe Wate Household, Longa Bay, Waihi Parish, Southern Region, Malaita

Marau Missionary Household, Guadalcanal

NAT Household, Mbokoniseu, Vutu, Ghaobata Parish, East Honiara, Guadalcanal

Sir Ellison L. Pogo Household, Honiara

Community Wares

Vestments, altar linen, weaving and crafts.

Associates: The supporters of the Community of the Sisters of Melanesia are called Associates, a group established in 1990. It is an organization for men and women, young and old, and has over one thousand members, including many young boys and girls. All promise to uphold the Sisters in prayer, and they are a great support in many ways. The Associates of the Community of the Sisters of Melanesia are in the Solomon Islands, Australia and Canada.

Bishop Visitor

Most Revd David Vunagi, Archbishop of Melanesia

Community of the Transfiguration

CT

Founded 1898

495 Albion Avenue
Cincinnati
Ohio 45246
USA
Tel: 513 771 5291
Fax: 513 771 0839
Email:
ctsisters@aol.com

Website www.ctsisters.org

Lauds, Morning Prayer
6.30 am

Holy Eucharist 7.00 am

Noon Office 12.30 pm

Evensong 5.00 pm

Compline 8.00 pm

Office Book
CT Office Book
& the
Book of Common Prayer

Community Publication
The Quarterly

Bishop Visitor
Rt Revd Christopher Epting

The Community of the Transfiguration, founded in 1898 by Eva Lee Matthews, is a Religious community of women dedicated to the mystery of the Transfiguration. Our life is one of prayer and service, reflecting the spirit of Mary and Martha, shown forth in spiritual, educational and social ministries. The Mother House of the community is located in Cincinnati, Ohio, where our ministries include a retreat and spirituality center, a school and a recreation center. The community also offers a retreat ministry on the West Coast; and in the Dominican Republic, the Sisters minister to malnourished children and their families through medical clinics and a school. The Sisters live their life under the vows of poverty, chastity and obedience. The motto of the community is Benignitas, Simplicitas and Hilaritas – Kindness, Simplicity and Joy.

Associates & Oblates
The Community has Associates and Oblates.

Other addresses

Transfiguration Spirituality Center, 469 Albion Avenue, Cincinnati, Ohio 45246, USA
Website: tscretreats.org

Bethany School, 555 Albion Avenue, Cincinnati, Ohio 45246, USA
Website: www.bethanyschool.org

Sisters of the Transfiguration, 1633 "D" Street, Eureka, California 95501, USA

St Monica's Recreation Center, 10022 Chester Road, Cincinnati, Ohio 45215, USA

Dominican Republic Ministry:
Sister Jean Gabriel CT, DMG # 13174 *or*
Sister Priscilla Jean CT, DMG # 19105
Agape Flights, 100 Airport Avenue,
Venice, Florida 34285, USA

Community history and books

Mrs Harlan Cleveland, *Mother Eva Mary CT: The story of a foundation,* Morehouse, Milwaukee, WI, 1929.

Sibyl Harton, *Windfall of Light: a study of the Vocation of Mother Eva Mary CT*, Roessler, Cincinnati, OH, 1968.

Guest and Retreat Facilities

Transfiguration Spirituality Center: 40 beds
Various guest houses and rooms: 16 beds.

Fikambanan'ny Mpanompovavin I Jesoa Kristy

(Society of the Servants of Jesus Christ)

FMJK

Founded 1985

Convent Hasina, BP 28
Ambohidratrimo 105
Antananarivo 101
MADAGASCAR

Bishop Visitor
Most Revd Ranarivello Samoelajaona, Archbishop of the Indian Ocean

The FMJK sisters were founded by Canon Hall Speers in 1985. They live in the village of Tsinjohasina, on the high plateau above the rice fields, situated some fifteen kilometres from Antananarivo, the capital of Madagascar. The sisters work in the village dispensary and are active in visiting, Christian teaching and pastoral work in the villages around. They are an independent community but have been nurtured by a connection with CSMV, Wantage, in the UK.

SISTER JACQUELINE FMJK
(*Masera Tonia, assumed office 5 June 2002*)
SISTER CHAPITRE FMJK *(Prioress)*

Sister Ernestine
Sister Georgette
Sister Isabelle
Sister Odette
Sister Voahangy
Sister Vololona
Sister Fanja

Novices: 1 (Angeline)
Postulants: 1 (Irène)

Community Wares: Crafts and embroidery.

Office Book: FMJK Office and Prayer Book

Other house
Antaralava, Soamanandray, BP 28, Ambohidratrimo 105, Antananarivo 101, MADAGASCAR

Little Brothers of Francis

LBF

Founded 1987

Franciscan Hermitage
"Eremophilia"
PO Box 162
Tabulam
NSW 2469
AUSTRALIA

We are a community of Brothers who desire to deepen our relationship with God through prayer, manual work, community, and times of being alone in our hermitages. We follow the Rule written by Saint Francis for Hermitages in which three or four brothers live in each fraternity. As others join us we envisage a federation of fraternities with three or four in each. Each Brother has responsibility for certain areas of community life. Decision-making is by consensus.

There are five sources of inspiration for the Little Brothers of Francis. They are:

The four Gospels: Matthew, Mark, Luke and John are central to our spirituality, and the main source material for our meditation and prayer life.

St Francis: Francis would recall Christ's words and life through persistent meditation on the Gospels for his deep desire was to love Christ and live a Christ-

Website: www.franciscanhermitage.org

Brothers have times of Solitude in their hermitage, which vary from a day to weeks or months, where they have their own personal rhythm of prayer and manual work.

Vigil Office followed by Lectio Divina (private) 2.00 am or 4.00 am

Meditation 6.00 am

Angelus and Mattins 7.00 am

Terce 9.00 am

Angelus and Sext 12 noon

None (private) 3.00 pm

Vespers 6.00 pm

Compline 8.00 pm

Office Book
LBF Office book, developed to provide for our needs as a Franciscan Hermitage

Bishop Protector
Rt Revd Godfrey Fryar, Bishop of Rockhampton, Qld

centred life. He was a man of prayer and mystic who sought places of solitude, and hermitages played a central role in his life. Though the early brothers embraced a mixed life of prayer and ministry, Francis wanted places of seclusion – hermitages, for the primacy of prayer, in which three or four brothers lived, and for which he wrote a rule.

St Francis's Rule for Hermitages: In his brief rule for life within the hermitage, Francis avoided a detailed document and set out the principles that are important: liturgy of the Hours is the focus, and sets the rhythm of the daily prayer; each hermitage was to have at the most four Brothers, which meant they would be both 'little' and 'fraternal'; within this framework, Brothers could withdraw for periods of solitude; the hermitages were not to be places or centres of ministry.

Desert Fathers: Their stories contain a profound wisdom for any who are serious about the inner spiritual journey. This is why they have held such prominence in monastic circles in both East and West down through the centuries, and why they are a priority source for us.

The Land: A strong connectedness to a spiritual and physical home has always been a part of our charism, not unlike St Francis' love for his 'Portiuncula' or Little Portion. In shaping and building our hermitage over the years our environment has shaped and formed us. Droughts, bushfires, floods and bountiful years have brought us into a real and living relationship with the land in this place.

Brother Howard LBF
Brother Wayne LBF
Brother Geoffrey Adam LBF

Friends
Friends are individuals, or self-organized groups, who value the contemplative life as lived by the Brothers and support them in various ways.

Contact person for Australia:
Father Dennis Claughton Email: parish@ang.org.au

Contact person for New Zealand:
Ian Lothian Email: ianlothian@xtra.com.nz

Community Publication: The *Bush Telegraph.*
Contact the Brothers for a subscription, which is by donation.

Community Wares: Hand-carved holding crosses, jam, marmalade, cards and honey.

Guest and Retreat Facilities: There is a guest hermitage for one person. A fee of $60 per night is negotiable.

The Melanesian Brotherhood

MBH

Founded 1925

Email: mbhches @solomon.com.sb

SOLOMON ISLANDS REGION
The Motherhouse of the Melanesian Brotherhood
Tabalia
PO Box 1479
Honiara
SOLOMON ISLANDS
TEL: +677 26355
FAX: +677 23079

PAPUA NEW GUINEA REGION
Dobuduru Regional Headquarters
Haruro
PO Box 29
Popondetta
Oro Province
PAPUA NEW GUINEA

SOUTHERN REGION
Tumsisiro Regional Headquarters
PO Box 05
Lolowai, Ambae
VANUATU

The Melanesian Brotherhood was founded by Ini Kopuria, a native Solomon Islander from Guadalcanal, in 1925. Its main purpose was evangelistic, to take and live the Gospel in the most remote islands and villages throughout the Solomon Islands, among people who had not heard the message of Christ. The Brotherhood's method is to live as brothers to the people, respecting their traditions and customs: planting, harvesting, fishing, house building, eating and sharing with the people in all these things. Kopuria believed that Solomon Islanders should be converted in a Melanesian way.

Today, the work of the Brotherhood has broadened to include work and mission among both Christians and non-Christians. The Melanesian Brotherhood now has three Regions in the Pacific: Solomon Islands (includes Brothers in the Philippines and Vancouver); Papua New Guinea; and Southern (Vanuatu, New Caledonia & the Diocese of Polynesia). There is a Region for Companions and any Brothers in Europe.

Following an ethnic conflict in the Solomon Islands 1998-2003, the Melanesian Brotherhood have been increasingly called upon as peace makers and reconcilers, work for which they were awarded the United Nations Pacific Peace Prize in 2004.

The Brotherhood has also led missions in New Zealand, Australia, Philippines and UK; their missionary approach includes music, dance and a powerful use of drama. There was a further mission in the UK in 2013 conducted with members of four Anglican Religious communities in Melanesia, entitled the Simply Living Mission. The Brothers and Sisters visited seven dioceses in England.

The Brotherhood aims to live the Gospel in a direct and simple way following Christ's example of prayer, mission and service. The Brothers take the vows of poverty, chastity and obedience, but these are not life vows but for a period of three years, which can be renewed. They train for four years as novices and normally make their vows as Brothers at the Feast of St Simon and St Jude. Most of the Brothers are laymen but a few are ordained.

THE MOST REVD DAVID VUNAGI,
ARCHBISHOP OF MELANESIA *(Father of the Brotherhood)*

BROTHER MATTHIAS TOVOTASI MBH
(Head Brother, assumed office October 2011)
BROTHER EZEKIEL TEMA MBH *(Assistant Head Brother)*

Timetable of the Main House

First Office and Mattins
5.50 am
(6.20 am Sun & holidays)

Holy Communion
6.15 am
(7.15 am Sun & holidays)

Morning Office
8.00 am

Midday Office
12 noon
(Angelus on Sun & holidays)

Afternoon Office
1.30 pm
(not Sun & holidays)

Evensong 5.30 pm
(6.00 pm Sun & holidays)

Last Office 9.00 pm

Office Book
Offices and Prayers of the Melanesian Brotherhood 1996
(not for public sale)

Website:
www.orders.anglican.org/mbh

SOLOMON ISLANDS REGION
THE MOST REVD DAVID VUNAGI,
ARCHBISHOP OF MELANESIA *(Regional Father)*
election pending for Regional Head Brother
Mr Alphonse Garimae *(Brotherhood Secretary)*
Brother Jesse Araiasi MBH *(Regional Secretary)*
Brother Nathan Kusa MBH *(Companions Chief Secretary)*
Brother Nelson Bako MBH *(Mission Coordinator)*
Brother Jeffrey Akoai MBH *(Chief Tutor)*

SOUTHERN REGION
THE RT REVD JAMES LIGO,
BISHOP OF VANUATU & NEW CALEDONIA
(Regional Father)
BROTHER OBED JOHNSON LERWELGAN MBH
(Regional Head Brother)
To be appointed (Regional Secretary)
To be appointed (Regional Companions Secretary)

PAPUA NEW GUINEA REGION
election pending for Archbishop of PNG
(Regional Father)
BROTHER JOHNSON INGAMAVU MBH
(Regional Head Brother)
Brother Martin Ogoba MBH *(Regional Secretary)*
To be appointed (Regional Companions Secretary)

EUROPE REGION *(for Companions)*
THE RT REVD DR ROWAN WILLIAMS, LORD WILLIAMS OF OYSTERMOUTH
former Archbishop of Canterbury
(Regional Father)

Professed Brothers: 280
(Solomon Islands: 148; PNG: 80: Southern Region: 49: Palawan: 3; Canada: 1)
Novices: 173
(Solomon Islands: 102; PNG: 12: Southern Region: 53; Palawan: 6)

Obituaries

16 Jan 2012 Brother Jacob Kivia MBH, years of service 2000-2012

16 Mar 2013 Brother Webster Diala MBH, aged 42, years of service 1997-2013

SOLOMON ISLANDS REGION

The Solomon Islands Region is divided into Sections according to each Diocese. Each Section has its own Section Father.

CENTRAL MELANESIA DIOCESAN SECTION

Section Father: The Most Revd David Vunagi, Archbishop of Melanesia
Address for all SI houses in this Section:

PO Box 1479, Honiara, Guadacanal, SOLOMON ISLANDS

BROTHER MICHAEL BOSAWAI MBH *(Section Elder Brother)*
BROTHER BRIAN DO'ORO MBH *(Elder Brother)*
Central Headquarters, Tabalia
BROTHER BEN ARIEL MBH *(Brother in charge)*
St Barnabas Cathedral Working Household, Honiara Tel: 24609 Fax: 23079
BROTHER THOMAS DAKATIA MBH *(Brother in charge)*
Bishopsdale Working Household, Honiara Tel: 27695 Fax: 23079
BROTHER SIMON PETER MBH *(Brother in charge)*
Iglesia Philipina Independiente (I.F.I.), De los Reyos Road 2, 5300 Puerto Princesa City, 5300 Palawan, PHILIPPINES

CENTRAL SOLOMONS DIOCESAN SECTION

Section Father: The Rt Revd Ben Seka, Bishop of Central Solomons
BROTHER CECIL MANEKETA MBH *(Section Elder Brother)*
BROTHER JOHN SELA MBH *(Elder Brother)*

Thomas Peo Section Headquarters,
c/o Central Solomons Diocesan Office, PO Box 52, Tulagi, Central Province

Address for other houses in this section:

c/o Central Headquarters, Tabalia, PO Box 1479, Honiara

BROTHER JEFFREY HAGAMAKARIA MBH *(Elder Brother)*
Ini Kopuria Household, Kolina, Guadalcanal
BROTHER ROBERT BEREOKA MBH *(Elder Brother)*
Olimauri Household, Mbambanakira, Guadalcanal
BROTHER NELSON BAIVALE MBH *(Elder Brother)*
Calvary Household, Surapau, Guadalcanal
BROTHER THOMAS KAULA MBH *(Brother in charge)*
Selwyn Rapu Working Household, Guadalcanal
BROTHER STEPHEN NAU MBH *(Brother in charge)*
Working Household, Bellona Island

MALAITA DIOCESAN SECTION

Section Father: The Rt Revd Samuel Sahu, Bishop of Malaita
Assistant Section Father: The Rt Revd Alfred Hou

All Households in Malaita are temporarily closed down except Apalolo and Tasman.

BROTHER DON SMITH BOLAMANA MBH *(Elder Brother)*

Apalolo Household, South Malaita
c/o Malaita Diocesan Office, PO Box 7, Auki, Malaita Province

BROTHER ALLEN KIKOA MBH *(Brother in charge)*

Tasman Working Household, Nukumanu Atoll (PNG), PO Box 1479, Honiara, Solomon Islands

YSABEL DIOCESAN SECTION

Section Father: The Rt Revd Richard Naramana, Bishop of Ysabel

Address for houses in this section:

c/o Ysabel Diocesan Office, PO Box 6, Buala, Isabel Province

BROTHER ISSCHER NICHOLSON MBH *(Section Elder Brother)*
BROTHER ISELWYN MANO MBH *(Elder Brother)*
Welchman Section Headquarters, Sosoilo
BROTHER JOHN MARK SELENI MBH *(Elder Brother)*
Poropeta Household, Kia
BROTHER JONATHAN LOKUMANA MBH *(Brother in charge)*
Alfred Hill Working Household, Jejevo
BROTHER NATHANIEL ROW MBH *(Brother in charge)*
Hulon Working Household, Yandina, Russell Islands
BROTHER REGINALD SADE MBH *(Elder Brother)*
John Pihavaka Household, Gizo
BROTHER ZEPHANIAH ZAZAGA MBH *(Brother in charge)*
Noro Working Household, New Georgia Island
BROTHER PHILIP HOUNIPUA MBH *(Brother in charge)*
Pupuku Working Household, Choiseul Province

HANUATO'O DIOCESAN SECTION

Section Father: The Rt Revd Alfred Karibongi, Bishop of Hanuato'o

Address for houses in this section:

c/o Hanuato'o Diocesan Office, Kirakira, Makira Province

BROTHER ROBERT HARRISON MBH *(Section Elder Brother)*
BROTHER NICKSON VAHI MBH *(Elder Brother)*
Fox Section Headquarters, Poronaohe, Makira
BROTHER HILTON SANAU MBH *(Elder Brother)*
Simon Sigai Household, Makira
BROTHER JAMES TATAHI MBH *(Brother in charge)*
Mumunioa Working Household, Makira
BROTHER CLEMENT BUBE MBH *(Brother in charge)*
John Hubert Waene Working Household, Makira

TEMOTU DIOCESAN SECTION

Section Father: The Rt Revd George Takeli, Bishop of Temotu

Address for houses in this section:

c/o Temotu Diocesan Office, Lata, Temotu Province

BROTHER PHILIP BULA MBH *(Section Elder Brother)*
BROTHER SIMON PETER KAKAI MBH *(Elder Brother)*
Makio Section Headquarters, Santa Cruz Island

BROTHER STANLEY OIGA MBH *(Brother in charge)*
Utupua Working Household, Utupua
BROTHER NELSON VAVIO MBH *(Brother in charge)*
Lata Working Household, Santa Cruz Island

SOUTHERN REGION

VANUATU SECTION

Section Father: The Rt Revd James Ligo, Bishop of Vanuatu & New Caledonia

Tumsisiro Regional Headquarters, Ambae
Saratabulu Household, West Ambae
Hinge Household, Lorevilko, East Santo
Suriau Household, Big Bay, Santo Bush
Caulton Weris Working Household
Patterson Household, Port Vila

BANKS & TORRES SECTION

Section Father: election pending, Bishop of Banks & Torres

Lency Section Headquarters, Vanua Lava Island
Towia Working Household

PAPUA NEW GUINEA REGION

POPONDOTA SECTION

Section Father: The Rt Revd Lindsley Ihove, Bishop of Popondetta
Dobuduru Regional Headquarters, Popondetta
Gorari Household; Nedewari Household; Domara Household

PORT MORESBY SECTION

Section Father: The Rt Revd Peter Ramsden, Bishop of Port Moresby

ATS Section Headquarters, Oro Village
Pivo Household; Moro Guina

DOGURA SECTION

Section Father: The Rt Revd Clyde Igara, Bishop of Dogura

Sirisiri Section Headquarters
Pumani Household; Podagha Project Household; Tabai Isu Working Household

AIPO RONGO SECTION

Section Father: The Rt Revd Nathan Ingen, Bishop of Aipo Rongo

Aiome Section Headquarters
Kumburub Household; Kuiyama Household; Saniap Working Household

NEW GUINEA ISLANDS SECTION

Section Father: The Rt Revd Allan Migi, Bishop of New Guinea Islands

Hosea Sakira Section Headquarters
Aseke Household; Saksak Household

Companions

The Melanesian Brotherhood is supported both in prayer, in their work and materially by the Companions of the Melanesian Brotherhood (C.O.M.B.). They have their own Handbook with both Pacific and Europe versions.

For more information about becoming a Companion, please contact:
Mrs Barbara Molyneux, 11 Milton Crescent, Heswall, Merseyside, CH60 5SS, UK
Tel: (0)151 342 6327 Email: bjmolyneux@hotmail.com

or Companions Chief Secretary, PO Box 1479, Honiara, Solomon Islands
or at the same address: Mr Alphonse Garimae, Secretary to the Brotherhood,
Tel: +677 26377 (8 am – 4 pm) Email: agarimae@yahoo.com

Alongside Companions, the Brotherhood also has associates whose ministry is more closely associated with the community, except that they do not take the threefold vow. They work voluntarily without wages just like the brothers.

Community Publications

Companions' Newsletter for the Europe Region (once a year)
– contact Mrs Barbara Molyneux, address under 'Companions' below.

Community History and other books

Brian Macdonald-Milne, *The True Way of Service: The Pacific Story of the Melanesian Brotherhood, 1925–2000,* Christians Aware, Leicester, 2003.

Richard Carter, *In Search of the Lost: the death and life of seven peacemakers of the Melanesian Brotherhood*, Canterbury Press, Norwich, 2006.

Charles Montgomery, *The Shark God: Encounters with myth and magic in the South Pacific,* Fourth Estate/Harper Collins, London, 2006.

Guest and Retreat Facilities

The Community offers hospitality ministry through Chester Rest House in Honiara, Solomon Islands. Two Brothers are mandated to welcome guests and offer a Christian welcome to any person who may want accommodation in their Rest House. This Rest House was funded by Chester Diocese in UK. It is an alcohol-free environment and every guest is ensured to be safe and enjoy the environment. It has 8 twin-bedded rooms, self-catering at £30 per room per night, and 8 self-contained single rooms, self-catering at £75 per room per night. A conference room to accommodate 10–15 people is also available at £10 per day, self-catering. Contacts for advance bookings can be made through email: mbhches@solomon.com.sb or telephone +677 26355.

All the Brotherhood's Headquarters and Section Headquarters can provide simple accommodation for visitors. Retreats can be made by prior arrangement with the relevant Chaplain at Central, Regional or Section headquarters. Tabalia Headquarters has a guest house with eight twin-bedded rooms, self-catering, no cost but a contribution is much appreciated. Meetings, workshops and Retreats can be made by prior arrangement with the Section Elder Brother/Elder Brother at Tabalia.

Women are not allowed to enter the Brotherhood square (St Simon & Jude), which usually is outside the chapel of every Brotherhood station (not in Honiara). Women are not allowed to enter Brothers' dormitories.

Order of the Holy Cross

OHC

Founded 1884

Holy Cross Monastery
PO Box 99
(1615 Rt. 9W)
West Park
NY 12493
USA
Tel: 845 384 6660
Fax: 845 384 6031

Email: superior@ gmail.com

Website: www. holycrossmonastery. com

Mattins 7.00 am

Holy Eucharist 9.00 am

Midday Prayer 12 noon

Vespers 5.00 pm

Compline 8.10 pm

Mondays are observed as a sabbath day on which there are no scheduled liturgies.

The Order of the Holy Cross is a Benedictine monastic community open to both lay and ordained. The principles governing the Order's life are those of *The Rule of St Benedict* and *The Rule of the Order of the Holy Cross*, written by its founder James Otis Sargent Huntington.

The liturgical life of each house centers around the corporate praying of the Divine Office and the celebration of the Holy Eucharist. Members also expected to spend time in private prayer and meditation.

The work of the Order is varied, depending on the nature of the household and the gifts and talents of its members. Houses vary from traditional monastic centers with active retreat ministries to urban houses from which brothers go forth to minister. A small number of brothers live independently as Monks Not In Residence.

Members are engaged in preaching, teaching, counseling and spiritual direction, parish and diocesan support work, the arts, evangelism, hospice care, and ministry with the homeless. The South African community administers educational and scholarship programs for local children and operates a primary school.

Other Addresses

Mount Calvary Monastery and Retreat House, PO Box 1296, Santa Barbara, CA 93102, USA
Tel: 805 682 4117
Website: www.mount-calvary.org

Holy Cross Priory, 204 High Park Avenue, Toronto, Ontario M6P 2S6, CANADA
Tel: 416 767 9081 **Fax: 416 767 4692**
Website: www.ohc-canada.org

Mariya uMama weThemba Monastery, PO Box 6013, Grahamstown 6141, SOUTH AFRICA
Tel: 46 622 8111 **Fax: 46 622 6424**
Website: www.umaria.co.za

Community Publications

Holy Cross News, published annually.
The following are three times a year (cost by donation):
Mundi Medicina (West Park, NY);
Uxolo (Grahamstown, South Africa);
Mount Calvary Community at St Mary's (Santa Barbara, CA);
Holy Cross Priory (Toronto, Ontario)

Office Book

A Monastic Breviary (OHC) or Lauds and Vespers (Camaldolese Monks OSB).

ROBERT LEO SEVENSKY OHC
(*Superior, assumed office 2008*)
SCOTT WESLEY BORDEN OHC (*Assistant Superior*)

Thomas Schultz
Christian George Swayne
Laurence Harms
Samuel DeMerell
Rafael Campbell-Dixon
Bede Thomas Mudge
Ronald Haynes
Brian Youngward
Nicholas Radlemiller
Roy Parker
Adrian Gill
David Bryan Hoopes
Adam McCoy
Carl Sword
William Brown
Timothy Jolley
James Robert Hagler
Leonard Abbah
Reginald-Martin Crenshaw
Richard Paul Vaggione
Lary Pearce
Andrew Colquhoun
John Forbis
Bernard Jean Delcourt
James Randall Greve
Daniel Ludik
Robert Magliula
James Dowd
Smache Josias Morobi
Charles Julian Mizelle
Roger Stewart
José Folgueira

Novices: 1

Associates

The Associates of Holy Cross are men and women of many different Christian traditions affliated to the Order through a Rule of Life and annual retreats and reports.

Guest and Retreat Facilities

WEST PARK: 39 rooms at US$75 per night ($95 weekends). Accommodations for couples and individuals. Closed Mondays.
SANTA BARBARA: 24 beds at US$90 per night ($100 weekends). Closed Mondays.
GRAHAMSTOWN: 19 rooms (doubles and singles). Apply to Guestmaster for rates. Closed Mondays.
TORONTO: 2 single rooms. Canadian $40 per night.

Community History

Adam Dunbar McCoy OHC, *Holy Cross: A Century of Anglican Monasticism,* Morehouse-Barlow, Wilton, CT, 1987.

Community Wares:
Incense and Publications (West Park).

Bishop Visitor:
Rt Revd Mark S Sisk

Order of the Holy Paraclete

OHP

Founded 1915

St Hilda's Priory
Sneaton Castle, Whitby
North Yorkshire
YO21 3QN
UK
Tel: 01947 602079
Fax: 01947 820854
Email: ohppriorywhitby @btinternet.com

Website:
www.ohpwhitby.org

Morning Prayer
7.30 am

Eucharist
7.45 am (Mon, Wed, Fri & Sat)
9.30 am (Sun)
12.30 pm (Thu)

Midday Office
12.40 pm
12.15 pm (Thu)
12 noon (Sat)

Vespers 6.00 pm
(4.30 pm Sun)

Compline 9.00 pm
(7.45 pm Fri)

No services in chapel on Tuesdays

Founded as an educational order, the sisters have diversified their work in UK to include hospitality, retreats and spiritual direction, hospital chaplaincy, inner city involvement, preaching and mission, and development work overseas.

The Mother House is at St. Hilda's Priory, Whitby. Some sisters work in the adjacent Sneaton Castle Centre, which caters for a wide variety of day and residential groups. Other UK houses are in York, Dormanstown (near Redcar), Bishopsthorpe and Sleights (near Whitby).

The Order has had a long-standing commitment to Africa since 1926. Most of the work begun by the sisters has been handed over to local people who continue to run the projects. Sister Benedicta continues to live and work in Manzini, Swaziland, raising school fees and helping with the education of orphans. The Order has two houses in Ghana. In Jachie, Sister Aba runs an eye clinic while Sister Alberta teaches in a kindergarten. In Sunyani, Sister Mavis acts as Bishop's secretary. She and Sister Sabina also make communion hosts, have a shop and are beginning a small vocational school teaching computer and crafts to girls who were unable to complete their education. Both houses still foster vocations to the Religious life.

Central to the Order's life in all its houses are the Divine Office and Eucharist, and a strong emphasis on corporate activity.

Houses in the UK

Beachcliff, 14 North Promenade, Whitby, N. Yorks YO21 3JX Tel: 01947 601968
Email: srmuriel@hotmail.co.uk

St Oswald's Pastoral Centre, Woodlands Drive, Sleights, Whitby, N Yorks YO21 1RY
Tel: 01947 810496 Email: ohpstos@globalnet.co

1A Minster Court, York YO7 2JJ
Tel: 01904 557276
Email: sistersohp@googlemail.com

3 Acaster Lane, Bishopsthorpe, York, N Yorks YO23 2SA Tel: 01904 777294
Email: ohpbishopsthorpe@archbishopofyork.org

All Saints House, South Avenue, Dormanstown, TS10 5LL Tel: 01642 486424
Email: sisteranita@btinternet.com

Houses in Africa

Resurrection House, PO Box 596, Sunyani, Brone Ahafo, GHANA Tel: 233 243 706840
Email: nyamebekyere2010@yahoo.com

Jachie, Convent of the Holy Spirit, PO Box AH 9375, Ahinsan, Kumasi Ashanti, GHANA, West Africa
Tel: 233 242 203432 Email: ohpjac@yahoo.com

Sister Dorothy Stella OHP
(Prioress, assumed office 15 July 2005)
Sister Heather Francis OHP *(Sub-Prioress)*

Sister Ursula
Sister Barbara Maude
Sister Olive
Sister Marjorie
Sister Janet
Sister Alison
Sister Michelle
Sister Mary Nina
Sister Muriel
Sister Anita
Sister Nancye
Sister Patricia
Sister Hilary Joy
Sister Grace
Sister Janette
Sister Janet Elizabeth
Sister Betty
Sister Benedicta
Sister Caroline
Sister Margaret Elizabeth
Sister Marion Eva
Sister Erika
Sister Maureen Ruth
Sister Margaret Anne
Sister Jocelyn
Sister Carole
Sister Mavis
Sister Linda
Sister Aba
Sister Pam
Sister Helen
Sister Karan
Sister Margaret
Sister Alberta
Sister Sabina
Sister Helena

Novices: 1

Obituaries

29 Dec 2011	Sister Heather, aged 82, professed 51 years
17 Feb 2012	Sister Stella Mary, aged 92, professed 52 years
31 Mar 2012	Sister Mary Margaret, aged 92, professed 50 years
10 Jul 2012	Sister Constance, aged 94, professed 58 years
14 Aug 2012	Sister Gillian, aged 74, professed 47 years

Tertiaries and Associates

The OHP Tertiary Order is a fellowship of women and men, united under a common discipline, based on the OHP Rule, and supporting one another in their discipleship. Tertiaries are ordinary Christians seeking to offer their lives in the service of Christ, helping the Church and showing love in action. They value their links with each other and with the Sisters of the Order, at Whitby and elsewhere, and when possible they meet together for mutual support in prayer, discussion and ministry. The Tertiary Order is open to communicant members of any Trinitarian Church.

The OHP Associates are friends of the Order who desire to keep in touch with its life and work while serving God in their various spheres. Many have made initial contact with the Sisters through a visit or parish mission, or via another Associate. All are welcome, married or single, clergy or lay, regardless of religious affiliation.

The Friends of OHP is a group open to men and women, of any religious affiliation or none, with an interest in OHP. The annual subscription of £10 includes a copy of the OHP newsletter and an invitation to an annual meeting.

Community Publication: *OHP Newsletter*, twice a year. Write to The Publications Secretary at St Hilda's Priory. Annual subscription: £4.50 for the UK, £5.50 for the rest of Europe and £7.00 for the rest of the world.

Community History

A Foundation Member, *Fulfilled in Joy,* Hodder & Stoughton, London, 1964.
Rosalin Barker, *The Whitby Sisters,* OHP, Whitby, 2001.

Community Wares: Cards and craft items. St Hilda's Priory has a shop selling books, cards, church supplies and religious artefacts.
Email: sneatonshop@btinternet.com

Guest and Retreat Facilities

St Hilda's Priory: six rooms (four single; one double; one twin) available in the Priory or nearby houses. Individuals or small groups are welcome for personal quiet or retreat, day or residential. If requested in advance, some guidance can be provided. There is no programme of retreats at the Priory. Contact the Guest Sister with enquiries and bookings.

Sneaton Castle Centre: seventy-one rooms (one hundred and twenty beds). The Centre has conference, lecture and seminar rooms with full audio-visual equipment, and recreational facilities. There are two spacious dining rooms and an excellent range of menus. Guests are welcome to join the community for worship or to arrange their own services in the Chapel.

Contact the Bookings Secretary, Sneaton Castle Centre, Whitby YO21 3QN.
Tel: 01947 600051 See also the website: www.sneatoncastle.co.uk

St Oswald's Pastoral Centre: 13 rooms (16 beds). 3 self-catering units.

Most convenient time to telephone:: 9 am – 5 pm, Mon-Fri; 10 am – 12 noon Sat

Registered Charity: No. 271117 **Office Book:** OHP Office

Bishop Visitor: Most Revd John Sentamu, Archbishop of York

Order of Julian of Norwich OJN

Founded 1985

2812 Summit Ave
Waukesha
WI 53188-2781
USA
Tel: 262 549 0452
Email: ojn@orderofjulian.org

The Order of Julian of Norwich is a contemplative semi-enclosed Religious order of nuns and monks in the Episcopal Church, living together in one house. We profess traditional vows of poverty, chastity, and obedience, with the added vow of prayer 'in the spirit of our Blessed Mother Saint Julian', the fourteenth-century English anchoress and our patron.

The ministry of the Order to the Church is to be a community of prayer and contemplative presence, expressed in communal liturgical worship in chapel and in the silence and solitude of the cell. Gregorian Chant is used for most of the four-fold Divine Office of the Book of Common Prayer. The Eucharist is the centre of our life, the genesis of our work of contemplative and intercessory prayer. This primary apostolate supports a limited exterior apostolate of spiritual direction, writing, and offering retreats.

Founded in 1985 by the Revd John Swanson, the Order was canonically recognized by the Episcopal Church in

1997, and is affiliated with the Conference of Anglican Religious Orders in the Americas. For further information on the Order or its affiliates, please address the Guardian.

Website
www.
orderofjulian.org

REVD MOTHER HILARY CRUPI OJN
(*Guardian, assumed office 30 April 2010*)
SISTER THERESE POLI OJN *(Warden)*
Revd Father John-Julian Swanson
Sister Cornelia Barry
Brother Barnabas Leben

Silent Prayer/ Morning Prayer
3.45 am

Mass
7.30 am

Midday Office
11.30 am

Silent Prayer/ Evensong
4.00 pm

Compline
7.00 pm

Office Book
The BCP of ECUSA with enrichments

Associates and Oblates

ASSOCIATES

Friends of the Order, desiring a spiritual bond with the Julian Community who keep a simple Rule (one daily Office, Sunday Mass, annual reports to the Warden of Associates) and pledge financial support for the Order.

OBLATES

Persons committed to live the Order's spiritual and contemplative charism in the world under an adaptation of regular vows. They have a Rule of: two BCP Offices daily; three per cent of their tithe to the Order; three hours contemplative prayer a week; a four-day silent retreat annually; Sunday Mass and seven Holy days of Obligation, etc. They make a semi-annual report to the Warden of Oblates.

Guest and Retreat Facilities

Three guest rooms. There is no charge.

Community Publication
Julian's Window quarterly.
Subscription free.
Contact
Sister Cornelia OJN

Community History and other books

Teunisje Velthuizen, ObJN, *One-ed into God: The first decade of the Order of St Julian of Norwich,* The Julian Press, 1996.

Gregory Fruehwirth OJN, *Words for Silence,* Paraclete Press, Orleans, MA, 2008.

John Julian Swanson OJN, *The Complete Julian,* Paraclete Press, Orleans, MA, 2009.

Bishop Visitor
Rt Revd
Wendell N. Gibbs, Jr.,
Bishop of Michigan

Community Wares

The Julian Shop has books, religious articles, many pamphlets written by members.
Email: julianshop@orderofjulian.org

Order of St Anne at Bethany

OSA

Founded 1910

25 Hillside Avenue
Arlington
MA 02476-5818
USA

Tel: 781 643 0921
Fax: 781 648 4547

Email: bethany convent@aol.com

Morning Prayer
7.00 am

Eucharist
8.00 am (Tue-Fri)
7.30 am (Sun)

Midday prayers
12 noon

Evensong 5.00 pm

Compline 7.30 pm

Office Book
SSJE Office Book

We are a small multi-cultural community of women committed to witnessing to the truth that, as Christians, it is here and now that we demonstrate to the Church and the world that the Religious Life lived in community is relevant, interesting, fulfilling and needed in our world and our times. We strive to recognize and value the diversity of persons and gifts. We believe that God has a vision for each one of us and that opportunities to serve the Church and the world are abundant. For this to become real, we know that our spirits and hearts must be enlarged to fit the dimensions of our Church in today's world and the great vision that God has prepared for our Order. We are especially grateful for our continuing ministry within the Diocese of Massachusetts.

The Rule of the Order of St Anne says our houses may be small, but our hearts are larger than houses. Our community has always been 'people-oriented' and we derive a sense of joy and satisfaction in offering hospitality at our Convent, at the Bethany House of Prayer and in our beautiful chapel. Always constant in our lives are our personal prayer and our corporate worship, our vows of Poverty, Celibacy and Obedience, our commitment to spiritual growth and development of mind and talents, and our fellowship with one another and other Religious communities, as friends and sisters.

Sister Ana Clara OSA
(Superior, assumed office 1992)

Sister Olga
Sister Felicitas
Sister Maria Agnes
Sister Maria Teresa

Associates
We have an associate program and continue to receive men and women into this part of our life.

Community Wares: Communion altar bread.

Community History
Sister Johanna OSA (editor), *A Theme for Four Voices,* privately printed, Arlington, Mass., 1985

Revd Charles C Hefling & Sister Ana Clara OSA, *Catch the Vision: celebrating a century of the Order of St Anne,* Order of St Anne-Bethany, Arlington, Mass., 2010

Bishop Visitor: Rt Revd M. Thomas Shaw SSJE,
Bishop of Massachusetts

Guest and Retreat Facilities
The Bethany House of Prayer, 181 Appleton Street, on the grounds of the Convent and Chapel, sponsors, coordinates and offers a variety of programs and events including Quiet Days, Special Liturgies, contemplative prayer, spiritual direction, day-retreats, hospitality and workshops. For more information call 781 648 2433.

Order of St Anne

Chicago

OSA

Founded 1910

1125 North LaSalle Blvd
Chicago
Illinois 60610
USA
Tel: 312 642 3638
Fax: 312 642 3638
Email: stannechicago@hotmail.com
Website: www.orderofstannechicago.org

Matins 6.40 am
Eucharist 7.00 am
(Church of the Ascension)
Terce 8.30 am
Sext 12 noon
Vespers 5.00 pm
Compline 7.00 pm

Office Book: Monastic Diurnal revised

The Order of St. Anne was founded in 1910 by Father Frederick Cecil Powell of the Society of St. John the Evangelist in Arlington Heights, Mass. The Sisters live a modified Benedictine Rule, dedicated to a life of prayer and good works beneficial to all people including children. The Sisters of St. Anne came to Chicago in 1921 invited by then rector of the Church of the Ascension, the Revd Stoskopf, to do parish work and other needed services in the Diocese of Chicago. The Chicago convent is autonomous, although Sisters live as part of the church of the Ascension.

According to our Rule "the Order of St. Anne cannot be designated as professing exclusively the contemplative, the mixed or active spirit" since all three may be found within the Order. The principal of the Order is the life of God within it and whatsoever He may say to us – whether to sit at His feet only or feed His lambs – which we must do. While our works are important, it must be kept in mind that God calls us to a life of prayer. The Sisters are involved in parish work, especially at the Church of the Ascension doing whatever is needed. The sisters also work with the homeless, alcoholics, addicts and other emotionally and mentally disturbed people. The sisters work as teachers, counsellors and hospital chaplains. A future plan is for a recovery home for addicts, alcoholics and emotionally disturbed women.

Sister Judith Marie OSA
(Superior, assumed office 2007)
Sister Barbara Louise OSA
Resident Companion: Ms Dorothy Murray

Obituaries
Nov 2009 Mother Mary Margaret *(former superior)*, aged 91

Associates
We have an associate program for men and women.

Community Publication: PROEIS

Guest and Retreat Facilities
Two guest rooms in Convent (women only). No charge, donations accepted. Individual retreats; spiritual direction and counselling available.

Bishop Visitor: Rt Revd Jeffrey Lee, Bishop of Chicago

Order of St Benedict

St Mark's Abbey, Camperdown

OSB

Founded 1975

Benedictine Abbey
PO Box 111
Camperdown
Victoria 3260
AUSTRALIA

Tel: 3 5593 2348
Fax: 3 5593 2887

Email: benabbey@dodo.com.au

Website: www.benedictineabbey.com.au

Vigils 4.30 am

Lauds 6.30 am

Terce & Conventual Mass 8.15 am

Sext 11.45 am

None 2.10 pm

Vespers 5.00 pm

Compline 7.30 pm

Office Book
Camperdown breviary

The community was founded in the parish of St Mark, Fitzroy, in the archdiocese of Melbourne on 8 November 1975. In 1980, after working in this inner city parish for five years, and after adopting the *Rule of Saint Benedict*, they moved to the country town of Camperdown in the Western District of Victoria. Here the community lives a contemplative monastic life with the emphasis on the balanced life of prayer and work that forms the Benedictine ethos. In 1993, the Chapter decided to admit women and to endeavour to establish a mixed community of monks and nuns. The community supports itself through the operation of a printery, icon reproduction, manufacture of incense, crafts and a small guest house.

In 2005, the Chapter petitioned the Subiaco Cassinese Congregation of the Benedictine Confederation for aggregation to the Congregation. After a period of probation, this was granted on the Feast of SS Peter and Paul 2007. The fruits of our association are already being shown forth.

THE RT REVD DOM MICHAEL KING OSB
(*Abbot, elected 11 July 2002*)

Dom Placid Lawson
Sister Mary Philip Bloore
Sister Raphael Stone
Brother Anselm Johns
Novices: 2

Oblates

There is a small group of clerics and lay people who form the Oblates of St Benedict attached to the community. The group numbers ninety persons from Australia, New Zealand and Canada following the Benedictine life according to their individual situations. Oblates usually visit the monastery once a year and keep in regular contact with the parent community.

Guest and Retreat Facilities

Small guest house (St Joseph's), accommodating 6 people, open to men and women, for private retreats and spiritual direction. Guests eat with the community and are welcome to attend the services in the church. A donation of $70.00 per day is suggested.

Community Publication: The Community produces a newsletter yearly in December.

Community Wares: Printing, icons, cards, incense, devotional items.

Abbot Visitor: Rt Revd Dom Bruno Martin OSB
Diocesan Bishop: Rt Revd Garry Weatherill

Order of St Benedict Community of St Mary at the Cross, Edgware

OSB

Founded 1866

Edgware Abbey
94A Priory Field Drive, Edgware
Middlesex
HA8 9PU
UK
Tel: 020 8958 7868
Fax: 020 8958 1920
Email: info@edgwareabbey.org.uk

Website: www.edgwareabbey.org.uk

Vigils (private)

Lauds 8.00 am

Midday Office 11.55 am (not Sun)

Vespers 6.00 pm
4.40pm Fri

Compline 8.00 pm

Mass weekdays:
7.45 am or 11.00 am
11 am (Sun & feast days)

Living under the Rule of St Benedict, and dedicated to St Mary at the Cross, the vocation of this community is to stand with Christ's Mother beside those who suffer; its heart in prayer, the Divine Office & the Eucharist are central to its life.

Beginning in Shoreditch, Mother Monnica Skinner and Revd Henry Nihill worked together, drawn to the desperate poverty and sickness around them. Awareness of the needs, especially of 'incurable children', led to the building of a hospital, marking the beginning of the community's life work. Developing to meet the needs of each generation, this ministry continues today in the provision of Henry Nihill House, a 30-bed care home with nursing for disabled and elderly frail persons, in the beautiful grounds of Edgware Abbey.

Edgware Abbey is a haven of peace which enfolds many visitors. All are offered Benedictine hospitality with space for rest and renewal. The small comfortable Guest Wing provides short stay retreat accommodation, and space for parish Away Days and Meetings. All guests are welcome to participate in the Community's offering of the Divine Office and Eucharist. Edgware Abbey is easily accessible from the M1, AI, tube and rail.

RT REVD DAME MARY THÉRÈSE ZELENT OSB
(Abbess, elected 30 March 1993)
Dame (Mary Eanfleda) Barbara Johnson

Oblates: Our Oblates are part of our extended Community family: living outside the cloister; following the spirit of the Holy Rule of St Benedict; bonded with the Community in prayer and commitment to service.

Community Publication: *Abbey Newsletter*, published yearly. There is no charge but donations are welcome. Obtainable from the Convent.

Guest and Retreat Facilities

The Guest Wing: 3 comfortable bedrooms for B & B retreat accommodation; guest reception area with kitchenette; space for small day groups & clergy groups, parish quiet day groups etc.; use of chapel and garden; small parking area.

Bishop Visitor: Rt Revd Peter Wheatley, Bishop of Edmonton

Office Book: Divine Office with own form of Compline.

Registered Charity: No. 209261

Order of St Benedict

Malling Abbey

OSB

Founded 1891

St Mary's Abbey
52 Swan Street
West Malling, Kent
ME19 6JX
UK
Tel: 01732 843309
Fax: 01732 849016

Website: www.
mallingabbey.org

Vigils 4.30 am (5.00 am Sun)

Lauds 6.50 am (8.10 am Sun)

Eucharist 7.30 am (9.00 am Sun)

Terce 8.45 am

Sext 12.00 noon

None 3.00 pm

Vespers 4.45 pm (5.00 pm Sun)

Compline 7.30 pm

Office Book
Malling Abbey Office

Christians are called to seek and serve God in many different ways. The *Rule of St. Benedict* provides a way of life for those whose vocation is to seek God through prayer and life in community. We express this Benedictine tradition in our daily Eucharist and seven-fold sung Office, in personal prayer and *lectio divina*. These are complemented by work in the house and large gardens and hospitality to our many guests. Times for recreation, study, literary and artistic work and various crafts complete a full and satisfying day. A newcomer who wishes to explore her vocation to the enclosed Benedictine life is welcomed, first for several weeks as an aspirant, then for at least six years of training and discernment before she makes her solemn life vows. Each novice is encouraged to make her own unique contribution to the common life, while also entering into the community's heritage and traditions. These include our concern for God's creation, our work for Christian unity and interfaith dialogue, and the practical care of the Abbey's Norman and medieval buildings.

MOTHER MARY DAVID BEST OSB
(Abbess, elected 16 September 2008)
SISTER MARY STEPHEN PACKWOOD OSB *(Prioress)*

Sister Macrina Banner
Sr Mary Mark Brooksbank
Sister Mary John Marshall
Sister Ruth Blackmore
Sister Mary Cuthbert Archer
Sister Mary Gundulf Wood
Sister Felicity Spencer
Sister Bartimaeus Ives
Sister Mary Michael Wilson
Sister Miriam Noke
Sr Mary Owen DeSimone
Sister Margaret Joy Harris
Sub-Prioress
Juniors: 1

Oblates

Oblates are men and women who feel called by God to follow the Benedictine way in their lives outside the cloister. After a two-and-a-half-year period of training and discernment they make a promise of the conversion of their life during the Eucharist and are then welcomed into the oblate family. Their commitment is expressed in a personal Benedictine rule of life, which balances their personal prayer, worship and lectio divina with their responsibility to family and work.

Community Wares
Cards and booklets printed and painted at the abbey are on sale at the Guest House.

Guest and Retreat Facilities
At the Abbey Guest House we can welcome ten residential guests in single rooms as well as a limited number of day guests. Our guests come to share in the worship and God-centred quiet, and to have the space and time for spiritual reflection and refreshment. There is no charge, though donations are welcome.
Monastic Experience We welcome enquiries from women who wish to deepen their spiritual lives by spending several months living alongside the community within the enclosure. This enables them to experience something of the common life according to the Rule of St. Benedict and the traditions of our community. There is no charge nor is there any wage. Further details from the Mother Abbess.
Most convenient time to telephone: 9.30 am – 11.00 am

Bishop Visitor: Rt Revd Laurie Green

Order of St Benedict

Busan

OSB

Founded 1993

810-1 Baekrok-ri
Habuk-myon
Yangsan-shi
Kyungnam 626-860
South Korea
Tel: 55 384 1560
Mobile: 010 93351560
Email: bundo1993 @hanmail.net

Morning Prayer
6.20 am

Eucharist
7.00 am (Wed only)

Day Office 12 noon

Evening Prayer
5.30 pm

Compline 8.00 pm

There has been an Anglican community in Seoul for many years, but it was the wish of Bishop Bundo Kim to establish a community in Busan – in the south of Korea. Thus it was that in 1993, the Order of St Benedict was founded in Busan City. In four years, sufficient money was raised by the Diocese to buy a more spacious, rural accommodation in Yangsan (to the north of Busan), offering more room for retreats, and for community and parish work.

Sister Martha Han OSB
(Senior Sister, assumed office 1998)
Sister Michaela

Associates
There is an informal group of Associates.

Community Publication
Summer and Christmas Newsletters. Contact Sister Martha re donations.

Guest and Retreat Facilities
There are three guest rooms for private retreats, with good kitchen and bathroom facilities. For larger groups, Korean-style accommodation is used. There are no restrictions on length of stay, and both men and women are welcome. There is no set charge but by donation only.

Most convenient time to telephone: 9.30 am – 7.00 pm

Office Book: Korean Common Prayer Book

Bishop Visitor: Rt Revd Solomon Yoon, Bp of Busan

Order of St Benedict Mucknell Abbey OSB

Founded 1941

Mucknell Abbey
Mucknell Farm Lane
Stoulton
Worcestershire
WR7 4RB
Tel: 01905 345900
Email: abbot@mucknellabbey.org.uk

Website
www.mucknellabbey.org.uk

Office of Readings 6.00 am

Lauds 7.00 am

Terce 8.45 am

Eucharist Noon (11 am Sun & solemnities)

None 2.15 pm

Vespers 5.30 pm

Compline 8.30 pm (8.00 pm in winter)

The contemplative community of monks and nuns sold their former monastery in Burford in 2008 and bought a farm near Worcester and transformed it into a monastery incorporating as many 'sustainable' features as possible. Having moved into their new home in November 2010, the Community is seeking to maintain an atmosphere of stillness and silence in which the Community and its guests are enabled to be open and receptive to the presence of God. The recitation of the Divine Office and the celebration of the Eucharist constitute the principal work of the Community. The ministry of hospitality, the development of the surrounding 40 acres of land (which comprises a large kitchen garden, orchard, newly-planted woodland and hay meadows), the production of incense for a world-wide market, and various income-generating crafts provide a variety of manual work for members of the Community and those guests who wish to share in it. The monastery seeks to celebrate the wonder and richness of Creation and to model a responsible stewardship. The Community's concern has always been to pray for Christian Unity, and it now rejoices in having a Methodist presbyter in its number. Dialogue with people of other faiths and those seeking a spiritual way, either within or outside an established religious tradition, is a priority.

Rt Revd Brother Stuart Burns OSB
(Abbot, elected 14 October 1996)
Brother Philip Dulson OSB *(Prior)*

Sister Mary Bernard Taylor	Brother Ian Mead
Sister Sue Allatt	Sister Sally Paley
Brother Thomas Quin	
Brother Anthony Hare	*Novices:* 3
Sister Mary Kenchington	

Obituaries

15 Nov 2011 Sister Scholastica Newman, aged 94, professed 54 years

Friends: There is a Friends' Association.
Contact: *friends@mucknellabbey.org.uk*

Community Wares

Incense: *incense@mucknellabbey.org.uk*
Hand-written icons, using traditional materials, and block mounted icon prints: *icons@mucknellabbey.org.uk*
Chinese brush painted cards: *cards@mucknellabbey.org.uk*

Office Book: Mucknell Abbey Office

Bishop Visitor: Rt Revd John Inge, Bishop of Worcester

Community publications
There are up-dates on the Community's website.
The Rule of St Benedict – inclusive translation by Abbot Stuart.

Registered Charity:
No. 221617

Guest and Retreat Facilities
Six guest rooms and one room for an individual having a quiet day. No groups.

Most convenient time to telephone:
9.30 am – 11.30 am; 2.30 pm – 3.45 pm. Email enquiries are preferred: *bookings@mucknellabbey.org.uk*

Order of St Benedict

Servants of Christ Priory OSB

Founded 1968

28 West Pasadena Avenue
Phoenix
AZ 85013 2002
USA
Tel: 602 248 9321
Email:
cderijk@cox.net

Morning Prayer
6.00 am

Mass 6.30 am

Midday Prayer
12 noon

Evening Prayer
4.30 pm

Compline 8.00 pm

A community united in love for God and one another following the Benedictine balance of prayer, study and work reflects the life of the monks. Outside engagements are accepted as long as they do not interfere with the monastic routine.

THE VERY REVD CORNELIS J. DE RIJK OSB
(*Prior, assumed office November 1985*)
The Revd Lewis H. Long

Oblates
Oblates follow a rule of life consistent with the *Rule of St Benedict* adapted to their lifestyle. Those in the metropolitan Phoenix area meet once a month at the monastery.

Community Wares: We have a gift shop which stocks prayer books, Bibles, hymnals, religious books and jewelry. We also supply altar bread and candles to numerous parishes. Through the sale of home-made bread, marmalade and jam, we raise funds for Navajo Indians, especially the seniors on the Reservations.

Guest and Retreat Facilities: We have two single rooms and two double rooms for individuals who wish to come and participate in our life. Day guests are also welcome. Guests have use of the grounds, the library, and share meals with the community. We are closed in August. There is a separate guest house with two double beds, sitting room, fireplace, kitchen and bahroom.

Office Book: The BCP of ECUSA

Bishop Visitor
Rt Revd Kirk Stevan Smith, Bishop of Arizona

Order of St Benedict Salisbury OSB

Founded 1914

St Benedict's Priory
19A The Close
Salisbury SP1 2EB
UK
Tel: 01722 335868
Email:
salisbury.priory@virginmedia.com

Vigils 5.30 am

Morning Worship & Eucharist
at Cathedral 7.30 am
(Eucharist 10.30 am Sun)

Lauds (at Priory)
8.00 am Sun & Thu
(with Eucharist Thu)

Terce 10.00 am

Midday Prayer
12.45 pm
(at Sarum College)
12.15pm Sat & Sun
(at Priory)

Evensong
at Cathedral
(times vary)

Compline 8.30 pm

The monastery aims to provide an environment within which the traditional monastic balance between worship, study and work may be maintained with a characteristic Benedictine stress upon corporate worship and community life. To this end, outside commitments are kept to a minimum.

VERY REVD DOM SIMON JARRATT OSB
(Conventual Prior, elected 13 December 2005)
(RT REVD) DOM KENNETH NEWING OSB *(Sub-Prior)*
Dom Francis Hutchison
Dom Bruce De Walt

Oblates
An extended confraternity of oblates, numbering over 250 men and women, married and single, seek to live according to a rule of life inspired by Benedictine principles. From the start, the community has believed in the importance of prayer for Christian unity and the fostering of ecumenism. Details can be obtained from the Oblate Master.

Community History
Petà Dunstan, *The Labour of Obedience,* Canterbury Press, Norwich, 2009

Community Publications
Books:
Augustine Morris, *Oblates: Life with Saint Benedict* £4.25.
Simon Bailey, *A Tactful God: Gregory Dix,* £12.99.

Guest and Retreat Facilities
The Community is currently extending the Priory to provide better facilities for day visitors. There are no facilities for residential guests, although Sarum College next door is open for bed & breakfast.

Most convenient time to telephone
9.00 am – 9.50 am; 10.30 am – 12.15 pm; 3.00 pm – 4.45 pm Tel: 01722 335868

Office Book: Own Office books at the Priory.

Bishop Visitor
Rt Revd Dominic Walker OGS

Registered Charity
Pershore Nashdom & Elmore Trust – No. 220012

St Gregory's Abbey Three Rivers OSB

Founded 1939

**St Gregory's Abbey
56500 Abbey Road
Three Rivers
Michigan
49093-9595
USA
Tel: 269 244 5893
Fax: 269 244 8712
Email: abbot@
saintgregorys
threerivers.org**

Website
www.saintgregorys
threerivers.org

Matins 4.00 am (5.30 am Sun & solemnities, with Lauds)

Lauds 6.00 am

Terce & Mass 8.15 am (8.30 am Sun & solemnities)

Sext 11.30 am (12 noon Sun & solemnities, with None)

None 2.00 pm

Vespers 5.00 pm

Compline 7.45 pm

St Gregory's Abbey is the home of a community of men living under the Rule of St Benedict within the Episcopal Church. The center of the monastery's life is the Abbey Church, where God is worshipped in the daily round of Eucharist, Divine Office, and private prayer. Also offered to God are the monks' daily manual work, study and correspondence, ministry to guests, and occasional outside engagements.

RIGHT REVD ANDREW MARR OSB
(*Abbot, elected 2 March 1989*)
VERY REVD AELRED GLIDDEN OSB (*Prior)*

Father Benedict Reid*	Brother Martin Dally
Father Jude Bell	Brother Abraham Newsom
Father William Forest	*Novices:* 1

**resident elsewhere*

Community Publications and History

Abbey Newsletter, published four times a year. Free

Singing God's Praises, published 1998. It includes articles from community newsletters over the past sixty years and also includes a history of St Gregory's. Copies can be bought from the Abbey, price $20 a copy, postpaid.

Come Let Us Adore: St Gregory's 1999-2011, a successor to the above. Published by iUniverse and available from online bookstores such as Amazon.

Andrew Marr OSB, *Tools for Peace: the spiritual craft of St Benedict and René Girard*, available from online bookstores.

Community Wares: The Abbey calendar.

Guest and Retreat Facilities

Both men and women are welcome as guests. There is no charge, but $40 per day is 'fair value for services rendered' that is not tax-deductible. For further information and arrangements, contact the guest master by mail, telephone or e-mail at *guestmaster@saintgregorysthreerivers.org*

Associates

We have a Confraternity which offers an official connection to the Abbey and is open to anyone who wishes to join for the purpose of incorporating Benedictine principles into their lives. For further information and an application form, please write the Father Abbot.

Office Book: The community uses home-made books based on the Roman Thesaurus for the Benedictine Office.

Bishop Visitor: Rt Revd Arthur Williams,
suffragan Bishop of Ohio (retired)

Order of St Helena

OSH

Founded 1945

Convent of St Helena
3042 Eagle Drive, Augusta GA 30906 USA
Tel: 706 798 5201
Fax: 706 796 0079

Email: augofficemgr @comcast.net

Website www.osh.org

Matins 7.30 am

Eucharist 8.00 am

Diurnum and intercessions noon

Vespers 5.00 pm

Compline 7.00 pm

Registered Charity No: US Government 501 (c)(3)

The Order of St Helena witnesses to a contemporary version of traditional monasticism, taking a threefold vow of Poverty, Celibate Chastity and Obedience. Our life in community is shaped by the daily Eucharist and fourfold Office, plus hours of personal prayer and study, and from this radiates a wide range of ministries.

As an Order, we are not restricted to any single area of work but witness and respond to the Gospel, with individual sisters engaging in different ministries as they feel called by God and affirmed by the community. Our work is thus wonderfully varied: sisters work in parishes as priests or as pastoral assistants; they lead retreats, quiet days and conferences; work with the national Church and various organizations; offer spiritual direction; are psychotherapists; teach; serve in hospital chaplaincies and community service programs. Seven sisters are ordained priests.

In 1997, the Order adopted a new style of governance and no longer has a superior or single sister as head. Instead, the Order was led by a four-member Leadership Council, with responsibility and ultimate authority vested equally in all four members. Since 2007, the Council has had three members.

In 2008, the sisters closed both their New York convents and consolidated into one house in Augusta, Georgia.

Leadership Council:

SISTER MARY LOIS MILLER OSH *(Administrator)*
REVD SISTER CAROL ANDREW OSH *(Pastoral)*
REVD DR ELLEN FRANCIS POISSON OSH *(Vocations/Formation)*

Sister Ruth Juchter
Sister Ellen Stephen
Sister Barbara Lee
Sister Benedicta
Sister Cintra Pemberton
Sister Elsie Reid
Revd Sister Rosina Ampah
Sister June Thomas
Sister Ann Prentice
Sister Linda Elston
Sister Faith Anthony
Sister Grace
Sister Miriam Elizabeth

Novices: 1

Obituaries

17 Jul 2011 Revd Sister Mary Michael Simpson, aged 85, professed 56 years

27 Nov 2012 Sister Cornelia, aged 83, professed 45 years, Superior 1985-97

Associates

ASSOCIATES – open to all women and men. Write to the Secretary for Associates at the Augusta Convent.

Guest and Retreat Facilities: Guest house with 11 single rooms

Community Publication: *saint helena,* published quarterly, free of charge. Sign up on the OSH website or write to the Convent of St Helena at Augusta for a subscription.

Community Wares and Books

Hand-made rosaries – write to Sister Mary Lois at the Augusta convent.
Icons and icon reproductions, by Ellen Francis, OSH (www.ellenfrancisicons.org)
Greeting cards, by Faith Anthony, OSH (see OSH website)
Sister Cintra Pemberton OSH, *Soulfaring: Celtic Pilgrimage then and now,* SPCK, London, & Morehouse, Harrisburg, PA, 1999.
Doug Shadel and Sister Ellen Stephen OSH, *Vessel of Peace: The voyage toward spiritual freedom,* Three Tree Press, 1999.
Sister Ellen Stephen, OSH, *The Poet's Eye: collected poetry,* Academica Press, 2012
Sister Ellen Stephen, OSH, *Some Antics,* Order of Saint Helena, 2012
Sister Rosina Ampah, *The Beautiful Cloth: stories and proverbs of Ghana,* Yellow Moon Press, 2010.
Sister Ellen Stephen OSH, *Together and Apart: a memoir of the Religious Life,* Morehouse, Harrisburg, PA, 2008.

Office Book: *The Saint Helena Breviary, Monastic Edition,* which includes all the music in plainchant notation, is now published. It follows closely the BCP of the Episcopal Church of the USA. The focus is on inclusive language and expanded imagery for God, following principles set forth by the Standing Commission for Liturgy and Music of the Episcopal Church, USA. The *Saint Helena Psalter*, extracted from the Breviary, was published in November 2004, *The Saint Helena Breviary, Personal edition,* in July 2006, both by Church Publishing Co., Inc.

Bishop Visitor: Rt Revd Neil Alexander, Bishop of Atlanta

Sisterhood of the Holy Nativity

SHN

Founded 1882

Bethlehem-by-the-Lake
W1484 Spring Grove Road
Ripon
WI 54971-8655
USA
Tel: 920 748 5332

Email: abizac50 @hotmail.com

Matins
7.30 am

Eucharist
8.00 am

Diurnum (Noonday Prayer)
12 noon

Vespers 5.30 pm (6.30 pm Sun)

Compline
8.00 pm

Office Book
The Monastic Breviary, published by the Order of the Holy Cross

Ours is a mixed life, which means that we combine an apostolic ministry with a contemplative lifestyle. The Rule of the Sisterhood of the Holy Nativity follows the model of the Rule of St Augustine of Hippo. As such, we strive to make the love of God the motive of all our actions. The 'charisms', which undergird our life, are Charity, Humility, Prayer, and Missionary Zeal. Our work involves us with children's ministries such as Sunday School, Summer Camp and Vacation Bible School, as well as ministry to those we meet in everyday life.

SISTER ABIGAIL SHN
(Revd Mother, assumed office 2012)
Sister Margaretta
Sister Columba
Sister Kathleen Marie
Sister Charis

Associates

ASSOCIATES are men and women who connect themselves to the prayer life and ministry of the community, and keep a Rule of Life.

Community Publication

We put out a newsletter occasionally. There is no charge. Anyone interested may contact us at the address above or by email.

Bishop Visitor

Rt Revd Russell E Jacobus, Bishop of Fond du Lac

Sisterhood of St John the Divine

SSJD

Founded 1884

St John's Convent
233 Cummer Ave
Toronto
Ontario M2M 2E8
CANADA
Tel: 416 226 2201
ext. 301
Fax: 416 222 4442
Emails:
convent@ssjd.ca
guesthouse@ssjd.ca
Website www.ssjd.ca

Morning Prayer
8.30 am

Holy Eucharist
12 noon (8.00 am Sun)

Mid-day Office
12 noon (when Eucharist not at noon)

Evening Prayer
5.00 pm

Compline 8.10 pm
(Tue, Wed, Thu & Fri)

Office Book
Book of Alternative Services 1985; SSJD Daily Office Binder with inclusive language psalter.

The Sisterhood of St John the Divine is a monastic community of women within the Anglican Church of Canada. Founded in Toronto, we are a prayer- and gospel-centred monastic community, bound together by the call to live out our baptismal covenant through the vows of poverty, chastity and obedience. These vows anchor us in Jesus' life and the transforming experience of the Gospel. Nurtured by our founding vision of prayer, community and service, we are open and responsive to the needs of the Church and the world, continually seeking the guidance of the Holy Spirit in our life and ministries.

St John's Convent nurtures and supports the life of the whole Sisterhood. Our guest house welcomes individuals and groups who share in the community's prayer and liturgy; offers regularly scheduled retreats and quiet days, spiritual direction, and discernment programs for those seeking guidance in their life and work; and provides Sisters to preach, teach, speak, lead retreats and quiet days. Our programs help people build bridges between secular culture, the Church, and the monastic tradition. The Sisterhood witnesses to the power of Christ's reconciling and forgiving love through the gospel imperatives of prayer, spiritual guidance, justice, peace, care for creation, hospitality, ministering to those in need, and promoting unity, healing, and wholeness.

The Sisters advocate for a vision of health care at the St. John's Rehab site of Sunnybrook Hospital which expresses SSJD's values in a multi-faith, multi-cultural setting. The Sisters provide spiritual and pastoral support for patients, staff and volunteers.

Other address

ST JOHN'S HOUSE, 3937 St Peter's Rd, Victoria, British Columbia V8P 2J9
Tel: 250 920 7787 **Fax: 250 920 7709**
E-mail: bchouse@ssjd.ca

A community of Sisters committed to being a praying presence in the Diocese of British Columbia. Prayer, intentional community, hospitality, and mission are at the heart of our life in the Diocese and beyond.

Community Wares

A variety of cards made by Sisters or Associates. Good selection of books on spiritual growth for sale at the Convent (not by mail) and a few CDs. Anglican rosaries made by the Sisters, some knitted items and prayer shawls.

Bishop Visitor: Most Revd Colin Johnson

Sister Elizabeth Ann Eckert SSJD
(*Reverend Mother, assumed office 13 April 2005, re-elected 13 April 2010*)
Sister Elizabeth Rolfe-Thomas SSJD *(Prioress)*

Sister Wilma Grazier
Sister Jean Marston
Sister Beryl Stone
Sister Merle Milligan
Sister Doreen McGuff *(Sub-Prioress)*
Sister Patricia Forler
Sister Jocelyn Mortimore
Sister Margaret Ruth Steele
Sister Sarah Jean Thompson
Sister Anitra Hansen
Sister Margaret Mary Watson
Sister Jessica Kennedy
Sister Constance Joanna Gefvert *(priest)*
Sister Brenda Jenner
Sister Anne Norman
Sister Helen Claire Gunter
Sister Susan Elwyn
Sister Louise Manson
Sister Dorothy Handrigan
Sister Amy Hamilton

Novices: 4

Obituaries

10 Jun 2011 Sister Madeleine Mary Salter, aged 90, professed 35 years
22 Mar 2013 Sister Joyce Bodley, aged 90, professed 64 years
2 Aug 2013 Sister Constance Murphy, aged 109, professed 76 years

Associates, Oblates and Alongsiders

Our approximately nine hundred **Associates** are women and men who follow a Rule of Life and share in the ministry of the Sisterhood. The Sisterhood of St John the Divine owes its founding to the vision and dedication of the clergy and lay people who became the first Associates of SSJD. A year of discernment is required before being admitted as an Associate to see if the Associate Rule helps the person in what she/he is seeking; and to provide the opportunity to develop a relationship with the Sisters and to deepen the understanding and practice of prayer. The Associate Rule provides a framework for the journey of faith. There are three basic commitments: belonging in a parish; the practice of prayer, retreat, study of scripture, and spiritual reading; and the relationship with SSJD. Write to the Associate Director nearest you for further information.

We have a small but growing number of **Oblates.** Oblates are women who wish to make a promise of prayer and service in partnership with the Sisterhood. Each Oblate develops her own Rule of Life in partnership with the Oblate Director, her spiritual director, and a support group. A year of discernment is also required, as well as an annual residency program. Write to The Reverend Mother at the Convent in Toronto for more information.

An **Alongsider** is a woman who lives "at the edge" of the community of the Sisterhood of St. John the Divine, moving back and forth between the monastery and the world outside. She lives outside the cloister in the convent's guest house but participates in many of the community activities (including common prayer in chapel and recreation) and shares in household tasks. Alongside the Sisters, she is committed to a daily practice of personal prayer, spiritual reading and reflection on sacred Scripture.

Community Publication: *The Eagle* (newsletter). Contact the Convent Secretary. Published quarterly. $10.00 suggested annual donation.

Community History and Books

Sister Eleonora SSJD, *A Memoir of the Life and Work of Hannah Grier Coome, Mother-Foundress of SSJD, Toronto, Canada,* OUP, London, 1933 (out of print).

The Sisterhood of St John the Divine 1884–1984, published 1931 as *A Brief History;* 4th revision 1984, (out of print).

Sister Constance Joanna SSJD, *From Creation to Resurrection: A Spiritual Journey,* Anglican Book Centre, Toronto, 1990.

Sister Constance SSJD, *Other Little Ships: The memoirs of Sister Constance SSJD,* Patmos Press, Toronto, 1997.

Sister Thelma-Anne McLeod SSJD, *In Age Reborn, By Grace Sustained,* Path Books, Toronto, 2007.

Dr Gerald D Hart, *St John's Rehab Hospital, 1885–2010, the Road to Recovery,*York Region Printing, Autora, ON, 2010

Guest and Retreat Facilities

Guest House has 37 rooms (42 people) used for rest, quiet time and retreats. Contact the Guest Sister at the Convent for details about private accommodation, scheduled retreats, quiet days and other programs.

The Sisters in Victoria also lead quiet days and retreats and have room for one guest. Please contact St John's House, BC, for detailed information.

Sisterhood of St Mary

SSM

Founded 1929

St Andrew's Mission
PO Haluaghat
Mymensingh
BANGLADESH

Prayer 6.30 am

Meditation 8.00 am

Prayers
9.00 am, 11.30 am,
3.00 pm, 6.00 pm

Compline 8.00 pm

The community is located on the northern border of Bangladesh at the foot of the Garo hills in India. The community was formed in Barisal at the Sisterhood of the Epiphany, and was sent here to work among the indigenous tribal people, side by side with St Andrew's membership of the Sisterhood has always been entirely indigenous. The first sisters were Bengalis. The present sisters are the fruit of their work – four are Garo, one is Bengali. They take the vows of Poverty, Purity and Obedience and live a very simple life. They lead a life of prayer and formation of girls. They also look after the Church and do pastoral work among women and children in the Parish.

SISTER MIRA MANKHIN SSM
(Sister Superior, assumed office 2002)
Sister Anita Raksam
Sister Bregita Doffo
Sister Mala Chicham
Sister Sobha Choudhury

Community Wares: Some handicrafts and vestments for church use and sale.

Office Book: Church of Bangladesh BCP & own book for lesser Offices

Bishop Visitor: Most Revd Paul Sarker, Bp of Dhaka

Sisters of Charity SC

Founded 1869

237 Ridgeway
Plympton
Plymouth
PL7 2HP
UK
Tel: 01752 336112
Email:
plymptonsisters@gmail.com

Morning Prayer
8.00 am

Vespers 5.00 pm

Compline 7.00 pm

Office Book
Daily Prayer

Bishop Visitor: Rt Revd Martin Shaw

Registered Charity:
No. X33170

A Community following the Rule of St Vincent de Paul and so committed to the service of those in need. The Sisters are involved in parish work and the Community also has a nursing home in Plympton.

MOTHER ELIZABETH MARY SC
(Revd Mother, assumed office 21 April 2003)
SISTER CLARE SC *(priest)* *(Assistant)*

Sister Theresa
Sister Angela Mary
Sister Mary Joseph
Sister Gabriel Margaret
Sister Mary Patrick

Obituaries
17 Aug 2011 Sister Hilda Mary, aged 89, professed 59 years
16 Jun 2012 Sister Rosamund, aged 91, professed 60 years

Oblates and Associate Members
The Community has a group of Oblates and Associate Members, formed as a mutual supportive link. We ask them to add to their existing rule the daily use of the Vincentian Prayer. Oblates are also asked to use the Holy Paraclete hymn and one of the Daily Offices, thereby joining in spirit in the Divine Office of the Community. Oblates are encouraged to make an annual retreat. Associate Members support us by their prayers and annual subscription.

Other address
Saint Vincent's Nursing Home, Fore Street, Plympton, Plymouth, PL7 1NE Tel: 01752 336205

Guest and Retreat Facilities
We welcome individuals for Quiet Days.
Most convenient time to telephone: 6.00 pm – 8.00 pm

Mother Elizabeth Mary *(right)* visits Sister Angela Mary on the latter's 94th birthday

Sisters of the Incarnation

SI

Founded 1981

The House of the Incarnation
6 Sherbourne Terrace
Dover Gardens
SA 5048
AUSTRALIA
Tel: 08 8296 2166
Email: sisincar @bigpond.com

Office Book
A Prayer Book for Australia (1995 edition) for Morning and Evening Prayer, and Compline; Midday Prayer is from another source.

The sisters live under vows of poverty, chastity and obedience in a simple life style, and seek to maintain a balance between prayer, community life and work for each member and to worship and serve within the church. They combine the monastic and apostolic aspects of the Religious Life. The monastic aspects include prayer, domestic work at home, community life and hospitality. The sisters are engaged in parish ministry.

The community was founded in the diocese of Adelaide in 1981 as a contemporary expression of the Religious Life for women in the Anglican Church. In 1988, the two original sisters made their Profession of Life Intention within the Sisters of the Incarnation, before the Archbishop of Adelaide, the Visitor of the community. One member was ordained to the diaconate in 1990 and the priesthood in 1993. The governing body of the community is its chapter of professed sisters, which elects the Guardian, and appoints an Episcopal Visitor and a Community Advisor.

REVD SISTER JULIANA SI
(*Guardian, assumed office 2013*)
Sister Patricia

Friends
The community has a group of Friends who share special celebrations and significant events, many of whom have supported the community from the beginning, while others become Friends as we touch their lives. There is no formal structure.

Bishop Visitor: Rt Revd Dr K Rayner

Sister Juliana presides at the Eucharist celebrating 20 years of her priesthood.

Sisters of Jesus Way

Founded 1979

Redacre
24 Abbey Road
West Kirby
Wirral
CH48 7EP
UK
Tel: 0151 6258775

Email:
sistersofjesusway@redacre.org.uk

Website:
www.redacre.org.uk

Morning Prayer
8.00 am

Intercessory prayer
(community only)
12.40 pm

Evening Prayer
7.00 pm

Registered Charity
No 509284

Two Wesley deaconesses founded the Sisters of Jesus Way. There have been many strands that have been instrumental in the formation of the community but primarily these have been the Gospels, the Charismatic Renewal, the teaching and example of the Pietists of the 17th and early 18th centuries as practised in some German communities and the lives of saints from many denominations.

Our calling is to love the Lord Jesus with a first love, to trust the heavenly Father as his dear children for all our needs both spiritual and material and to allow the Holy Spirit to guide and lead us. Prayer, either using the framework of a simple liturgy or informal, is central to all that we do. We make life promises of simplicity, fidelity and chastity. Our work for the Lord varies as the Holy Spirit opens or closes doors. We welcome guests, trusting that as the Lord Jesus lives with us, they will meet with him and experience his grace. Music, some of which has been composed by the sisters, is very much part of our life. We work together, learning from the Lord to live together as a family in love, forgiveness and harmony.

SISTER MARIE
(Little Sister, assumed office 1991)
SISTER SYLVIA *(Companion Sister)*

Sister Hazel	Sister Susan
Sister Florence	Sister Louise
Sister Beatrice	

Associates
The Followers of the Lamb are a small group of women following a simple Rule of Life and committed to assisting the Sisters. A resident Follower of the Lamb Brother works alongside the community: Brother Elliot.

Bishop Guardian
Rt Revd Dr Peter Forster, Bishop of Chester

Guest and Retreat Facilities
6 single rooms, 4 double rooms. Several rooms for day visitors and small groups.

Most convenient time to telephone:
9.40am – 12.40pm; 2.15pm – 5.45pm; 7.20pm – 8.45pm

Community Publication: Twice-yearly teaching and newsletter. Contact Sr Louise.

Community History
Published by the Sisters of Jesus Way and available from the Community:
The Beloved Community – Beginnings; A Time to Build;
Circles of Love – the Life and Work of the Sisters of Jesus Way

Society of the Holy Cross

SHC

Founded 1925

3 Jeong-dong
Jung-ku
Seoul 100-120
Korea
Tel: 2 735 7832
or 2 735 3478
Fax: 2 736 5028
Email:
holycross25@
yahoo.com

Website
www.sister.or.kr

Morning Prayer
6.15 am

Holy Eucharist
6.45 am

Midday Prayer
12.30 pm
(12 noon Sun & great feast days)

Evening Prayer
5.00 pm

Compline 8.00 pm

Office Book
Revised Common Prayer for MP & EP and Compline; & SHC material for Midday Office

The community was founded on the feast day of the Exaltation of the Holy Cross in 1925 by the Rt Revd Mark Trollope, the third English bishop of the Anglican Church in Korea, admitting Postulant Phoebe Lee and blessing a small traditional Korean-style house in the present site of Seoul. The Community of St Peter, a nursing order in Woking, Surrey, England, sent eighteen Sisters as missionaries to Korea between 1892 and 1950, who nourished this young community for a few decades. Sister Mary Clare CSP, who was the first Mother Superior of this community, was persecuted by the North Korean communists and died during the 'Death March' in the Korean War in 1950. This martyrdom especially has been a strong influence and encouragement for the growth of the community.

Our spirituality is based on a modified form of the Augustinian Rule harmonized with the Benedictine one. Bishop Mark Trollope, the first Visitor, and Sister Mary Clare CSP compiled the Divine Office Book and the Constitution and Rule of the Community. The activities that are being continuously practised even now include pastoral care in parishes, running homes for the elderly and those with learning difficulties, conducting Quiet Days, and offering people spiritual direction. We run a programme for vocation one weekend each month, and a spiritual prayer meeting and workshop monthly with people who want to improve their faithful life. We lead contemplation based on Ignatian Spirituality or Lexio Divina. We also have a programme of Biblio Drama for young people, clergy wives and laity.

Sister Alma SHC
(Reverend Mother, assumed office 1 Jan 2010, re-elected 2013)
Sister Helen Elizabeth SHC *(priest) (Assistant Superior)*

Sister Monica
Sister Phoebe Anne
Sister Edith
Sister Cecilia
Sister Maria Helen
Sister Etheldreda
Sister Catherine *(priest)*
Sister Maria Clara
Sister Pauline
Sister Angela
Sister Theresa
Sister Grace
Sister Helen Juliana
Sister Lucy Edward
Sister Martha
Sister Prisca

Novices: 2

Friends and Associates

Friends are mostly Anglicans who desire to have a close link with the community. They follow a simple Rule of

Life, which includes praying for the Sisters and their work. Friends also form a network of prayer, fellowship and mutual support within Christ's ministry of wholeness and reconciliation. About one hundred members gather together for the annual meeting in May in the Motherhouse. The committee members meet bi-monthly at the convent in Seoul.

ASSOCIATES: forty-five friends have been trained for admission and vow-taking for full membership between 2005 and 2011.

Other Addresses

St Anne's Nursing Home for Elderly People,
619–28 Onsuri, Kilsang, Kangwha, Inch'on, 417-840 South Korea
Tel: 32 937 1935 Fax: 32 937 0696 Email: anna1981@kornet.net
Website: www.oldanna.or.kr

St Bona House for Intellectually Handicapped People,
2–4 Neamni, Kadok, Chongwon, Chungbuk 363-853, South Korea
Tel: 43 297 8348 Fax: 43 298 3156 Email: sralma@naver.com
Website: www.bona.or.kr

Community Publication: *Holy Cross Newsletter*, published occasionally, in Korean. Sister Catherine SHC, *Holy Vocation* (booklet for the SHC 75th anniversary, 2000)

Community History

Jae Joung Lee, *Society of the Holy Cross 1925–1995*, Seoul, 1995 (in Korean).
Sisters Maria Helen & Catherine, *The SHC: the First 80 Years*, 2005
Sister Helen Elizabeth (ed), *Fragrance of the Holy Cross,* 2010 (story of Sister Mary Clare in Korean)

Guest and Retreat Facilities: The Community organizes Retreats and Quiet Days monthly for Associates and groups and individuals.

Community Wares: Wafers and wine for Holy Eucharist.

Bishop Visitor: Rt Revd Paul Kim, Bishop of Seoul *(assumed office 15 Jan 2009)*

Society of the Precious Blood

(UK)

SPB

Founded 1905

Burnham Abbey
Lake End Road
Taplow, Maidenhead
Berkshire SL6 OPW
UK

Tel & Fax:
01628 604080

Email:
burnhamabbey@btinternet.com

Website: www.burnhamabbey.org

Lauds 7.30 am

Eucharist 9.30 am

Angelus & Sext 12.00 noon

Vespers 5.30 pm

Compline 8.30 pm

Office Book
SPB Office Book

Bishop Visitor
Rt Revd
Stephen Cottrell,
Bishop of Chelmsford

Registered Charity
No. 900512

We are a contemplative community whose particular work within the whole body of Christ is worship, thanksgiving and intercession. Within these ancient Abbey walls, which date back to 1266, we continue to live the Augustinian monastic tradition of prayer, silence, fellowship and solitude. The Eucharist is the centre of our life, where we find ourselves most deeply united with Christ, one another and all for whom we pray. The work of prayer is continued in the Divine Office, in the Watch before the Blessed Sacrament and in our whole life of work, reading, creating, and learning to live together. This life of prayer finds an outward expression in welcoming guests, who come seeking an opportunity for quiet and reflection in which to deepen their own spiritual lives, or to explore the possibility of a religious vocation.

Sister Victoria Mary SPB
(Reverend Mother, assumed office 6 August 2011)

Sister Margaret Mary	Sister Mary Philip
Sister Mary Bernard	Sister Mary Benedict
Sister Dorothy Mary	Sister Miriam Mary
Sister Jane Mary	Sister Elizabeth Mary
Sister Mary Laurence	Sister Grace Mary

Companions and Oblates: Oblates are men and women who feel drawn by God to express the spirit of the Society, united with the Sisters in their life of worship, thanksgiving and intercession. They live out their dedication in their own situation and make a yearly Promise.

Men and women who desire to share in the prayer and work of the Society but cannot make as full a commitment to saying the Office may be admitted as Companions.

Community History
Sister Felicity Mary SPB, *Mother Millicent Mary,* 1968.

Booklets and leaflets on the history and life of the Abbey.

Community Wares: We have a small shop for cards.

Community Publications: *Newsletter,* yearly at Christmas. *Companions/Oblates Letter,* quarterly.

Guest and Retreat Facilities: We have a small guest wing with three single en suite rooms for individual (unconducted) retreats. We also have rooms available for Quiet Days or groups of up to twenty.

Most convenient time to telephone: 10.30 am – 11.45 am; 3.30 pm – 4.30 pm; 7.00 pm – 8.00 pm

Society of the Precious Blood (southern Africa)

SPB

Founded 1905

St Monica's House of Prayer
46 Green Street
West End
Kimberley, 8301
SOUTH AFRICA
Tel: 00275 38 331161
Email: spbmasite@leo.co.ls

Morning Prayer 7.00 am

Eucharist 7.30 am

Terce 10.00 am

Midday Office 12 noon

Evening Prayer 5.30 pm

Compline 8.00 pm

Office Book
Daily Prayer & An Anglican Prayer Book 1989, CPSA

Bishop Visitor
Rt Revd Adam Taaso, Bishop of Lesotho

Five Sisters of the Society of the Precious Blood at Burnham Abbey came to Masite in Lesotho in 1957 to join with a community of African women, with the intention of forming a multi-cultural contemplative community dedicated to intercession. In 1966, this community at Masite became autonomous, although still maintaining strong ties of friendship with Burnham Abbey. In 1980, a House of Prayer was established in Kimberley in South Africa, which has developed a more active branch of the Society. Sadly, due to diminishing numbers, health issues and finance, the Lesotho Priory will close on 1 March 2014 and the sisters there disperse. The Kimberly house will continue its ministry.

SISTER ELAINE MARY SPB
(Prioress, assumed office 24 September 1997) *(at Kimberley)*

Sister Josephine Mary *(at Kimberley)*
Sister Theresia Mary *(in Lesotho)*
Sister Lucia Mary *(in Lesotho)*
Sister Diana Mary *(in UK)*
Sister Camilla Mary *(at Kimberley)*
Intern Oblates: 1 *(at Kimberley)*

Obituaries
25 Oct 2011 Sister Cicily Mary, aged 71, professed 28 years

Oblates and Companions
The Community has thirteen oblates (in Lesotho, South Africa, Zambia, New Zealand and the UK), and eighty-six Companions and Associates (in Lesotho, South Africa and the UK). All renew their promises annually. Oblates are sent prayer material regularly. Companions and Associates receive quarterly letters and attend occasional quiet days.

Community Publication
Annual *Newsletter;* apply to the Prioress. No charge.

Community Wares: Cards, crafts, religious booklets.

Community History and books
Sister Theresia Mary SPB, *Father Patrick Maekane MBK*, CPSA, 1987
Evelyn Cresswell (Oblate SPB), *Keeping the Hours,* Cluster Pubs, Pietermaritzburg, 2007

Other Address (only until 1 March 2014)
Priory of Our Lady Mother of Mercy, PO Box 7192, Maseru 100, Lesotho Tel: 00266 5885 9585

Society of the Sacred Advent

SSA

Founded 1892

Community House
18 Petrie Street
Ascot
QLD 4007
AUSTRALIA
Tel: 07 3262 5511
Fax: 07 3862 3296

Email:
eunice@
stmarg.qld.edu.au

Quiet time 6.00 am

Morning Prayer
6.30 am
(7.00 am Sun & Mon)

Eucharist 7.00 am
(7.30 am Sun)

Midday Prayer
12 noon

Evensong 5.30 pm

Compline 7.30 pm
(8.00 pm Wed & Sat)

Bishop Visitor
Rt Revd GodfreyFryar, Bishop of Rockhampton

The Society of the Sacred Advent exists for the glory of God and for the service of His Church in preparation for the second coming of our Lord and Saviour Jesus Christ.

Members devote themselves to God in community under vows of poverty, chastity and obedience. Our life is a round of worship, prayer, silence and work. Our Patron Saint is John the Baptist who, by his life and death, pointed the way to Jesus. We would hope also to point the way to Jesus in our own time, to a world which has largely lost touch with spiritual realities and is caught up in despair, loneliness and fear.

As part of our ministry, Sisters may be called to give addresses, conduct Retreats or Quiet Days, or to make themselves available for spiritual direction and parish work. The aim of the Community is to grow in the mind of Christ so as to manifest Him to others. The Society has two Schools, St Margaret's and St Aidan's and two Sisters are on each of the School Councils.

SISTER EUNICE SSA
(*Revd Mother, assumed office 21 March 2007)*

Sister June Ruth
Sister Sandra
Sister Beverley
Sister Gillian

Fellowship and Company

THE FELLOWSHIP OF THE SACRED ADVENT
Since 1925, the work of the Community has been helped by the prayers and work of a group of friends known as the Fellowship of the Sacred Advent. They have a simple Rule of Life.

THE COMPANY OF THE SACRED ADVENT began in 1987. This is a group of men and women, clergy and lay, bound together in love for Jesus Christ and His Church in the spirit of St John the Baptist. It seeks to proclaim the Advent challenge: 'Prepare the Way of the Lord.' Members have a Rule of Life and renew their promises annually.

Members of the Fellowship and Company are part of our extended Community family. The Sisters arrange Retreats and Quiet Days and support them with their prayers, help, or spiritual guidance, as required.

Other address

Society of the Sacred Advent, 261 Anduramba Road, Crows Nest, Queensland 4355, AUSTRALIA

Community Publication
There is a Newsletter, twice yearly. For a subscription, write to Sister Sandra SSA. The cost is A$5 per year.

Community History
Elizabeth Moores, *One Hundred Years of Ministry,* published for SSA, 1992.
Ray Geise, *Educating Girls since 1895,* Victory Press, Bribie Island, QLD, 2012.

Community Wares: Cards and crafts.

Guest and Retreat Facilities
Brisbane – day groups or quiet days
Crows Nest – day groups or quiet days; and cottage for retreats with three bedrooms

Office Book
A Prayer Book for Australia; *The Daily Office SSF* is used for Midday Prayer.

Society of the Sacred Cross

SSC

Founded 1914 (Chichester); to Wales in 1923

Tymawr Convent
Lydart
Monmouth
Gwent
NP25 4RN
UK

Tel: 01600 860244

Email: tymawrconvent @btinternet.com

The community, part of the Anglican Church in Wales, lives a monastic, contemplative life of prayer based on silence, solitude and learning to live together, under vows of poverty, chastity and obedience, with a modern rule, Cistercian in spirit. At the heart of our corporate life is the Eucharist with the daily Office and other times of shared prayer spanning the day. All services are open to the public and we are often joined by members of the neighbourhood in addition to our visitors. Our common life includes study, recreation and work in the house and extensive grounds. It is possible for women and men, married or single, to experience our life of prayer by living alongside the community for periods longer than the usual guest stay. Hospitality is an important part of our life at Tymawr and guests are most welcome. We also organise and sponsor occasional lectures and programmes of study for those who wish to find or develop the life of the spirit in their own circumstances. The community is dedicated to the crucified and risen Lord as the focus of its life and the source of the power to live it.

Community Wares
Colour photographs cards of Tymawr available at 60p each (including envelope).

Community Publication: *Tymawr Newsletter*, yearly at Advent. Write to the above address.

Community History
Sister Jeanne SSC, *A Continuous Miracle,* (privately printed)

Sister Gillian Mary SSC
(Revd Mother, assumed office 2010)
Sister Veronica Anne SSC *(Assistant)*
Sister Lorna Francis*
Sister Heylin Columba*
Sister Rosalind Mary
Sister Elizabeth
Sister Danielle

Novices: 1
Postulants: 1

** Living the contemplative life away from Tymawr*

Website
www.
tymawrconvent.org

Morning Prayer
7.15 am

Terce 8.45 am

Eucharist
12.00 noon

Evening Prayer
5.15 pm

Silent Corporate Prayer
7.45 pm

Compline 8.15 pm

Office Book
CCP, with additional SSC material.

Bishop Visitor
Rt Revd Dominic Walker OGS, Bishop of Monmouth

Registered Charity:
No. 1047614

Companions, Oblates and Associates
There are 7 Companions; 46 Oblates, living in their own homes, each having a personal Rule sustaining their life of prayer; 114 Associates, women and men, who have a simple commitment.

Guest and Retreat Facilities
The community offers facilities for individual guests and small groups. There are five rooms (one double) in the guest wing of the Main House for full board. Michaelgarth, the self-catering guest house offers facilities for individuals or groups (five singles and two doubles), and also for day groups. The Old Print House offers full facilities for day groups of up to eight. Individuals may have private retreats with guidance from a member of the community. The community occasionally organises retreats and study days. Pilgrimages round the grounds, on a variety of themes, can be arranged. Please write with a stamped addressed envelope for details.

Most convenient time to telephone: 6.45 pm – 8.00 pm only, except Mondays, Fridays and Sundays.

Society of the Sacred Mission

SSM

Founded 1893

Office Book
Celebrating Common Prayer

Bishops Visitor
Rt Revd
John Pritchard,
Bishop of Oxford
(PROVINCE OF EUROPE)

Most Revd
Philip Freier,
Archbishop of Melbourne
(SOUTHERN PROVINCE)

Most Revd
Thabo Makgoba,
Archbishop of Cape Town
(SOUTHERN AFRICAN PROVINCE)

Founded in 1893 by Father Herbert Kelly, the Society is a means of uniting the devotion of ordinary people, using it in the service of the Church. Members of the Society share a common life of prayer and fellowship in a variety of educational, pastoral and community activities in England, Australia, Japan, Lesotho, and South Africa.

PROVINCE OF EUROPE

COLIN GRIFFITHS SSM
(*Provincial, assumed office April 2010*)

Frank Green
Ralph Martin
Andrew Muramatsu
Jonathan Ewer
Edmund Wheat
Mary Hartwell
Margaret Moakes

Associates:
Paul Golightly
Elizabeth Baker
Robin Baker
Marcus Armstrong
Joan Golightly
Karen Walker

Obituaries

19 Oct 2012 Elizabeth Macey, aged 83, professed 14 years

Associates and Companions (applicable to all provinces)

ASSOCIATES: are men and women who share the life and work of a priory of the Society.

COMPANIONS: are men and women who support the aims of the Society without being closely related to any of its work. They consecrate their lives in loving response to a vocation to deepen their understanding of God's will, and to persevere more devotedly in commitments already made: baptism, marriage or ordination.

Addresses

Provincial & Administrator:

The Well, Newport Road, Willen MK15 9AA, UK
Tel: 01908 241974 Email: ssmlondon@yahoo.co.uk

St Antony's Priory, Claypath, Durham DH1 1QT, UK Tel: 0191 384 3747
Email: durham.ssm@which.net

1 Linford Lane, Milton Keynes, Bucks MK15 9DL, UK Tel: 01908 663749

Community History

Herbert H Kelly SSM, *An Idea in the Working,* SSM Press, Kelham, 1908.

Alistair Mason, *SSM: History of the Society of the Sacred Mission*, Canterbury Press, Norwich, 1993.

Community Publication: *SSM News* (newsletter of the Province of Europe) The Secretary, SSM Newsletter, The Well, Newport Road, Willen MK15 9AA, UK

Australian Province

Christopher Myers SSM
(*Provincial, assumed office November 2009*)

Laurence Eyers	*lay members:*	Joyce Bleby Lewis
David Wells	Geoff Pridham	Judith Nurton Smith
Dunstan McKee	Stuart Smith	Iris Trengrove
Matthew Dowsey	Lynne Rokkas	Sue Ballett
Margaret Dewey	Joy Freier	Helen Starr
Steven de Kleer	John Lewis	
Gregory Stephens	Des Benfield	

Obituaries
18 Nov 2012 Henry Arkell, aged 85, professed 58 years

Addresses
St John's Priory, 14 St John's Street, Adelaide, South Australia 5000
Tel: 8 8223 1014 Fax: 8 8223 2764
Email: ssm.adelaide@bigpond.com

St Michael's Priory, 75 Watson's Road, Diggers Rest, Victoria 3427, Australia Tel: 03 9740 1618 Fax: 03 9740 0007
Email: ssm.melbourne@bigpond.com

Community Publication:
Sacred Mission (newsletter of the Southern Province): Editor, St John's Priory, 14 St John's Street, Adelaide, South Australia 5000

Southern African Province

(re-founded September 2004)

Tanki Mofana SSM
(Provincial, assumed office January 2013)

Michael Lapsley	Moeketsi Ernest Mototjane	Samuel Monyamane
William Nkomo		Mosuoe Rakuoane
Robert Stretton	Moeketsi Khommonngoe	
Mosia Sello	Moiloa Mokheseng	*Novices*: 4

Addresses
33 Elgin Road, Sybrand Park, Cape Town, South Africa, 7708
Tel: 21 696 4866 Email: michael.lapsley@attglobal.net

SSM Priory, PO Box 1579, Maseru 100, Lesotho
Tel: 22315979 Fax: 22310161 Email: priorssm@ilesotho.com

Community Publication
Michael Lapsley SSM, *Redeeming the Past: my journey from Freedom Fighter to Healer*, Orbis, 2012.

Society of St Francis SSF

Founded 1919 (USA)
1921 (UK)

Minister General
Email: clark.berg@ s-s-f.org

Minister Provincial (European Province)
Email: ministerssf@ franciscans.org.uk

European Province
Website: www. franciscans.org.uk

Office Book
The Daily Office SSF (revised edition 2010)

Bishop Protector
Rt Revd Michael Perham, Bishop of Gloucester

Community History
Petà Dunstan
This Poor Sort
DLT, London, 1997
£19.95 + £2 p&p

European Province SSF Registered Charity:
No. 236464

The Society of St Francis has diverse origins in a number of Franciscan groups which drew together during the 1930s to found one Franciscan Society. SSF in its widest definition includes First Order Brothers, First Order Sisters (CSF), Second Order Sisters (OSC) and a Third Order (TSSF). The First Order shares a common life of prayer, fraternity and a commitment to issues of justice, peace and the integrity of creation. In its larger houses, this includes accommodation for short-term guests; in the city houses, the Brothers are engaged in a variety of ministries, chaplaincies and care for the poor and marginalised. They are also available for retreat work, counselling and sharing in the task of mission in parishes and schools. They also work in Europe and have houses in the Americas, Australasia, the Pacific, and Korea.

CLARK BERGE SSF
(Minister General, assumed office 1 November 2007)

EUROPEAN PROVINCE

BENEDICT SSF
(Minister Provincial, assumed office June 2012)
PHILIP BARTHOLOMEW SSF *(Assistant Minister)*

Amos
Angelo
Anselm
Austin
Benjamin
Christian
Damian
David Jardine
Desmond Alban
Donald
Edmund
Giles
Hugh
James William
Jason Robert
John
Julian
Kentigern John
Kevin
Malcolm
Martin
Martin John
Nicholas Alan
Peter
Raphael
Raymond Christian
Reginald
Samuel
Thomas Anthony
Vaughan
Vincent

Novices: 7

Obituaries
2 Aug 2011 Colin Wilfred, aged 73, professed 39 years
31 May 2012 Nathanael, aged 82, professed 47 years
17 Aug 2012 Arnold, aged 92, professed 61 years
4 Oct 2012 Wilfrid, aged 96, professed 60 years
13 Jan 2013 Ronald, aged 100, professed 70 years
2 Aug 2013 Andrew, aged 85, professed 58 years

Companions: Companions are individual Christians who wish to associate themselves with the Society through prayer, friendship and in seeking to live the spirit of the Gospel in the way of St Francis. For more information about becoming a Companion contact: The Secretary for Companions at Hilfield Friary.

Third Order: see separate entry, page 162.

Addresses All email addresses are @franciscans.org.uk

The Friary, Alnmouth, Alnwick, Northumberland NE66 3NJ
Tel: 01665 830213 Fax: 01665 830580 Email: alnmouthssf

St Matthias' Vicarage, 45 Mafeking Road, Canning Town, London E16 4NS Tel: 020 7511 7848

The Master's Lodge, 58 St Peter's Street, Canterbury, Kent CT1 2BE
Tel: 01227 479364 Email: canterburyssf

St Mary-at-the-Cross, Glasshampton, Shrawley, Worcestershire WR6 6TQ
Tel: 01299 896345 Fax: 01299 896083 Email: glasshamptonssf

The Friary, Hilfield, Dorchester, Dorset DT2 7BE
Tel: 01300 341345 Fax: 01300 341293 Email: hilfieldssf

25 Karnac Road, Leeds LS8 5BL Tel: 0113 226 0647 Email: leedsssf

House of the Divine Compassion, 42 Balaam St, Plaistow, London E13 8AQ Tel: 020 7476 5189 Email: plaistowssf

St Anthony's Friary, St Anthony's Vicarage, Enslin Gardens, Newcastle upon Tyne, NE6 3SRT

Anglican Chaplaincy, Via San Gabriele dell'Adorata 12, 06081 Assisi (Pg), ITALY Bookings: passf@franciscans.org,uk

Community Publications: *franciscan,* three times a year – annual subscription is £8.00. Write to the Subscriptions Secretary at Hilfield Friary. Books available from Hilfield Friary book shop include: *The Daily Office SSF,* £10 + £2 p&p.

Community Wares: Hilfield Friary shop has on sale 'Freeland' cards, SSF publications and books of Franciscan spirituality and theology, as well as traidcraft goods. Alnmouth Friary and Glasshampton Monastery also have small shops selling cards.

Guest and Retreat Facilities

HILFIELD: The friary guest house has eight bedrooms (two twin-bedded) for men and women guests and two self-catering houses of six bedrooms each for the use of families and groups. Individually-guided retreats are available on request. There are facilities for day guests and for groups of up to forty. The brothers living at Hilfield are now joined by lay people, men and women, including families, who together comprise the Hilfield Friary Community, an intentional Franciscan community focussing on peace, justice and the integrity of creation. The Hilfield Peace and Environment Programme is an annual programme of courses & events which shares Franciscan insights on the care of creation and reconciliation. *(www.hilfieldfriary.org.uk).* The Friary is normally closed from Sunday afternoon until Tuesday morning.

ALNMOUTH: The Friary has twelve rooms (including one twin-bedded) for men or women guests. Conducted retreats are held each year and individually-guided retreats are available on request. The recently-innovated chalet is available for families and

Little Portion Friary
PO Box 399
Mount Sinai
NY 11766/0399, USA
Tel: 631 473 0533
Fax: 631 473 9434
Email: mtsinaifriary@s-s-f.org

San Damiano
573 Dolores Street
San Francisco
CA 94110, USA
Tel: 415 861 1372
Fax: 415 861 7952
Email: judehillssf@aol.com

St Francis Friary
2449 Sichel Street
Los Angeles
CA 90031, USA
Tel: 323 222 7495

Divine Providence Friary
Rua José Pedro de Carvalho Lima 180
333 Morumbi
São Paulo-SP
05712-080
BRAZIL
Tel: (11) 3672 5454

Minister Provincial
Tel: 415 861 7951
Fax: 415 861 7952
Email: judehillssf@aol.com

Website
www.s-s-f.org

groups in particular need referred by churches and social services. The Friary is closed for twenty-four hours from Sunday afternoon.

GLASSHAMPTON: This has a more contemplative ethos. The guest accommodation, available to both men and women, comprises five rooms. Groups can visit for the day, but may not exceed fifteen people. The friary is closed from noon on Mondays for twenty-four hours and at Christmas time.

PROVINCE OF THE AMERICAS

The Province of the Americas of SSF was founded as the Order of St Francis in 1919 by Father Claude Crookston, who took the name Father Joseph. Under his leadership the community developed, based first in Wisconsin and then on Long Island, New York.

The Order originally combined a monastic spirituality with a commitment to missions and evangelizing. In 1967, the OSF friars amalgamated with the Society in the UK and became the American Province of SSF.

Our lives are structured around our times together of formal prayer and the Eucharist, which give our lives a focus. Brothers engage in a wide variety of ministries: community organizing, missions, work in parishes and institutions, counselling and spiritual direction, study, the arts, serving the sick and infirm and people with AIDS, the homeless, workers in the sex industry, political work for the rights of people who are rejected by society. We come from a wide variety of backgrounds and cultural traditions. Living with each other can be difficult, but we work hard to find common ground and to communicate honestly with each other. God takes our imperfections and, in the mystery of Christ's body, makes us whole.

JUDE SSF
(Minister Provincial, assumed office May 2005)
THOMAS SSF *(Assistant Minister)*

Ambrose-Christobal
Antonio Sato
Clark Berge *(Minister General)*
Derek
Dunstan
Eric Michael
Ivanildo
James

Jonathan-Guthlac
Leo-Anthony
Maximilian Kolbe
Robert Hugh
Simon

Novices: 3
Postulants: 0

Obituaries
22 Jun 2012 Richard Jonathan, aged 60, professed 8 years

Community Publication: *The Little Chronicle,* electronic now. Write to: The Editor TLC, PO Box 399, NY 11766/0399, USA.

Guest and Retreat Facilities: There is a guest house at Little Portion Friary (Mount Sinai address), with twelve rooms, accommodating a maximum of sixteen guests. It is closed on Mondays. If there is no answer when telephoning, please leave a message on the answering machine.

Office Book: SSF Office Book

Bishop Protector: Rt Revd Jon Bruno, Bp of Los Angeles

The Province of Divine Compassion

SSF friars went from England to Papua New Guinea in the late 1950s and the first Australian house was established in 1964. The first New Zealand house followed in 1970. In 1981, the Pacific Province was divided into two: Australia/New Zealand and the Pacific Islands. The latter was divided again in 2008 into Papua New Guinea and the Solomon Islands. Since 1993 when the first Korean novices were admitted to form the Korean Franciscan brotherhood, they were linked by covenant to SSF and became part of SSF at our Provincial Chapter in 2010. We have reached a consensus to change the name of the province to The Divine Compassion.

Addresses for the Province of Divine Compassion

The Hermitage
PO Box 46
Stroud
NSW 2425
AUSTRALIA
Tel: 2 4994 5372
Fax: 2 4994 5527

Email: ssfstrd@bigpond.com

The Friary
PO Box 6134
Buranda
Brisbane
QLD 4102
AUSTRALIA
Tel: 7 3391 3915
Fax: 7 3391 3916

Website: www.franciscan.org.au

Friary of the Divine Compassion
PO Box 13-117
Hillcrest
Hamilton 3251
AOTEOROA NEW ZEALAND
Tel: 7 856 6701

Email: friary@franciscan.org.nz

Website: www.franciscan.org.nz

CHRISTOPHER JOHN SSF
(Minister Provincial, assumed office 2012)
BRUCE-PAUL SSF *(Assistant Minister)*

Alfred BoonKong	James Andrew	Simone
Bart	Lawrence	Stephen
Brian	Lionel	William
Damian Kenneth	Nathan-James	
Daniel	Noel-Thomas	*Novices:* 1
Donald Campbell	Raphael Suh	

Guest and Retreat Facilities

There is limited accommodation for short stay guests in the Brisbane, Stroud, Hamilton and Korea houses. In all cases, payment is by donation. Additionally, in Korea larger numbers can be accommodated at the nearby Diocesan Retreat House managed by the Brothers.

At Stroud, the old monastery of the Community of St Clare is also available for accommodation. The booking telephone number is: 2 4960 7100.

The Friary
156 Balsan-Ri
Nam-Myeon
Chuncheon 200-922
Republic of Korea
Tel: 33 262 4662
Fax: 33 262 4068

Email:
kfb1993@kornet.net

Website:
www.francis.or.kr

Office Book
The Daily Office SSF

Community Publication
New Zealand: *Franciscan Angles (4 per year)*
Australia: *Franciscan Angles, (3 per year)*
Korea: *newsletter* in Korean (quarterly)
All are available on the relevant websites or by email. To subscribe to printed copies, please contact the Hamilton, Brisbane or Korea address as appropriate. In all cases, subscription is by donation.

Community Wares
Holding Crosses (Stroud, Brisbane & Korea)
Block-mounted religious prints (Korea)

Bishops Protector
Most Revd Roger Herft, Archbishop of Perth *(Protector General)*
To be appointed *(Deputy Protector for New Zealand)*
Most Revd Paul Kim, Bishop of Seoul *(Deputy Protector for Korea)*

Brother Simone SSF of the Province of Divine Compassion

Papua New Guinea Province

Oswald Dumbari SSF
(*Minister Provincial, assumed office July 2012*)

Albert Bobogara
Anthony Kambuwa
Charles Iada
Clement Vulum
Collin Velei
Ham Kevaja
Jerry Ross
John Gai
Laurence Hauje
Lester Meso
Lindsay Ijiba
Nathaniel Gari
Peter Kevin
Reuben Arthur
Rhoy Wadidika
Wallace Yovero
Willbert
Worrick Marako

Novices: 3

Bishop Protector
Most Revd Joseph Kopapa, Archbishop of PNG & Bishop of Popondota

Addresses in PNG

Saint Mary of the Angels Friary, Haruro, PO Box 78, Popondetta 241, Oro Province Tel: 329 7060

Geoffrey's Friary, Katerada, PO Box 78, Popondetta 241, Oro Province

Saint Francis Friary, Koki, PO Box 1103, Port Moresby, NCD Tel & fax: 320 1499 Email: ssfpng@daltron.com.pg

Martyrs' House, PO Box 35, Popondetta, Oro Province Tel & fax: 3297 491

Philip Beawa Friary, Ukaka, PO Box 22, Alotau, Milne Bay Province

Province of the Solomon Islands

Clifton Henry SSF
(*Minister, assumed office March 2012*)

Athanasius Faifu	Francis Ngofia	Luke Manitara	Stephen Watson Hovu
Andrew Laukiara	Hilton Togara	Manasseh Birahu	Thomas Hereward Peleba
Andrew Manu	Ini Mumua	Martin Tawea	
Benjamin Tabugau	John Kogudi	Matthew Sikoboki	
Caspar Gu'urau	John Mark Ofu	Noel Pwetus	
Commins Romano	John Rare	Patrick Paoni	*Novices:* 14
Elliott Faga	Jonas Balugna	Samson Amoni	
Ellison Ho'asepepe	Judah Kea	Samson Siho	
Ellison Sero	Lent Joseph Fugui	Selwyn Tione	

Bishop Protector: Rt Revd Richard Naramana, Bishop of Ysabel

Addresses in the Solomon Islands

Patteson House, PO Box 519, Honiara, Guadalcanal Tel: 22386 Regional Office tel & fax: 25810

St Bonaventure Friary, Kohimarama Theological College, PO Box 519, Honiara, Guadalcanal Tel: 50128

Saint Francis Friary, PO Box 7, Auki, Malaita Province Tel: 40054

San Damiano Friary, Diocese of Hanuato'o, Kira Kira, Makira Ulawa Province

Michael Davis Friary, PO Box 519, Honiara, Guadalcanal

La Verna Friary/Little Portion, Hautambu, PO Box 519, Honiara, Guadalcanal

Holy Martyrs Friary, Luisalo, PO Box 50, Lata, Temotu Province

Society of St John the Divine

SSJD

Founded 1887

Cottage 252
Umdoni
Retirement Village
PO Box 300
Pennington 4184
KwaZulu Natal
SOUTH AFRICA

Tel: +27
039 975 9552

Emails:
maryevelyncoffee
@gmail.com

hil64337
@gmail.com

Angelus
& Morning Prayer
8.15 am

Angelus
& Midday Office
12.15 pm

Angelus
& Evening Prayer
5.00 pm

Compline
7.30 pm

Prayer Time
taken privately

The Society has never been a large community, with just sixty professions over a century, and has always worked in Natal. Originally the community ran schools and orphanages. In 1994, after the death of the older Sisters, the four of us who remained moved to a house that was more central in Durban.

We moved to Umdoni Retirement Village in Pennington in 2003. Our involvement outside the village involves being on the Board of Governors of our school, St John's Diocesan School for Girls in Pietermaritzburg, and all our Associates, Friends and Oblates worldwide. Sister Mary Evelyn is a Layminister and exercises her ministry within Umdoni. Sister Margaret Anne is now resident in a nursing home in Pennington.

Sister Mary Evelyn SSJD
Sister Margaret Anne SSJD
Sister Sophia SSJD
Sister Hilary SSJD

Oblates and Associates: These are people who are linked with us and support us in prayer.
Oblates: There is one, non-resident, and she renews her oblation annually.
Associates: There are over a hundred, some overseas. They have a Rule of Life and renew their promises annually.
Friends: They have a Rule of Life and like the Associates and Oblates meet with the Sisters quarterly, and they renew their promises annually.
Friends and Associates meet quarterly in a different area group.

Community Publication
One newsletter is sent out each year to Oblates, Associates and friends in Advent.

Community History and books
Sister Margaret Anne SSJD, *What the World Counts Weakness,* privately published 1987 (now out of print).

Sister Margaret Anne SSJD, *They Even Brought Babies,* privately published.

Bishop Visitor
Rt Revd Rubin Phillip,
Bishop of Natal, Dean of the Province

Office Book
An Anglican Prayer Book 1989 (South African) for Morning & Evening Prayer.
Our own SSJD book for Midday Office & Compline.

Society of St John the Evangelist

(UK)

SSJE

Founded 1866

Email: superior@ssje.org.uk

A Registered Charity.

The Society of Saint John the Evangelist is the oldest of the Anglican orders for men, founded at Cowley in Oxford in 1866 by Father Richard Meux Benson. From it grew the North American Congregation and we were also involved in the founding of several other Communities around the world both for men and women. SSJE worked as a Missionary Order in several countries, most notably India and South Africa. In 2012 the English Congregation closed its last House in London and went into retirement where they continue to live out their vows.

FATHER PETER HUCKLE SSJE
(Superior, assumed office 7 March 2002)
Father Peter Palmer
Brother James Simon

The Fellowship of St John: Email: superior@ssje.org.uk

Bishop Visitor: Rt Revd Dominic Walker OGS

Society of St John the Evangelist

(North American Congregation)

SSJE

Founded 1866

The Monastery
980 Memorial Drive
Cambridge
MA 02138
USA
Tel: 617 876 3037

Email: monastery@ssje.org

The Society of St John the Evangelist was founded in the parish of Cowley in Oxford, England, by Richard Meux Benson in 1866. A branch house was established in Boston in 1870. The brothers of the N. American Congregation live at the monastery in Cambridge, Massachusetts, near Harvard Square, and at Emery House, a rural retreat sanctuary in West Newbury, Massachusetts. They gather throughout the day to pray the Divine Office, and live under a modern Rule of Life, adopted in 1997, which is available online at www.ssje.org. At profession, brothers take vows of poverty, celibacy and obedience.

SSJE's guesthouses offer hospitality to many. Young adults may serve for year as Monastic Interns. Guests may come individually or in groups for times of silent reflection and retreat. SSJE brothers lead retreats and programs in their own houses and in parishes, dioceses throughout North America. SSJE brothers also serve as preachers, teachers, spiritual directors and confessors. One of the brothers, Thomas Shaw, is Bishop of Massachusetts. Each year, SSJE brothers serve as chaplains for pilgrimages in Israel/Palestine sponsored by St George's College, Jerusalem. In recent years, brothers have been leading retreats and teaching in Anglican churches and seminaries in Kenya and Tanzania. Nearer to home, they are engaged in part-time ministries with students and young adults, the Deaf, Asian-Americans, and those in Twelve-step Programs.

BROTHER GEOFFREY TRISTRAM SSJE
(*Superior, assumed office 4 May 2010*)
BROTHER JAMES KOESTER SSJE *(Deputy Superior)*
BROTHER DAVID VRYHOF SSJE *(Assistant Superior)*

David Allen
John Oyama *(in Japan)*
Bernard Russell
Thomas Shaw
John Goldring *(in Canada)*
Jonathan Maury
Eldridge Pendleton

Curtis Almquist
Mark Brown
Robert L'Esperance
Luke Witewig

Novices: 4
Postulants: 2

Obituaries

23 Sep 2011 John Mathis, aged 88 professed 17 years

Associates

The Fellowship of Saint John is composed of men and women throughout the world who desire to live their Christian life in special association with the Society of Saint John the Evangelist. They have a vital interest in the life and work of the community and support its life and ministries with their prayers, encouragement and gifts. The brothers of the Society welcome members of the Fellowship as partners in the gospel life, and pray for them by name during the Daily Office, following a regular cycle. Together they form an extended family, a company of friends abiding in Christ and seeking to bear a united witness to him as "the Way, the Truth and the Life", following the example of the beloved Disciple. For further information, or to join the Fellowship, visit the Society's website: www.ssje.org.

Other address

Emery House, 21 Emery Lane, West Newbury, MA 01985, USA Tel: 978 462 7940

Community Publication: Cowley: a quarterly newsletter. Available online (www.ssje.org) or in printed form (contact monastery@ssje.org). For a subscription, write to SSJE at the Cambridge, Massachusetts, address. The suggested donation is US$20 annually.

Guest and Retreat Facilities

MONASTERY GUESTHOUSE in Cambridge, MA – 16 rooms.
EMERY HOUSE in West Newbury, MA – 6 hermitages, 3 rooms in main house.
At both houses: US$100 per night/ US$50 for full-time students (closed in August).

Morning Prayer
6.00 am

Eucharist
7.45 am

Midday Prayer
12.30 pm

Evening Prayer
6.00 pm

Compline
8.30 pm

(The schedule varies slightly during the week. The complete schedule can be found on the community's website.)

Office Book
BCP of ECUSA, and the Book of Alternate Services of the Anglican Church of Canada

Website
www.ssje.org

Cowley Publications
Website:
www.cowley.org

Community History
This is now being written.

Bishop Visitor
Rt Revd
Frank T. Griswold, III

Society of St Margaret

(Duxbury)

SSM

Founded 1855
(US Convent founded 1873)

St Margaret's Convent
50 Harden Hill Road
PO Box C
Duxbury
MA 02331-0605
USA
Tel: 781 934 9477
Fax: 781 934 0837

Email: convent@ssmbos.org

Website
www.ssmbos.org

Morning Prayer
6.00 am

Eucharist 7.30 am

Noon Office
12 noon

Evening Prayer
5.00 pm

Compline 7.30 pm

Office Book
BCP
of ECUSA

The Sisters of St Margaret are an Episcopal Religious Order of women called to glorify God and proclaim the gospel of Jesus Christ through our worship and work, prayer and common life. Our commitment to God and to one another is expressed through vows of poverty, celibate chastity and obedience.

The Eucharist is central to our lives. From the center we go forth to celebrate the diversity, fullness and creativity of the people of God. We reverence all, seeking the living Christ in one another and in all creation. We strive for a spirit of fearlessness in Christian service, encouraged and empowered by the presence of the Spirit.

Our Sisters minister in many places: schools, prisons, parishes, nursing homes and homeless shelters. Our Houses offer hospitality to guests, retreatants, parish and civic groups, and all who long for a contemplative space in their lives. As a Community we will deepen our commitment to prayer, inviting others to join us in seeking greater intimacy with God. We live out our values in ministry with the poorest of the poor in Haiti; at the crossroads of urban life in lower Manhattan; and in Boston and its suburbs.

SISTER ADELE MARIE SSM *(priest)*
(*Mother Superior, assumed office March 2011*)
SISTER CAROLYN SSM (*Assistant Superior)*

Sr Catherine Louise (*priest*)
Sister Marjorie Raphael
Sister Marion
Sister Emily Louise
Sister Gloria
Sister Marie Margaret
Sister Ann
Sister Claire Marie
Sister Mary Gabriel
Sister Adele
Sister Julian
Sister Christine
Sister Marie Thérèse
Sister Brigid
Sister Promise
Sister Grace
Sister Sarah Margaret *(priest)*
Sister Kristina Frances
Sister Kethia

Obituaries

15 Jun 2011 Sister Bernardine, aged 95, professed 70 years
21 Jun 2011 Sister Lucy Mary, aged 94, professed 66 years
23 Aug 2011 Sister Mary Michael, aged 95, prof. 52 years
5 Sep 2011 Sister Jane Margaret, aged 90, prof. 62 years

Community Publication: *St Margaret's Quarterly*. Issues available free on our website or by email. For information, contact communications@ssmbos.org. The subscription rate is $10 for mailed copies.

Associates
Associates of one Convent of the Society of St Margaret are Associates of all. They have a common Rule, which is flexible to circumstances. They include men and women, lay and ordained. No Associate of the Society may be an Associate of any other community.

Addresses of other houses

Sisters of St Margaret, 375 Mount Vernon Street, Apt 611, Boston, MA 02125, USA Tel: 617 533 7742 Email: srmgssm@yahoo.com

St Margaret's Convent, Port-au-Prince, Haiti
Mailing address: **St Margaret's Convent, Port-au-Prince, c/o Agape Flights, Inc., 100 Airport Avenue, Venice, FL 34285-3901, USA**
Tel: 011 509 3443 3683 Email: mariemargaretssm@yahoo.com

Neale House, 50 Fulton Street #2A, New York, NY 10038-1800, USA
Tel: 212 619 2672 Email: annwhitaker1942@gmail.com

Community History
Sister Catherine Louise SSM, *The House of my Pilgrimage: a History of the American House of the Society of Saint Margaret,* privately published, 1973.
Sister Catherine Louise SSM, *The Planting of the Lord: The History of the Society of Saint Margaret in England, Scotland & the USA;* privately published, 1995.
Contact communications@ssmbos.org to order. $6 US each, plus $4 US shipping and handling.

Guest and Retreat Facilities
Limited guest facilities. Contact the Duxbury convent for more information.

Bishop Visitor: Rt Rev David B. Joslin, Bishop of Central New York, Res.

Society of St Margaret

(Hackney)

SSM

Founded 1855
(St Saviour's Priory 1866)

Website: www.stsavioursprioty.org.uk

St Saviour's Priory is one of the autonomous Houses which constitute the Society of St Margaret founded by John Mason Neale. Exploring contemporary ways of living the Religious life, the community seeks, through a balance of prayer and ministry, to respond to some of the needs that arise amongst the marginalised in East London. The Office is four-fold and the Eucharist is offered daily. The Sisters' outreach to the local community includes: working as staff members (lay or ordained) in various parishes; supporting issues of justice and racial equality; supporting the gay community; Sunday Stall and Drop in Centre; Dunloe Centre for the homeless and alcoholics; complementary therapy; individual spiritual direction and retreats; dance workshops; art work and design. The Sisters also share their community building and resources of worship and space with individuals and groups.

St Saviour's Priory
18 Queensbridge Road
London E2 8NS
UK
Tel: 020 7739 9976
Email: ssmpriory@aol.com

Leader of the community
020 7613 1464

Guest Bookings
020 7739 6775
Fax: 020 7739 1248

(Sisters are not available on Mondays)

Morning Prayer
7.15 am
(7.30 am Sun)
followed by
Eucharist
(12.15 pm on major feasts)

Midday Office
12.45 pm

Evening Prayer
5.00 pm

Night Prayer
8.30 pm

Office Book
Celebrating Common Prayer

Registered Charity
No 230927

LEADERSHIP ELECTION DUE 2013

Sister June Atkinson
The Revd Sister Judith Blackburn SSM *(priest)*
Sister Frances (Claire) Carter
Sister Elizabeth Crawford
Sister Pauline (Mary) Hardcastle
Sister Anna Huston
Sister Enid Margaret Jealous
Sister Moira Jones
The Revd Sister Helen Loder SSM *(priest)*
The Revd Sister Sue Makin *(deacon)*
Sister Pamela Radford

Associates and Friends

ASSOCIATES make a long term commitment to the Society of St Margaret, following a Rule of Life and helping the Community where possible. An Associate of one SSM house is an Associate of all the houses. There are regular quiet days for Associates who are kept in touch with community developments.

FRIENDS OF ST SAVIOUR'S PRIORY commit themselves to a year of mutual support and friendship and are invited to regular events throughout the year.

Community Publication: *The Orient*, yearly. Write to The Orient Secretary at St Saviour's Priory. Brochures about the Community are available at any time on request.

Community Wares

Cards, books and religious items for sale.

Community History

Memories of a Sister of S. Saviour's Priory, Mowbray, 1904.

A Hundred Years in Haggerston, published by St Saviour's Priory, 1966.

Sister Catherine Louise SSM, *The Planting of the Lord: The History of the Society of Saint Margaret in England, Scotland & the USA;* privately published, 1995.

Guest and Retreat Facilities

Six single rooms for individual guests. Excellent facilities for non-residential group meetings.

Most convenient time to telephone

10.30 am – 1.00 pm (Not Mondays).

Bishop Visitor

Rt Revd Jonathan Clark, Bishop of Croydon

Society of St Margaret (Uckfield) SSM

Founded 1855

**St Margaret's Convent
Hooke Hall
250 High Street
Uckfield
East Sussex
TN22 1EN
UK
Tel: 01825 766808**

**Emails:
uckfieldssm@hotmail.co.uk**

egmotherssm@hotmail.com

Eucharist 8.00 am (9.30 am Sun & 11 am Wed in the parish church)

Matins 9.15 am (8.00 am Sun & Wed)

Midday Office & Litany of the Holy Name 12.30 pm

Vespers 5.00 pm (4.45 pm Sun)

Compline 8.00 pm

Office Book
'A Community Office' printed for St Margaret's Convent, East Grinstead

The Convent at Hooke Hall is one of the autonomous Convents which constitute the Society of St Margaret, founded by John Mason Neale. The Sisters' work is the worship of God, expressed in their life of prayer and service. They welcome visitors as guests and retreatants, and are involved in spiritual direction and parish work. At Chiswick they care for elderly people in a nursing home and have guests. There is a semi-autonomous house and a branch house in Sri Lanka.

MOTHER CYNTHIA CLARE SSM
(Mother Superior, assumed office 2 March 2000)
SISTER MARY PAUL SSM *(Assistant Superior)*

Sister Raphael Mary	Sister Lucy
Sister Mary Michael	Sister Barbara
Sister Rita Margaret	Sister Mary Clare
Sister Jennifer Anne	Sister Sarah

Obituaries
14 Sep 2012 Sister Elizabeth, aged 86, professed 20 years

Associates: Associates observe a simple Rule, share in the life of prayer and dedication of the community, and are welcomed at all SSM convents.

Other address:
St Mary's Convent & Nursing Home, Burlington Lane, Chiswick, London W4 2QE, UK
Tel: 020 8 994 4641 Fax: 020 8995 9796

Community Publication
St Margaret's Chronicle, Newsletter twice a year. Write to the Editor at St Margaret's Convent. £4.00 per annum, including postage and packing.

Community History: Sister Catherine Louise SSM, *The Planting of the Lord: The History of the Society of Saint Margaret in England, Scotland & the USA;* privately published, 1995.

Pamela Myers & Sheila White, *A Legacy of Care: St Mary's Convent and Nursing Home, Chiswick, 1896 to 2010,* St Mary's Convent, Chiswick, 2010.

Doing the Impossible: a short sketch of St Margaret's Convent, East Grinstead 1855–1980, privately published, 1984. Postscript 2000.

Guest and Retreat Facilities
There are 3 beds primarily for individual retreats. Day retreatants are welcome: both as individuals and in groups of up to twelve people. Some Sisters are available for

Bishop Visitor
Rt Revd Martin Warner, Bishop of Chichester

Registered Charity:
No. 231926

support in these retreats. Donations are appreciated. Quiet afternoons are arranged on a regular basis.

Most convenient time to telephone:
10.00 am – 12 noon, 7.00 pm – 8.00 pm.

SEMI-AUTONOMOUS HOUSES OVERSEAS

St Margaret's Convent
157 St Michael's Road
Polwatte
Colombo 3
SRI LANKA

The Sisters run a Retreat House, a Hostel for young women, a Home for elderly people, and are involved in parish work and church embroidery.

SISTER CHANDRANI SSM
(Sister Superior, assumed office 2006)
Sister Lucy Agnes
Sister Jane Margaret
Sister Mary Christine

Bishop Visitor
Rt Revd Dhiloraj Canagasaby, Bishop of Colombo

Other address
A children's home:
St John's Home, 133 Galle Rd, Moratuwa, SRI LANKA

Society of St Margaret

(Walsingham)

SSM

Founded 1855
(Walsingham Priory founded 1955)

The Priory of Our Lady
Bridewell Street
Walsingham
Norfolk
NR22 6ED
UK
Tel: 01328 820340 (Revd Mother)
Tel: 01328 820901 (Sisters & guests)

In January 1994, the Priory of Our Lady at Walsingham reverted to being an autonomous house of the Society of St Margaret. The Sisters are a Traditional Community whose daily life is centred on the Eucharist and the daily Office, from which flows their growing involvement in the ministry of healing, and reconciliation in the Shrine, the local parishes and the wider Church. They welcome guests for short periods of rest, relaxation and retreat, and are available to pilgrims and visitors. They also work in the Shrine shop and the Welcome Centre.

SISTER MARY TERESA SSM
(Reverend Mother, installed 30 May 2011)

Sister Alma Mary
Sister Francis Anne
Sister Columba
Sister Phyllis *(in care)*

Novices: 1

Obituaries

8 Jan 2012 Sister Mary Joan, aged 93, professed 19 years
2 Nov 2012 Sr Christina Mary, aged 84, professed 56 years

Emails:
Mother: teresa@prioryofourlady.uk.com
Bursar: bursar@prioryofourlady.uk.com

Bishop Visitor
Rt Revd Peter Wheatley, Bishop of Edmonton

Readings & Morning Prayer
7.00 am

Mass 9.00 am
(on Thu, followed by Exposition to 10.00 am) (No Mass on Sun in Sisters' Chapel)

Exposition of the Blessed Sacrament
10.30 am – 12.30 pm
(except Sun & Thu)

Midday Prayer
12.45 pm

Evening Prayer
5.00 pm

Night Prayer
8.45 pm
(7.00 pm Sun)

Associates
There are Associates, and Affiliated Parishes and Groups.

Community Publication: Community booklet, *Wellspring*, published annually in the autumn. Write to the Priory for information. £3.50, including postage.

Community History
Sister Catherine Louise SSM, *The Planting of the Lord: The History of the Society of Saint Margaret in England, Scotland & the USA;* privately published, 1995.

Community Wares
Cards (re-cycled) and embroidered; books; Religious objects (statues, pictures, rosary purses etc).

Guest and Retreat Facilities: St Margaret's Cottage, (self-catering) for women and men, families and small groups. One single room (bed sit, ensuite) on the ground floor, suitable for a retreatant, and three twin rooms upstairs.

Most convenient time to telephone: 10.30 am – 12.30 pm; 2.30 pm – 4.30 pm; 6.30 pm – 8.30 pm.

Office Book: The Divine Office

Registered Charity: No. 25515

Society of St Paul

SSP

Founded 1958

2728 Sixth Avenue
San Diego
CA 92103-6397
USA
Tel: 619 542 8660
Email: anbssp@societyofstpaul.com

Bishop Visitor
Rt Revd
James R Mathes,
Bishop of San Diego

The Society of St Paul began in Gresham, Oregon in 1958. Early ministry included nursing homes, a school, and commissary work in the Mid-East and Africa. In 1959, SSP was the first community for men to be recognized by the canons of ECUSA. The brothers live a life of prayer and are dedicated to works of mercy, charity and evangelism. In 1976, the order moved to Palm Desert, California, providing a retreat and conference center until 1996. In 2001, the brothers moved to St Paul's Cathedral in San Diego. In particular, we are involved at St Paul's Senior Homes and Services, the Uptown Faith Community Services, Inc., Dorcas House, a foster home for children whose parents are in prison in Tijuana, Mexico, and St Paul's Cathedral ministries.

THE REVD CANON BARNABAS HUNT SSP
(*Rector, assumed office 1989*)
THE REVD CANON ANDREW RANK SSP (*Associate Rector*)

Fellowship of St Paul
The Fellowship of St Paul, our extended family, is an association of Friends, Associates and Companions of the Society of St Paul, who live a Rule of Life centered on the Glory of God.

Society of the Sisters of Bethany

SSB

Founded 1866

7 Nelson Road
Southsea
Hampshire
PO5 2AR
UK
Tel: 02392 833498
Email: ssb@sistersofbethany.org.uk

Website: www.sistersofbethany.org.uk

Mattins 7.00 am

Mass 7.45 am (8.00 am Sun; 9.30 am Wed & alternate Sats)

Terce 9.15 am

Midday Office 12 noon

Vespers 5.00 pm

Compline 8.00 pm

Office Book
Anglican Office book with adaptations

Registered Charity:
No. 226582

By prayer and activity, the Sisters seek to share in the work of reconciling the divided Churches of Christendom and the whole world. At the heart of each Sister's vocation is a call to prayer. The Community prays daily for the unity of Christians. The intention of the Eucharist every Thursday is for Unity and is followed by their Office for Unity. On Fridays a three-hour Prayer Watch is kept in Chapel, and in addition each Sister has her own special intentions. The Sisters' online ministry using Twitter (**twitter.com @bethanysister**) and Facebook (**facebook.com@sisters .ofbethany**) engages with nearly 3,000 people meeting them where they are and helping them see that God really is in the 'everyday'. Each Sister makes the offering of herself in the hidden life of prayer within the Community, in the belief that God desires and accepts that offering. They are encouraged to persevere by some words of Abbé Paul Couturier with which he concluded one of his letters to the Community: "In Christ let us pray, pray, pray for Unity." The work of the Sisters includes giving hospitality for those seeking spiritual or physical refreshment and arranging retreats and quiet days.

MOTHER RITA-ELIZABETH SSB
(Reverend Mother, assumed office 22 October 2009)
SISTER MARY JOY SSB *(Assistant Superior)*

Sister Katherine Maryel
Sister Ruth Etheldreda
Sister Florence May
Sister Ann Patricia
Sister Gwenyth
Sister Joanna Elizabeth
Sister Elizabeth Pio

Associates

The Associates are a body of close friends who unite their life of prayer to that of the Community and who are accepted as members of an extended Community family. They live in their own homes and accept a simple rule of life which is the expression of a shared concern to love and serve God and one another after the example of Martha, Mary and Lazarus.

Community Wares: Cards.

Community Publication: Associates' magazine, Jul & Dec

Guest and Retreat Facilities: 6 rooms (1 twin-bedded). Individual retreatants welcome. Closed at Christmas.

Most convenient time to telephone:
9.30 am – 11.45 am, 1 pm – 4 pm, 6 pm – 7.45 pm

Bishop Visitor: Rt Revd Trevor Willmott, Bp of Dover

Some other Communities

Africa

Benedictine Sisters of Bethany (EBSB) **Bamenda, Cameroon**

The EBSB sprang fom the Emmanuel Sisterhood, a community of sisters that was founded in 1971 in Makak, among members of the Eglise Presbyterienne du Cameroon (EPC). The sisters moved to Bafut in 1975, a year after they had transferred to the Presbyterian Church in Cameroon (PCC). Their foundress, Sister Madeleine Marie Handy, was the first women ordained in the PCC (in 1978). She died in 1999 and was succeeded by Sister Judith Ngo Nyemb.

One of the Emmanuel sisters, Sister Jane Manka'a, who had joined the community aged just 16, had a vision of working with the many homeless and orphaned street children found in Bamenda. To this end, she left the Emmanuels and became an Anglican. She started the Good Shepherd Home in Bamenda, which cares for 35 children, who would otherwise have nowhere to go and no one to look after them. The new community is called the Benedictine Sisters of Bethany.

Asia

The Order of Women, Church of South India

18, CSI Women's House, Infantry Road, Bengaluru, Karnataka 560001, India

Soon after the inauguration of the CSI in 1948, a Religious Order for women was organized under the initiative and leadership of Sister Carol Graham, a deaconess in the Anglican Church before 1948. The Order has both active and associate members. The former take a vow of celibacy, observe a rule of life and are engaged in some form of full-time Christian service. The Order is a member of the Diakonia World Federation. The Sisters are dispersed among the twenty-one dioceses of the CSI.

Sisters of St Francis (SSF)

206 Eoamri, Miwonmyeon, Cheongwongun, Chungcheonbukdo 363-872, Republic of Korea Tel: (043) 225 6856

Australasia and the Pacific

Congregation of the Sisters of the Visitation of Our Lady (CVL)

Convent of the Visitation, Hetune, Box 18 , Popondetta, Oro Province, PNG

Europe

Society of the Franciscan Servants of Jesus and Mary (FSJM)

Posbury St Francis, Crediton, Devon, EX17 3QG, UK

Society of Our Lady of the Isles (SOLI)

Lark's Hame, Aithness, Isle of Fetlar, Shetland ZE2 9DJ, UK Tel: 01957 733303
https://sites.google.com/site/societyofourladyoftheisles/

North America and the Caribbean

Order of the Teachers of the Children of God (TCG)

5870 East 14th Street, Tucson, AZ 85711, USA

Society of Our Lady St Mary (SLSM)

Bethany Place, PO Box 762, Digby, Nova Scotia, BOV 1AO, Canada

SINGLE CONSECRATED LIFE

One of the earliest ways of living the Religious life is for single people to take a vow of consecrated celibacy and to live in their own homes. This ancient form of commitment is also a contemporary one with people once again embracing this form of Religious life. Some may have an active ministry, others follow a contemplative lifestyle, some are solitaries, and others are widows or widowers. In 2002, the Advisory Council (for Religious Communities in the Church of England) set up a Personal Vows group in response to enquiries from bishops and others to advise those who wish to take a vow of consecrated celibacy. In 2011 the Advisory Council approved a constitution for the network, and a leadership team was elected which now provides support for those who have professed this vow and arranges gatherings. In the Roman Catholic Church, this form of living the consecrated life was affirmed by Vatican II, which re-established the Order of Consecrated Virgins (OCV) and now an order of Widows is also emerging.

People exploring this call should be single, widowed, widowered or divorced, mature Christians (men or women) already committed to a life of prayer and willing to undertake a period of discernment before taking a temporary vow which may precede a life vow. An appropriate spiritual director and support from association with a Religious Community or through the Single Consecrated Life network is important to ensure adequate formation. We also have a group of Friends who support us in prayer.

The vow is received by a person's bishop. The bishop (or their appointee) becomes the 'guardian of the vow' and the act of consecration is registered with SCL for the Advisory Council.

SUE HARTLEY *(Coordinating Dean)*
BEVERLEY SMITH *(Dean of Sisters)* PHILLIP TOVEY *(Dean of Brothers)*

Persons in Life Vows: 22 Persons in First Vows: 9
Seekers: 13

For further information contact:
Sue Hartley SCL
272 New North Road
Ilford IG6 3BT
UK
Email: suemhartley@btinternet.com

Website: http://singleconsecratedlifeanglican.org.uk/index.html

A group at an SCL meeting in the garden at CSJD in Birmingham.

Directory of dispersed celibate communities

In this section are communities that from their foundation have lived as dispersed communities. In other words, their members do not necessarily live a common life in community, although they do come together for chapter meetings and other occasions each year.

Like traditional communities, they do take vows that include celibacy.

OGS worldwide Brethren in Chapter, Ditchingham, UK, 2011

Oratory of the Good Shepherd

OGS

Founded 1913

Website
www.ogs.net

Bishop Visitor
Rt Revd Jack Nicholls

The Oratory of the Good Shepherd is a society of priests and laymen founded at Cambridge (UK), which now has provinces in North America, Australia, Southern Africa and Europe. Oratorians are bound together by a common Rule and discipline; members do not generally live together in community. The brethren are grouped in 'colleges' and meet regularly for prayer and support, and each province meets annually for retreat and chapter. Every three years, the General Chapter meets, presided over by the Superior of the whole Oratory, whose responsibility is to maintain the unity of the provinces.

Consecration of life in the Oratory has the twin purpose of fostering the individual brother's personal search for God in union with his brethren, and as a sign of the Kingdom. So through the apostolic work of the brethren, the Oratory seeks to make a contribution to the life and witness of the whole Church.

In common with traditional communities, the Oratory requires celibacy. Brothers are accountable to their brethren for their spending and are expected to live simply and with generosity. The ideal spiritual pattern includes daily Eucharist, Offices, and an hour of prayer. Study is also regarded as important in the life. During the time of probation which is for two years, the new brother is cared for and nurtured in the Oratory life by another brother of his College. The brother may then, with the consent of the province, make his first profession, which is renewed annually for at least five years, though with the hope of intention and perseverance for life. After five years, profession can be made for a longer period, and after ten years a brother may, with the consent of the whole Oratory, make his profession for life.

Companions and Associates
The Oratory has an extended family of Companions, with their own rule of life, and Associates. Companionship is open to men and women, lay or ordained, married or single.

Community History
George Tibbatts, *The Oratory of the Good Shepherd: The First Seventy-five Years,* The Almoner OGS, Windsor, 1988.

Obituaries
25 Dec 2012 David Jowitt, aged 87, professed 47 years, Superior 1975-81

PETER HIBBERT OGS
(*Superior, assumed office August 2011*)
2 Blossom Road, Erdington, Birmingham, B24 0UD, UK
Tel: 0121 382 7286

The Community in Australia

KEITH DEAN-JONES OGS
(*Provincial, assumed office 2011*)
St John's Rectory, 294 Victoria Street, Taree, NSW, AUSTRALIA
or PO Box 377, Taree, NSW, AUSTRALIA
Tel: (0) 26552 1310 Email: kdean-jones@ogs.net

Michael Boyle
Trevor Bulled
Robert Braun
Michael Chiplin
Barry Greaves
Charles Helms
Ronald Henderson
Roger Kelly
Kenneth Mason
John Stevenson
Geoffrey Tisdall

Probationers: 0

The Community in North America

PHILIP HOBSON OGS
(*Provincial, assumed office August 2005*)
151 Glenlake Avenue, Toronto, Ontario, M6P 1E8, CANADA
Tel: (0) 416 604 4883 Email: phobson@ogs.net

David Brinton
Gregory Bufkin
William Derby
Carlson Gerdau
Michael Moyer
Walter Raymond
Edward Simonton

Probationers: 1

The Community in southern Africa

JOHN SALT OGS
(*Provincial, assumed office 2010*)
"Palmers", 5 Common Place, Walsingham, Norfolk, NR22 6BW, UK
Tel: 01328 820823 Email: jsalt@ogs.net

Tammy Masikane
James Mvuba
Thanda Ngcobo
Jabulani Ngidi
Douglas Price
Thami Shange
Mlungisi 'Dicky' Shozi

Probationers: 5

The Community in Europe

MICHAEL BARTLETT OGS
(*Provincial, assumed office August 2011*)
Cobblers Cottage, 3–5 Park Road, Sandy, Bedfordshire, SG19 1JB, UK
Tel: 01767 683951 Email: mbartlett@ogs.net

Peter Baldwin
Alexander Bennett
Michael Bootes
Michael Bullock
Malcolm Crook
Peter Ford
Nicholas Gandy
David Johnson
Brian Lee
Robert Pipes
Christopher Powell
Lindsay Urwin
Dominic Walker
Peter Walker

Probationers: 3

Directory of acknowledged Communities

In this section are communities that are 'acknowledged' by the Church as living out a valid Christian witness, but whose members do not all take traditional Religious vows. Some communities expect their members to remain single whilst others may include members who are married: some have both members who remain celibate and those who do not. The specific vows they take therefore will vary according to their own particular Rule. However, communities in this section have an Episcopal Visitor or Protector. Some are linked to communities listed in section 1, others were founded without ties to traditional celibate orders. This section also includes some ashrams in dioceses in Asia.

In the Episcopal Church of the USA, these communities are referred to in the canons as 'Religious communities' – as distinct from those in section 1 of this *Year Book*, which are referred to as 'Religious orders'. However, this distinction is not used in other parts of the Anglican Communion where 'communities' is also used for those who take traditional vows.

Brotherhood of Saint Gregory

BSG

Founded 1969

Brotherhood of Saint Gregory
PO Box 57
White Plains
NY 10602
USA

Email:
Servant@gregorians.org

Website
www.gregorians.org

Office Book
The Book of Common Prayer (1979)

The Brotherhood of Saint Gregory was founded on Holy Cross Day 1969, by Richard Thomas Biernacki, after consultation with many Episcopal and Roman Catholic Religious. The first brothers made their profession of vows in the New York monastery of the Visitation Sisters. Later that year, Bishop Horace Donegan of New York recognized the Brotherhood as a Religious community of the Episcopal Church.

The community is open to clergy and laity, without regard to marital status. Gregorian Friars follow a common Rule, living individually, in small groups, or with their families, supporting themselves and the community through secular or church-related employment.

The Rule requires the Holy Eucharist, the four Offices of the Book of Common Prayer, meditation, theological study, Embertide reports, the tithe, and participation in Annual Convocation and Chapter.

The Postulancy program takes a minimum of one year; Novitiate at least two years, after which a novice may make First Profession of Annual Vows. Members are eligible for Life Profession after five years in Annual Vows.

Gregorian Friars minister in parishes as liturgists, musicians, clergy, artists, visitors to the sick, administrators, sextons, and teachers. A number serve the diocesan and national church. For those in secular work the 'servant theme' continues, and many are teachers, nurses, or administrators, sharing the common goal of the consecration of each brother's lifetime through prayer and service.

Community Publications & Wares

The Brotherhood produces a quarterly newsletter titled *The Servant*. Subscription is US$8.00 per year. An order blank is available by mail or via our website.

There are a number of Brotherhood publications – please write or visit our website for further details regarding placing an order.

Community History

Karekin Madteos Yarian BSG, *In Love and Service Bound: The First 40 years of the Brotherhood of Saint Gregory,* BSG, 2009.

Bishop Visitor

Rt Revd Rodney R Michel,
assisting Bishop of Pennsylvania

Brother Richard Thomas Biernacki, BSG
(Minister General and founder, assumed office 14 September 1969)

Brother James Teets
Brother Luke Antony Nowicki
Brother William Francis Jones
Brother Stephen Storen
Brother Tobias Stanislas Haller *(priest)*
Brother Edward Munro *(deacon)*
Brother Donovan Aidan Bowley
Brother Christopher Stephen Jenks
Brother Ciarán Anthony DellaFera
Brother Richard John Lorino
Brother Ronald Augustine Fox
Brother Maurice John Grove
Brother Charles Edward LeClerc *(deacon)*
Brother Virgilio Fortuna *(deacon)*
Brother Gordon John Stanley *(deacon)*
Brother Karekin Madteos Yarian
Brother William David Everett
Brother Thomas Bushnell
Brother Robert James McLaughlin
Brother Peter Budde
Brother John Henry Ernestine
Brother Francis Sebastian Medina
Brother Aelred Bernard Dean
Brother Joseph Basil Gauss
Brother Mark Andrew Jones *(priest)*
Brother Richard Matthias
Brother William Henry Benefield
Brother Nathanael Deward Rahm
Brother Thomas Lawrence Greer
Brother Enoch John Valentine
Brother Ron Fender
Brother David Luke Henton
Brother David John Battrick *(priest)*
Brother Will Harpest
Brother Bo Alexander Armstrong
Brother Francis Jonathan Bullock
Brother Blane Frederick van Pletzen-Rands *(priest)*
Brother James Patrick Hall
Brother Millard Cook

Novices: 3
Postulants: 2

Obituaries

8 Feb 2012 Brother Michael Elliott *(priest)*, aged 72, professed 2 years

Church Army

CA

Founded 1882

Acknowledged as
a mission community
2012

Church Army
Wilson Carlile Centre
50 Cavendish Street
Sheffield
S3 7RZ

Tel: 0300 123 2113

Email:
missioncommunity@churcharmy.org.uk

Website
www.churcharmy.org.uk

Daily prayers at 12 noon

Community history
Videos and articles about the history of the Church Army can be found on our website here: *http://www.churcharmy.org.uk/pub/aboutus/125/125home.asp*

Registered Charity Nos.
No. 226226
and SC040457

Our vision is of a movement of Christ's disciples who are so set on fire by the love of Jesus that they go to the margins of society, beyond the reach of most of the Church, showing that love through both words and actions. It is for people like this that the Church Army Mission Community exists; to be a home for those with a passion for evangelism.

It is a family where they can be resourced and encouraged, a place where they can cry together and laugh together, celebrate God's goodness and stand with each other in the difficulties. It is not an organisation so much as a movement that focuses on relationships rather than rules. It is held together by a commitment to Christ, to the gospel and to holiness of life. Though coming from within the Anglican Church, it has an inclusive ethos and is open to those from other churches.

It is a vision of a community of love sustained by prayer and the grace of God. Our mission flows out from this Mission Community seeing transformed by Christ.

CANON MARK RUSSELL
(Community Leader, assumed office September 2012)
SISTER VANESSA KIRBY *(Dean of Community)*

Around 250 members

Community Publications
Shareit! Magazine that goes out to individual supporters and churches. It is full of real life storics of the work of the Church Army and our partners.
Inspire This is the UK's biggest reach Christian magazine going FREE to UK churches, with a circulation of 50,000-55,000 and a readership of at least 200,000.
Church Army's daily prayer diary.

Guest and Retreat Facilities
20 single, 10 double rooms. No restrictions.
£30 + VAT per single room per night; £40 + VAT per double room per night.

Most convenient time to telephone:
9.00 am – 5.00 pm

Bishop Visitor: awaiting appointment

Church Mission Society

CMS

Founded 1799

Acknowledged as a mission community 2008

CMS
Watlington Road
Oxford
OX4 6BZ

Tel: 01865 787400
Fax: 01865 776375

Email:
info@cms-uk.org

Website:
www.cms-uk

Bishop Visitor
Rt Revd Dr
Christopher Cocksworth,
Bishop of Coventry

Registered Charity No.
No. 1131655
Company No. 6985330

CMS is a community of people in mission obeying the call of God to proclaim the Gospel in all places and to draw all people into fellowship with the Lord Jesus Christ. Its founders wanted social reform at home and a missionary movement to take the Gospel beyond the boundaries of Europe. CMS has always had a significant community feel about it: some members even refer to CMS as their "family". A transforming community life was also part of CMS mission service, in mission compounds, schools and hospitals and training colleges. CMS had a major influence in forming the Anglican Communion, about two-thirds of whose Churches trace their origins to the missionary movement fostered by CMS or have had CMS contributions to their early growth and development. Over its 200-year existence, CMS has sent out about 10,000 people in mission.

Under a new constitution, approved in 2009, community members affirm seven promises, including a commitment to participating in mission service, regular prayer, bible reading, study, reflection, supporting the Church's mission, and mutual encouragement.

CMS supports people in mission in over thirty-five countries in Africa, Asia, Europe (including the UK), the Middle East and Latin America.

JOHN RIPLEY *(Chair of Trustees)*
THE REVEREND CANON PHILIP MOUNSTEPHEN
(Community Leader/Executive Director)

Membership: 2,500+

Community Publications: *Connect*, three times a year, distributed free to members. Occasional monographs on mission themes through the CMS Crowther Centre for Mission Education. See CMS website for more news and information about regular printed publications.

Community Wares: See the website for free resources for prayer, group study and seasons of the Christian year plus books, resources and craft products for sale from the CMS shop: www.shop.org.uk.

Conference Facilities
CMS in Oxford has excellent modern conference facilities for meetings from 2 to 150 people. See www.cms-uk.org/conferencing for details.

Community of St Denys

CSD

Founded 1879

contact address:

57 Archers Court
Castle Street
Salisbury
SP1 3WE
UK

Email: junewatt@ internet.com

Most convenient time to telephone
9am – 1pm

Website
www.ivyhouse.org

Bishop Visitor
Rt Revd
Nicholas Holtam,
Bishop of Salisbury

Registered Charity
No 233026

The Community was founded for mission work at home and overseas. The remaining Sisters live in individual accommodation. The present dispersed community of men and women live with a Rule of Life based on the monastic virtues and a particular ministry towards encouragement in the practice of prayer and active service. The Retreat centre at Ivy House, Warminster, continues actively under a secular Warden and staff, providing hospitality for retreats and conferences for groups and individuals. There is a Board of Trustees responsible for financial matters.

MRS JUNE WATT
(Leader, assumed office October 2010)

Committed members: 28
among whom the professed sisters are:
Sister Margaret Mary Powell
Sister Frances Anne Cocker *(priest)*
Sister Elizabeth Mary Noller *(priest)*

Obtuaries
Jul 2012 Sister Phyllis Urwin, aged 94, professed 49 years

Fellowship
CSD has a fellowship (friends).

Community History
CSD: The Life & Work of St Denys', Warminster to 1979, published by CSD, 1979 *(out of print).*

Community Publication
Annual *Newsletter* and quarterly prayer leaflet. Write to the Leader (address above). A suggested donation of £5.00 is welcome.

Guest and Retreat Facilities
St Denys Retreat Centre, Ivy House, is available for various types of retreat and conferences. Guests are also welcome. It has 22 rooms, 6 of which are double. (Closed during the Christmas period.)

Bookings to the Warden,
Ivy House, 2/3 Church Street, Warminster
BA12 8PG
Tel: 01985 214824
Email: stdenys@ivyhouse.org

Companions of St Luke, OSB

Founded 1992

Companions of St Luke, OSB
PO Box 332
Spring Grove
Illinois 60081
USA

Email:
csl91.membership@gmail.com

Website
www.csl-osb.org

Office Book
BCP
(Episcopal Church of the USA)

Community Publication
The Community has a quarterly newsletter called *Value Nothing Whatever Above Christ Himself.* It is available upon request from csl91membership@gmail.com

Bishop Visitor
Rt Revd Dean Wolfe, Episcopal Diocesan of Kansas

The Companions of St Luke OSB is a Benedictine community as defined by the Canons of the Episcopal Church. As such, it incorporates vowed members and Oblates who may be married or partnered as well as celibates, those who live dispersed and those who are called to live in community. Our stability is in Christ and the Community, and our cloister is in the heart.

From our foundation, it has been the intention of the Companions to live the Benedictine life in a manner consistent with our time under the Benedictine Rule and our vows of Obedience, Stability, and Conversion of Life. Further, we are an intentional hybrid of 'Christian Community' and traditional monastic order, a dynamic tension that informs our commitment to "prefer nothing whatever to Christ, that He may bring us all together to everlasting life" [RB 72]. We are knit together with Christ and each other through our commitment to pray regular, daily Offices, spending time in contemplative prayer, and ongoing study. We live in the world, working to frame our secular lives around our love of God and our prayers.

BROTHER ROBERT COTTON OSB
(assumed office October 2010)
SISTER MONICA RUTH MULLEN OSB *(Prioress)*

Brother Matthias Smith
Brother David Gerns *(Dean of Formation)*
Sister Anna Grace Madden *(Dean of Finance)*
Brother Camillus Converse
Sister Martha Lamoy
Brother Luke Doucette
Sister Jan Korver
Sister Mary Francis Deulen
Brother Kenneth Maguire
Brother Bede Leach
Brother Joshua Kingsley
Brother Basil Edwards
Brother Stephan Francis Arnold
Sister Bernadette Barrett
Sister Veronica Taylor
Brother Dunstan Townsend

Novices: 2 *Postulants:* 7

Oblates and Companions: The Companions of St Luke has an Oblate program. Oblates are considered by this community to have a 'full and authentic' vocation with its own formation. Oblates sit with their vowed counterparts in the Office, have voice and seat in Chapter.

Community Publication
Brother David Gerns OSB (editor), *Reflections on Benedictine Life in the Modern World* – a small booklet of reflections on Benedictine Life in a dispersed community by members of the Companions of St Luke. It is available upon request from csl91membership@gmail.com.

Company of Mission Priests

CMP

Founded 1940

Warden's address:

**St Mary Magdalene's Vicarage
Wilson Street
Sunderland
SR4 6HJ
Tel & Fax:
0191 565 6318
Email: frskelsmm
@btinternet.com**

Website: www.
missionpriests.com

Associates
Laymen closely associated with the Company in life and work may be admitted as Associates.

Community Publication:
Occasional Newsletter

Office Book:
The Divine Office (Vincentian calendar)

Bishop Visitor
Rt Revd
Lindsay Urwin OGS

The Company of Mission Priests is a dispersed community of male priests of the Anglican Communion who, wishing to consecrate themselves wholly to the Church's mission, keep themselves free from the attachments of marriage and the family, and endeavour to strengthen and encourage each other by mutual prayer and fellowship, sharing the vision of Saint Vincent de Paul of a priesthood dedicated to service, and living in a manner prescribed by our Constitution, and with a Vincentian rule of life. For many years the company, although serving also in Guyana and Madagascar, was best known for its work in staffing 'needy' parishes in England with two, three, or more priests who lived together in a clergy house. Although this is rarely possible nowadays, because of the shortage of priests, we encourage our members who work in proximity to meet as often as practicable in order to maintain some elements of common life. The whole company meets in General Chapter once a year, and the Regional Chapters more frequently.

We were among the founding members, in the year 2000, of the Vincentians in Partnership, which works in accordance with the principles established by St Vincent de Paul, to support and empower those who are poor, oppressed, or excluded.

FATHER BERESFORD SKELTON CMP
(Warden, assumed office 2012)

Michael Whitehead
Anthony Yates
Allan Buik
John Cuthbert
Peter Brown
Michael Shields
David Beater
Michael Gobbett
John Vile
Ian Rutherford
Andrew Collins Jones
James Geen
Tim Pike
Philip North
Mark McIntyre
Alan Watson
Simon Atkinson
Peter Bostock
Jonathan Kester
Robert Martin
Christopher Buckley
Kevin Palmer
Andrew Welsby
Derek Lloyd
Alexander Lane
James Hill

Probationers: 2
Aspirants: 5

Obituaries

6 Sep 2012 Brian Godsell, aged 72, professed 44 years

Little Sisters of Saint Clare

LSSC

Founded 2002

Mother Guardian
19334 King's Garden Dr. N., Shoreline WA 98370 USA
Tel: 206 533 0884
Email: motherguardian@gmail.com

LSSC Office Mail and Seattle Chapter House, St. Andrew's Episcopal Church, 111 Northeast 80th Seattle WA 98115 USA

Website: www.stclarelittlesisters.org

Services at St Andrew's Episcopal Church. Call for times.

Office Books
BCP, SSF Office for Franciscan saints, Holy Women, Holy Men Celebrating the Saints

The Little Sisters of St. Clare is a dispersed women's Franciscan community that seeks to live a contemporary expression of the rule of St. Clare in the world. We desire to live a simple and consecrated life but do not live in a common house. We strive always to be mindful of our vocation to contemplative and intercessory prayer, carefully maintaining the challenging balance between secular and Religious life.

Our first focus is to order our own lives to live under a common Rule. Each of us is responsible for our own financial support and livelihood. We support ministries to the poor in our local communities and serve in our local parish churches within the Diocese of Olympia, Washington, USA.

We use our discernment and formation program is to encourage and equip women who are called by God to our community. Our formation program is designed from our experience living the Gospel. It provides a supportive study program, time for reflection and conversation about Christian living and spiritual practices. Our curriculum is offered to all members in our local Chapters. They are all within a 100 miles from Seattle.

Sister Dorothy-Anne Kiest, LSSC
(Mother Guardian, assumed office October 2006)

Sisters:
Sr Mary-Agnes Staples
Sr Mary-Louise Sulonen
Sr Marie-Elise Trailov
Sr Jeanne-Marie Williamson
Sr Kathryn-Mary Little
Sr DedraAnn Bracher
Sr Mary-Olivia M. Stalter

Companions:
Tovi Andrews
Nora Blum
Marcia Bracher
Laura Carroll
Grace Grant
Nancy Jones

Associates LSSC: 9

Novices: 2
Sr Priscilla Kaufmann
Sr Jami Ortung

Obituaries

18 Jan 2012	Abbess Gloria-Mary Goller PCLS, aged 96, professed 22 years
26 Jan 2012	Revd Bridget Moore, Companion, aged 88
19 Dec 2012	Joan Lindall, Companion, aged 78

Episcopal Visitor
Rt Revd Sanford Z K Hampton, *retd*

Companions and Associates

We have various categories of membership. Companions are welcomed as they take a service role working closely with the Sisters. Associate membership is a way to stay connected with the community intercessory prayer requests. Companions and Associates may elect to participate in our Chapter formation program. This is an opportunity to spend time in prayer and learn about spiritual practices that are central to the Franciscan ethos and contemplative living. Inquiries may be made to Sr. DedraAnn Bracher, Vocations Director at bracherd@gmail.com or Sr. Kathryn-Mary Little, Director of Associates at kathylynnelittle@gmail.com.

Guest and Retreat Facilities

No retreat facilities. Spiritual direction available. Call Mother Guardian.

Most convenient time to telephone:

Pacific Time, USA : 9.00 am – 11.30 am, 2.00 pm – 4.00 pm

Community Book

We have self published a little book called *Holy Weavings – A Tapestry of Reflections* by The Little Sisters of Saint Clare. We offer this to others for a donation of $15 to cover our costs and shipping. Write: LSSC, c/o St. Andrew's Episcopal Church (see address above).

Abbess Gloria Mary Goller PCLS
– for obituary see page 180

Order of the Community of the Paraclete

OCP

Founded 1971

Reformed Chapter of Pentecost 1991

PO Box 61399
Seattle
WA 98141
USA

Website
www.
theparacletians.org

Monthly gathering at 2212 NE 125th Street, Seattle, WA

Monthly gathering at St Michael's Episcopal Church, Yakima, WA

Eucharist, meal, study and fellowship, every third Friday
5.30 pm – 9.00 pm

Office Book
Book of Common Prayer

The Community of the Paraclete is an apostolic community offering an authentic Religious life of prayer and service. We were recognized by the Episcopal Church in 1992. The Paracletians are self-supporting women and men, lay and ordained, who have committed themselves to live under the Paracletian Rule and constitution. Our vision: we are a network of Paracletian communities learning how to grow spiritually and exercising our gifts in ministry. We stand with and serve anyone who is broken in mind, body or spirit.

BROTHER JOHN RYAN OCP
(Minister, assumed office June 2009)
Email: BrjohnPastoralServices@gmail.com

BROTHER MARVIN TAYLOR OCP *(Vice-Minister)*

Brother Douglas Campbell
Sister Ann Case
Sister Susanne Chambers
Brother Carle Griffin
Sister Barrie Gyllenswan
Sister Patricia Ann Harrison
Brother Timothy Nelson
Sister Martha Simpson

Novices: 2

Friends, Associates and Companions
FRIEND: any baptized Christian, with the approval of chapter.
ASSOCIATE: confirmed Episcopalian, active member of an Episcopal parish, or church in communion with the Episcopal Church or the Episcopal See of Canterbury; six months' attendance at local chapter, and the approval of chapter.
COMPANION: Any person who is a benefactor of the Order.

Other Addresses
Members are in the states of Arizona, Florida and Washington, USA.

Community Publication
Paracletian Presence, distributed free

Bishop Visitor
Rt Revd Nedi Rivera, Bishop of Eastern Oregon

The Sisters of Jesus

Founded 2000

34 Eaton Road
Bowdon
Altrincham Cheshire
WA14 3EH
Tel: 0161 233 0630
(evenings)

E-mail:
(Foundation Sister)
**susangabriel@
btinternet.com**

Website:
www.sistersofjesus.
org.uk

Bishop Visitor
Rt Revd
Richard Blackburn,
Suffragan Bishop of
Warrington

Registered Charity No.:
The Gettalife Project.
Charity number
1131341.
See the Sisters of Jesus website for more information

The core of our vocation is the call to the Religious Life, not living in community but in the midst of everyday circumstances. It is to have our first priority a search for the reality of the living God as Ignatius of Loyola put it, to 'know God in all things' and to live out a life of kinship based on this call of our shared life in Christ and therefore Sisters of him and of each other.

The first vows were taken by the Foundation Sister before Bishop Christopher Mayfield, the Bishop of Manchester, on the festival of St Michael and All Angels, 2000. The community was acknowledged by the Advisory Council in July 2011. At present, this pilot light, newly-acknowledged dispersed community comprises three Sisters, two Sisters in temporary vows. The Foundation Sister took permanent vows in 2007. One sister is called to a partly solitary life. There is one person exploring whether to take first temporary vows in January 2014.

Revd Dr Susan Gabriel Talbot
(Foundation Sister)
Claire Sherman *(Assistant)*

Office book
We have developed our own liturgies for morning and evening worship as well as using the traditonal Compline.

Associates and Friends
It is possible to join as an Associate Sister or Friend should that be appropriate for the candidate and according to our Constitution. There are guidelines for Associates which can be discussed with any interested party.

Guest and Retreat Facilities
It is possible to stay for a time of quiet at the main house,which is a period terrace with one guest room. The 24 hour or 48 hour stay would be as the Foundation Sister's guest. It can be directed or just 'time-out' (women only). Costs, depending on circumstance, but full board for 24 hours £25–30. £15 for a day with soup, bread and cheese lunch.

Sisters of Saint Gregory

SSG

Founded 1987 as the Companion Sisterhood of Saint Gregory by the Brotherhood of Saint Gregory. Achieved autonomy in 1999 as The Sisters of Saint Gregory.

Contact address for the Treasurer, who receives and routes all communications:

Sister Susanna Bede Caroselli, SSG
505 Allenview Drive
Mechanicsburg
PA 17055
Tel: (717) 697 7040

E-Mail:
SusannaCaroselli@verizon.net

Website:
www.sistersofsaintgregory.org

The Sisters of Saint Gregory is a women's community canonically recognized by the Episcopal Church. The community is comprised of lay and clergy, young and old, regardless of marital status. Called together by God to the vowed life in the world, we live intentionally dispersed, some individually and some with our families, supporting ourselves and the community through secular or church-related employment performed in a spirit of service. Sisters are also encouraged to serve their parishes and dioceses and other church-sponsored or civic outreach programs. We follow a Rule of Life that requires the Daily Offices in the Book of Common Prayer, prayer and meditation, the Holy Eucharist, Embertide reports, a tithe, and participation in an annual convocation and chapter for retreat, business, fellowship and worship. The formation program includes a one-year postulancy and two-year novitiate with spiritual and theological study. After five years in annual vows, a Sister may elect to make life profession.

SISTER CARIN BRIDGIT DELFS, SSG *(priest)*
(Leader, assumed office 1 January 2013)
SISTER LAURIE JOSEPH NIBLICK, SSG *(Administrator)*

Sister Lillian-Marie DiMicco
Sister Helen Bernice Lovell
Sister Susanna Bede Caroselli
Sister Connie Jo McCarroll *(deacon)*
Sister Eugenia Theresa Wilson *(deacon)*
Sister Michael Julian Davidson

Novices: 1
Postulants: 2

Office Book: Book of Common Prayer (1979)

Bishop Visitor: Rt Rev. Laura J. Ahrens,
Bishop Suffragan of Connecticut

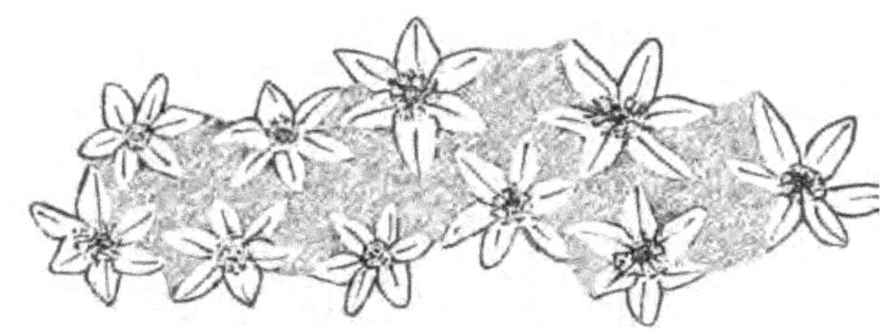

Society of the Community of Celebration SCC

Founded 1973

**809 Franklin Avenue
Aliquippa
PA 15001-3302
USA
Tel: 724 375 1510
Fax: 724 375 1138**

Email: mail@communityofcelebration.com

Website: communityofcelebration.com

Morning Prayer
8.00 am

Noonday Prayer
12.30 pm

Evening Prayer
5.30 pm

Compline (seasonal)
9.00 pm

Conventual **Eucharist** is celebrated on Saturday evenings at 5.30 pm, and Saints' days as applicable. Monthly service Taizé worship (except February).

The Community of Celebration is a life-vowed, contemporary residential community whose roots stretch back to the renewal of the Church of the Redeemer, Houston, Texas, in the 1960s. Today the Community resides in Aliquippa (near Pittsburgh), Pennsylvania. Members are women and men, single and married, adults and children, lay and ordained. Following the *Rule of St Benedict*, members live a rhythm of prayer, work, study, and recreation.

Our ministry is to be a Christian presence among the poor, responding to the needs around us by offering safe, affordable housing; serving with neighborhood organizations concerned with the revitalization of Aliquippa, and providing hospitality, retreats, sabbaticals, and conferences. We provide various chaplaincies, supply clergy, liturgical consultants, worship leadership and speakers for conferences.

BILL FARRA
(Primary Guardian, assumed office 1995)
MAY MCKEOWN *(Guardian for Vocations)*

Mimi Farra	Joe Beckey
Revd Steven McKeown	Revd Phil Bradshaw
James von Minden	Margaret Bradshaw

Associates: Companions of the Community of Celebration follow the Rule of Life for Companions.

Other address
UK house, c/o Revd Phil Bradshaw, 35 Cavendish Road, Redhill, Surrey RH1 4AL, UK
Website: ccct.co.uk

Guest Facilities: We offer a chapel, meeting and dining spaces, and overnight accommodation for 13–17 people (one guesthouse can be self-catering for 4–5 people). We welcome individual retreatants and groups, men and women. For further information contact Celebration's hospitality director by mail, telephone or email.

Most convenient time to telephone:
9.00 am – 5.00 pm Eastern Time (Mon–Fri)

Community Wares: Music and worship resources, including CDs, songbooks, liturgical music, children's music, *A Pilgrim's Way* study manual (English & Spanish) – see website store.

Office Book: Book of Common Prayer

Bishop Visitor: Rt Revd C. Christopher Epting

Community Publication: *News from Celebration* – once a year. Contact Bill Farra for a free subscription.

Community books

W Graham Pulkingham, *Gathered for Power*, Hodder & Stoughton, London, 1972
Michael Harper, *A New Way of Living*, Hodder & Stoughton, London, 1972
W Graham Pulkingham, *They Left their Nets,* Hodder & Stoughton, London, 1973
Betty Pulkingham, *Mustard Seeds,* Hodder & Stoughton, London, 1977
Faith Lees with Jeanne Hinton, *Love is our Home,* Hodder & Stoughton, London, 1978
Maggie Durran, *The Wind at the Door,* Kingsway Publications/Celebration, 1986
David Janzen, *Fire, Salt, and Peace,* Shalom Mission Communities, 1996
Phil Bradshaw, *Following the Spirit,* O Books, 2010
Betty Pulkingham, *This is my story, this is my song,* WestBow Press, 2011

Society of St Luke SSL

Founded 1994

32b Beeston Common
Sheringham
NR26 8ES
Tel: 01263 825623

Emails
ssluke@ btinternet.com
andrewssl@me.com

Morning Prayer & Eucharist 8.30 am

Midday Prayer & Meditation 12.15 pm

Evening Prayer 5.00 pm

Night Prayer 9.00 pm

Registered Charity No.: 1107317

The Society of St. Luke was established by the Christian Deaf Community (CDC) of the Middle East. CDC is an Anglican Religious Community within the Province of Jerusalem. Initially SSL focused upon the two schools for deaf youngsters situated in Beirut (Lebanon) and Salt (Jordan.) Times have changed since those roots were set down. The Society today, while remembering the schools in prayer and where possible giving financial support to them, has broadened its mission. It became a charity in 2004 with its primary aims of providing 'prayer for the suffering world' and 'relief and support to those who come for help and counsel.' These aims reflect the Anglican Church's mission of 'care and prayer'.

FATHER ANDREW LANE SSL
(Superior, assumed office 18 October 1994)
Sister Julie Wiseman Sister Penny Daniels

Associates: 25 Associates (Oblates) who take vows of Simplicity and to keep the Aims of the Society.

Community Publication
Newsletter at the Feast of St Luke, Christmas & Easter. Contact the Community; donations invited.

Community Wares: Notelets, marmalade & pickles

Guest and Retreat facilities: One double room for an individual or couple, donations invited.

Most convenient time to telephone:
Any time as answer phone is available.

Office Book: Common Worship

Bishop Visitor
Rt Revd Graham James, Bishop of Norwich

The Third Order, Society of Saint Francis

TSSF

Founded:

1920s
Americas

1930s
Europe

1975
Africa

1959
Australia with
East Asia & PNG

1962
Aoteoroa-New Zealand
with Melanesia

The Third Order of the Society of Saint Francis consists of men and women, ordained and lay, single or in committed relationships, who believe that God is calling them to live out their Franciscan vocation in the world, living in their own homes and following ordinary professions. Like the First Order members, members (called Tertiaries) encourage one another in living and witnessing to Christ through a Rule of Life that includes prayer, study and work. The Third Order is worldwide, with a Minister General, and five Ministers Provincial to cover their respective Provinces.

KENNETH E. NORIAN TSSF
(Minister General, assumed office September 2011)
45 Malone Street, Hicksville, NY 11801, USA
Tel: +1 917 416 9579 Email: ken@tssf.org

REVD JOHN HEBENTON TSSF
(Assistant Minister General)
15 Farm Street, Mt. Maunganui, NEW ZEALAND
Tel: 07 575 9930 (home); 07 578 7916 (work);
021679202 (mobile) Fax: 07 574 0079
Email: john.hebentontssf@gmail.com
***or* jbheb@clear.net.nz**

Statistics for the whole community

	Professed	*Novices*
Americas	420	30
Europe	1862	138
Australia & E Asia	279	99
Africa	101	30
NZ-Aoteoroa	172	57
Total	**2834**	**354**

Bishop Protector General
The Most Reverend
Roger Herft,
Archbishop of Perth,
Western Australia

Office Book
Third Order Manual
The Manual includes a form of daily prayer called 'The Community Obedience'. Members are encouraged to use this in the context of Morning or Evening Prayer. This may be from:

Provincial Books of Common Prayer
Daily Office SSF
CSF Office Book

Province of the Americas

Revd John Brockmann TSSF *(Minister Provincial)*
130 Chapel Street, Norwood, MA 02062, USA
Tel: +1 443 553 0378
Email: jbrockma@english.udel.edu

Website of Province: www.tssf.org

Statistics of Province

Professed: 420; *Novices:* 30; *Postulants:* 13

Deaths since last Year Book

Carole Watson (19 May 2011); Rita Tolomeo (2 Sep 2011); Robert Ripson (8 Nov 2011); John Peter Bennett (2011); Judy Schmidt (9 Feb 2012); Adilson Ferreira da Silva (13 Feb 2012); Eunice Edwards (6 Mar 2012); Laselve Stanley Davis (10 Mar 2012); Arthur Wolsoncraft (28 Mar 2012); David Nard (26 Apr 2012); Dianne Varty (15 Jun 2012); Ann Elliot (22 Jun 2012); Janet Chaudruc (5 Aug 2012); Jan Meikle (1 Jun 2012); Kathryn George (12 Jun 2012); Corinne Rice (16 Nov 2012); Robert Teudesman

Associates of the Society of Saint Francis

Welcomes men and women, lay or clergy, single or in committed relationships, young and old, to join us as Associates in our diverse Franciscan family.

Provincial Publication

The Franciscan Times. Available online at www.tssf.org/archives.shtml

Bishop Protector: Rt Revd Gordon P Scruton

Province of Europe

Averil Swanton TSSF *(Minister Provincial)*
11, The Grange, Fleming Way, Exeter EX2 4SB, UK
Tel: +44 1392 430355
Email: ministertssf@franciscans.org.uk

Administrator: **Howard McFadyen, Les Standous, La Fontade 46300, Gourdon, France** **Email: handjmcfadyen@gmail.com**

Website of Province: www.tssf.org.uk

Statistics of Province: *Professed:* 1862; *Novices:* 138

RIPs for In Memoriam at 2012 October Chapter

Isobel Alder (Yorks North & East); Margaret Booker (Wyevern); William Chapman (Blackmore Vale); Ted Cosens (Sussex); Andrew Cribb (Cumbria/Lancashire); Joan Eskdale (Solent); Miriam Fitter (Devon); Pat Gathercole (Guildford); Molly Grimshaw (Sussex); Jennifer Gunraj (Oxford); Kingsley Halden (Notts & South Derbyshire); Freda Hibbs (Somerset); Joan Highet (Guildford); Barbara Keddie

(Yorks West & Skipton); Sue Midwood (Yorks North & East); Pat Moore (Notts & South Derbyshire); Sixten Nyblom (Sweden); Diana Sanders (East Anglia); Bill Simmons (Northants); Christopher Sinclair (East Anglia); Frances Stanjer (London West); Barbara Thatcher (Scotland); Alastair Todd (Sussex); Lesley Warren (Cambridge); Paul Wilson (Solent); Anne Winton (Wales).

Provincial Publication
The Little Portion (twice yearly), also available on TSSF Website
Third Order News (three times a year); Contact: Communications Officer
Chris Petrie, 55 Briardene Crescent, Newcastle upon Tyne, Tyne & Wear, NE3 4RX, UK. Tel: +44 191 2855131 Email: Chris.Petrie@Newcastle.ac.uk.

Bishop Protector: Rt Revd Michael Perham, Bishop of Gloucester

Province of Australia

Colin Fidock TSSF *(Minister Provincial)*
11 Francis St, St Agnes, South Australia 5097, Australia.
Tel: +61 (0)8 8396 3602 Email: provincial.minister@tssf.org.au

Website of Province: www.tssf.org.au

Statistics of Province:
Professed: 297 *Novices:* 99

Deaths since last Year Book

26 Mar 2012	Mrs Estmere Busch, professed 24 years
6 Jun 2012	Dr Norma Kent, professed 1 year
2012	Mr Bill Pearson, professed 12 years
29 Jan 2013	Revd Fleming Beicher, professed 22 years

Provincial Publication: *Quarterly Newsletter* – available on request from the Provincial Secretary, David White TSSF, or from the website www.tssf.org.au/Newsletter/
Email: provincial.secretary@tssf.org.au

Community History: Denis Woodbridge TSSF, *Franciscan Gold: A history of the Third Order of the Society of St Francis in the Province of Australia, Papua New Guinea and East Asia: Our first fifty years: 1959–2009.* Available from the Provincial Secretary.

Bishop Protector: Rt Revd Godfrey Fryar, Bishop of Rockhampton, Queensland

Province of Africa

Revd Nolan Tobias TSSF *(Minister Provincial)*
PO Box 285, Simon's Town, South Africa
Tel: +2721 786 3564 (work) Email: nolantobias@mweb.co.za

Website: www.tssf.org.za

Statistics of Province

Professed	*Novices*
101	30

Bishop Protector: *vacancy*

Provincial Publication

Pax et Bonum (published three times a year). Available free of charge from provincial Publications Officer: Alan Rogers TSSF Email: alanrs@telkomsa.co.za
Or the Newsletter Editor: The Rev Canon Roy Snyman TSSF
Email: fr.roy@telkomsa.net

PACIFIC PROVINCE

REVD JOHN HEBENTON TSSF *(Minister Provincial)*
15 Farm Street, Mt. Maunganui, New Zealand
Tel: 07 575 9930 (home); 07 578 7916 (work); 021679202 (mobile)
Fax: 07 574 0079
Email: john.hebentontssf@gmail.com or jbheb@clear.net.nz

Website of Province: www.franciscanthirdorder.godzone.net.nz

Statistics of Province

	Professed	*Novices*
New Zealand	94	11
Melanesia	78	46
TOTAL	**172**	**57**

Provincial Publication: *TAU* Available from the Provincial Secretary:
Terry Molloy Email: tharmolloy@xtra.co.nz

Community History

Booklets by Chris Barfoot: *Beginnings of the Third Order in New Zealand 1956–74; Peace and Joy : Part 2 of the History of the Third Order, Society of St Francis in New Zealand*

Bishops Protector

Rt Revd Philip Richardson, Bishop of Waikato
Rt Revd Richard Naramana, Bishop of Ysabel *(for Melanesia)*

The Worker Sisters and Brothers of the Holy Spirit

WSHS & WBHS

Founded 1972 (Sisters) & 1979 (Brothers)

Contact addresses:

Sr Deborah WSHS (Canadian Director) 711 McMurtry Road Midland, ON CANADA L4R 0B9 Tel: 647 965 3196 Email: strdeborah @hotmail.com

Sr Christine WSHS, (American Director) 528 First Street Windsor CO 80550 USA Tel: 970 686 7135 Email: casturges @gmail.com

Website: www. workersisters.org & www. workerbrothers.org

The Worker Sisters and Brothers of the Holy Spirit is a Covenant Community which seeks to respond to God's call through the power of the Holy Spirit, participate in Jesus Christ's vision of unity, become his holy people, show forth Fruit, and in obedience to his command, go forth into the world. It offers women and men, regardless of marital status, a path for individual spiritual growth through a life commitment to a Rule which provides an opportunity to experience prayer, worship, becoming, discovery, belonging, relating, commitment and mission. Membership is made up of:

First Order: Sisters – Lay Workers and Lay Sisters;
Second Order: Brothers – Lay Workers and Lay Brothers;
Third Order: Clergy Sisters and Clergy Brothers;
Companions: Lay and Clergy Persons;
Friends: Lay and Clergy Persons

The first three Orders are bound together under a Life Commitment to a common Rule which is Benedictine in orientation. Members do not live together, yet are not separated by geographical boundaries.

SISTER DEBORAH WSHS *(Canadian Director)*
SISTER CHRISTINE WSHS *(American Director)*
(Co-Directors, assumed office April 2010)

Members: 135
Novices: 2 *Postulants:* 1

Obituaries

16 Jan 2012	Sr Jane Barnabas WSHS, professed 38 years
14 Oct 2012	Sr Angela, *Founder* WSHS, professed 50 years
20 Oct 2012	Sr Catharine WSHS, professed 34 years
16 Dec 2012	Sr Beth Evelyn WSHS, professed 24 years

Companions and Friends

COMPANIONS make a Life of Commitment to a Rule of Life. FRIENDS share in the prayer and spiritual journey of the Community.

Other Address

Sister Kathleen Rachel WSHS, Director of Admissions, **2601 Sungold Dr, Las Vegas, NV 891134, USA**

Office Book: Book of Common Prayer

Community Ecclesiastical Visitors

CANADA: Rt Revd Philip Poole, Friend WSHS/ WBHS, Diocese of Toronto

USA: Rt Revd Barry Howe, Friend WSHS/ WBHS, Diocese of West Missouri, *(retired)*

Ashrams & other Communities

Bethel Ashram

Warickadu, Kuttapuzha P.O., Tiruvalla, Pathanamthitta District, Kerala, India Tel: 09562 335401

The Ashram is a part of Madhya (Central) Kerala Diocese, CSI. Located in Warickad, since 1926 the Ashram has run a school, looked after orphans and run a dispensary. Today its ministry includes a small geriatric care ward, a retirement home for monastic sisters of the Church of South India, and a boarding school. It is also used as a place of retreat for the diocese.

Achamma George *(Mother)*

Christa Kulu Ashram

Tirupattur, Vellore, Tamil Nadu 635602, India

The Christu Kula Ashram was among the earliest Christian Ashrams, starting in 1921. This was one of the first Protestant Ashrams and it aimed to promote equality between Europeans and Indians, and to give an Indian presentation of Christian life and worship. It is in Vellore Diocese, CSI, and is linked to the National Missionary Society of India.

Christa Prema Seva Ashram

Shivajinagar, Pune – 411 005, India Tel: 20 553 9276

Founded as the Ashram for the Christa Seva Sangha in 1922 by Jack Winslow to create a community of Indian and British members living in equality, the original community ceased in the early 1960s. Some members of this group were influential in the formation of the Third Order SSF *(see entry elsewhere)*. A decade later, a multi-denominational group of Religious began to reside here. This group too did not continue and the Ashram is now the focus of a non-celibate community.

Revd B L Sojawal *(Acharya)*

Christa Sevakee Ashram

Karkala, Karnataka, India

Started in 1950 in Karnataka (Southern) Diocese, CSI, this Ashram runs a home for aged men and two homes for aged women, altogether caring for fifty elderly people, who are deserted, poor or without relatives. The institution has completed its Golden Jubilee of service. This Ashram is also functioning as a self-employment training centre, a centre for retreats and conferences, and as a short-term stay home for deserted women or women in distress.

Community of St Stephen

4 Rajput Road, Delhi 110 054, India Tel: 11 2396 5437

St Stephen's Community, for women, began as St Stephen's Home in 1871 and formally became a community in 1886. In the 1940s, it came to consist of those Indian and English women who wished to live together as a community under a simple rule of prayer and life.

Mrs S M Rao *(Head)*

Christavashram

Manganam P.O., Kottyam District, Kerala 686 018, India
Email: christavashram@gmail.com
Website: manganam.tripod.com/ashram/index.html

Christavashram (Society of St Thomas) is an active Christian community for service, founded in 1934, based on Christian principles with the motto "Thy Kingdom Come". It is in Madhya (Central) Kerala Diocese, CSI.

The Community consists of 120 people, including members, staff and children of the Kerala Balagram, staff and trainees of the Gurukul Ecumenical Institute and Peace Centre staying in the campus, and 30 Associate members living outside.

The sources of income for the Community are its agricultural and dairy farms, and contributions from Associate members and friends. All members are committed to contributing "Bread labour", and all earnings go to a common pool from where the needs of members are met. Any honorarium received either from the Ashram's own institutions or from outside goes to the "Common purse".

Chapel: It is an open and ecumenical chapel, welcoming people for meditation and prayers, besides daily common prayers in the morning and noon, Sunday communion services are held in different denominations' rites at 7.30 am.

Guests: The Ashram welcomes visitors from India and abroad. participants from abroad for the Gurukal ccourses, peace studies and seminars are welcome. As a simple life style is followed with vegetarian food, the cost of food and accommodation is kept to a minimum. Yoga practice is offered at the Ashram. Smoking and consumption of alcohol is not permitted in the Ashram premises.

Devasevikaramaya

Devasevikaramaya 31, Kandy Road, Kurunegala, Sri Lanka
Tel: 0094 372 221803

An order for women, founded by the first Bishop of Kurunegala, Rt Revd Lakdasa de Mel, in the 1950s. A picture from Devasevikaramaya is below.

Some other communities

This section includes communities, either monastic or acknowledged, that whilst not Anglican in ecclesiastical allegiance are in communion with Anglicans.

There is also here a community in the USA, inter-denominational in its origins, which includes Lutherans as well as Anglicans, as the ELCA is now in full communion with the Episcopal Church of the United States.

The third cross of the Stations in the grounds at CCK, Australia, surrounded by grazing Dorpor sheep.

Mar Thoma Syrian Church

Mar Thoma Dayaraya

Founded 1996

Plachery PO (Kalayanad) Punalur 691 331 Kerala, INDIA Tel: 04742222282 Email: rev.alexa@ gmail.com

Night Prayer & Morning Prayer 5.00 am
3rd Hour 9.00 am
6th Hour 12 noon
9th Hour 3.00 pm
Evening Prayer 6.00 pm
Night Prayer 9.00 pm

This is one of four monastic communities of the Mar Thoma Syrian Church (a Church in Full Communion). It is a part of a monastic movement that goes alongside the better-known Ashram movement. There are six brothers and their monastery is in the hill ranges of Kerala. They live on a rubber plantation donated to the church by Captain Thomas Alexander in 1929 to run an orphanage of 30 boys now managed by the brothers. Their life is one of contemplative prayer and witness to those around by service in the orphanage and outreach in mission parishes in the local villages. They also take in ordinands and aspirants for ordination for experience of the life of prayer.

FATHER ALEXANDER ABRAHAM
Acharya (Abbot)

Brother Isaac Matthew
Father P Philip
Brother Sanil Alexander
Brother Reji Kuriakose
Brother Anish Thomas

Office Book
The Community uses a reformed version of the Shimtho in Malayalam.

Guest facilities: There is a guesthouse with five rooms as well as facilities for larger groups for a day.

MAR THOMA SANYASINI SAMAOHAM
Elanthor P.O., Pathanamthitta District, INDIA Tel: 0468 2361972
Sister P.T. Mariamma *(Superior)*

CHRISTA PANTHI ASHRAM
Darsani P.O., Sihora – 483 225, INDIA Tel: 07624 260260
Christa Panthi Ashram, Sihora, was established in 1942 under the leadership of Revd K T Thomas, Mr John Varghese and Mr M P Mathew, who both later became ordained. Today there are more than forty members, including permanent workers and volunteers. In addition to Gospel work, the activities of the Ashram include hospital work, village schools, a home for the destitute, agricultural work and a rural development programme.

Revd James Idiculla *(Acharya)*

CHRISTA MITRA ASHRAM
P.B. No. 3, Ankola P.O., North Kanara, Karnataka – 531 314, INDIA
Tel: 08388 230392, 230287 (0)
Started in 1940, an ashrams of the Mar Thoma Evangelistic Association.

CHRISTU DASA ASHRAM
Olive Mount P.O., Palakkad – 678 702, INDIA Tel: 0492 272974
Started in 1928 as an Ashram with celibate members, it is located in the north-eastern part of Kerala near the Tamil Nadu border.

Miss Mariyamma Thomas *(Superior)*

SANTHIGIRI ASHRAM
11/488, Edathala North, Aluva, Kerala – 683 564, INDIA
Tel: 0484 2639014, 2839240
Email: santhigiriasram@yahoo.co.uk Website: www.santhigiri.in/index.html
This is a holistic healing and meditation centre.

SUVARTHA PREMI SAMITHI
Munsiari, Ranthi P.O., Pithorragarh, Uttar Pradesh, INDIA
Revd A K George and two lady workers went to Tejam and Munsiari on the border of Tibet and started work among the Bothi community. The Bhotias used to trade with Tibet until the 1949 invasion by China. The missionaries hoped to reach Tibet with the help of the Bhotias. Some from the Bhotia community accepted the Gospel and congregations have been founded at Munsiari and Tejam. At present, two groups are working here.

Communities in Churches who have signed the Porvoo agreement

Porvoo created a community of Churches, the members of which have signed an agreement to "share a common life in mission and service". Anglicans in the British Isles and Iberia are currently members, with Lutherans from Denmark, Estonia, Finland, Iceland, Lithuania, Norway and Sweden.

ÖSTANBÄCK MONASTERY Founded 1970, Benedictine monks
733 96 Sala, SWEDEN Tel: 0224 25188 Email: caesarius@swipnet.se

COMMUNITY OF THE HOLY TRINITY Founded 1993
Mount Foundation, 795 91 Rättvik, SWEDEN Tel. 0248 79 7170

MARY MAGDALENE SISTERS
Henriksdalsringen 9, 4th floor, 131 32 Nacka, SWEDEN Tel. 08 714 7751

MARY DAUGHTERS OF THE EVANGELICAL MARIAVÄGEN Founded 1964
Maria Farm at Vallby Church, 745 98 Enköping, SWEDEN

SANKT SIGFRID SISTERS
Sjöborgen, Old Växjövägen 5, 360 44 Ingelstad, SWEDEN Tel 0470 30128

THE RISEN SAVIOUR SISTERHOOD
Overselo Abbey Farm, 640 61 Stallarholmen, SWEDEN Tel: 0152 41116

Sisters of the Holy Spirit in Alsike kloster

Helgeandssystrarna

Founded 1965

Alsike Kloster
SE – 741 92
Knivsta
SWEDEN

Tel: 46 (0) 1838 3002

Emails:
systrarna@ alsikekloster.org
or
syster.marianne @gmail.com

Website:
www.alsikekloster.org

Lauds 7.00 am

Terce 9.00 am

Midday prayer
12 noon

None 3.00 pm

Vespers 6.00 pm

Compline/Vigils
8.00 pm

The monastic family of the Holy Spirit Sisters at Alsike Kloster is one of the fruits of the re-awakening of monastic life which started in the first half of the 20th century in the Reformation churches in Europe. This movement touched the Swedish Church in the 1940s-1950s.

In 1948, Sister Marianne Nordström was invited by the Order of the Holy Paraclete to test her vocation. Having returned to Sweden in 1954, she and Sister Ella Persson started a common life in the Diocese of Stockholm, moving to Uppsala in 1856 on the invitation of the then Dean, Olof Herrlin (later Bishop of Visby) to take up work among the university students. In 1964 the community moved to Alsike, twenty kilometres south of Uppsala, continuing their life of prayer and hospitality in the old schoolhouse close to the parish church. During this period novices came and went. In 1983, Sister Karin Johansson was received as a postulant and made her final profession in 1995. By then, Archbishop Gunnar Weman had succeeded Bishop Herrlin as Visitor, and the community, having become involved in refugee work since 1978, was declared the Sanctuary of the diocese by him. The years of crisis in the Swedish Church brought them into contact with the Evangelical Lutheran Church of Kenya, where they have found a response for their way of life and a new hope of growth. There are now plans to erect a kind of monastic village for work with refugee children, students and mission.

SISTER MARIANNE NORDSTRÖM
(Prioress, assumed office 1965)
Sister Ella Persson
Sister Karin Johansson

Community Publication
Meddelande till S:t Nicolai Vänkrets (twice a year)

Guest & Retreat Facilities
According to plans for the "monastic village", there will be five rooms, free of charge.

Most convenient time to telephone: between Offices.

Oblates and Friends
The community has Oblates and 'Friends of St Nicolas'.

Office Book: adjusted Benedictine Office

Bishop Visitor: Rt Revd Göran Beijer

Chaplain: Rt Revd Gunnar Weman

Sisters of Saint Francis

Helige Franciskus Systraskap

Founded 1979

Klaradals kloster
Lindåsvägen 22
SE 443 45 Sjövik
SWEDEN
Tel:+46 302 43260

Email:
porten@klaradalskloster.se

Lauds
6.45 am

Sext
12 noon

Vespers
5.30 pm

Compline
8.30 pm

Mass
Tuesday 6.30 pm
Thursday 8.00 am
Friday 8.00 am

Helige Franciskus Systraskap (Sisters of Saint Francis) is a community in the Swedish Lutheran Church. We follow an adapted version of the Catholic Rule for the Third Order Regular of St Francis.

Our convent is situated 40 kilometres north east of Göteborg. Our life has its center in prayer, community life and meeting others either in our guest house, in the village or when invited to parishes, prayer groups, networks and other gatherings.

SISTER INGER JOHNSSON
(Leader, assumed office 13 January 2011)

Sister Lena Pettersson
Sister Hanna Söderberg
Sister Gundega Petrevica

Guest & Retreat Facilities
Five rooms.
For organized retreats we welcome both men and women, otherwise women only
We take guests in periods, normally two weeks per month.
Guests leave a gift for food and lodging.

Most convenient time to telephone
Weekdays 9.30 am – 11.30 am

Bishop Visitor
Rt Revd Biörn Fjärstedt (retired bishop of Visby).

Brothers of Saint John the Evangelist (OSB)

EFSJ

Founded 1972

1787 Scenic Avenue
Freeland
WA 98249
USA
Tel: 360 320 1186
Email:
efsj@whidbey.com

Website: www.
brothersofsaintjohn
.org

Morning Prayer
8.45 am

Noonday Prayer
12 noon

Vespers 5.30 pm

Office book
Book of Common Prayer

Bishop Visitor
Rt Revd
Sanford Z K Hampton,
Diocese of Olympia

The community strives to promote interest, study and understanding of the vocation to the Religious life, and to sustain a Religious community on South Whidbey Island, WA. This monastic community is guided by the venerable *Rule of St Benedict.*

The Ecumenical Fellowship of Saint John was founded in Los Angeles in the spring of 1972 by five men – clergy and lay – from the Episcopal, Lutheran and Roman Catholic Communions of the Church. On Saint John's Day 1973, four of the founding group (two Lutherans and two Roman Catholics) made Promises of Commitment at Saint John's Episcopal Church in Los Angeles. After some years in Fallbrook, San Diego County, the Community moved to Whidbey Island in 1990. In 2000, we were blessed with the gift of ten secluded and wooded acres, donated by Judith P Yeakel of Langley. Here the monastic house was built, and blessed on Holy Cross Day 2003. The 'Called to Common Mission' declaration of ELCA and TEC made it easy for Lutherans and Episcopalians to become one. We were officially recognised as a canonical Religious community at the Diocesan Convention 2010.

BROTHER RICHARD TUSSEY EFSJ
(Superior, assumed office December 1973)
BROTHER DAVID MCCLELLAN EFSJ *(Prior)*

Sr Julian of Norwich DiBase
Brother Aidan Shirbroun
Brother Thomas Langler
Sister Frideswide Dorman
Sister Hildegard Babson
Sister Agnes Steele
Novices: 1

Obituaries
6 Dec 12 Brother Alcuin Vandegrift, aged 88, professed 17 months

Associates: We currently have three Associates.

Community Publication: *Benedicite.* Contact us via email or post; no charge other than freewill offering. It is also available via email and as part of our website.

Community Wares: "Tanglewood Treats": jam, pecan pie, etc. (Tanglewood is the name of our monastery.)

Guest and Retreat Facilities: No overnight guests at present. We do have a building fund.

Most convenient time to telephone
10 am – 12 noon, 2 pm – 3 pm

Remembering and thanksgiving

Sister Sheila CSJB (1918–2010)

Sister Sheila CSJB (Winifred Sheila Mary O'Brien) has a unique place in CSJB, directly descended from the brother of the Founder, Mother Harriet. Born in England, Sheila spent three years in India before returning to London aged eight. After school, she trained as a secretary. In 1939 she enlisted with the Auxiliary Territorial Service where she served until 1945 and then trained as an almoner. Admitted as a postulant of CSJB in April 1956, she was professed in 1958 and life professed in 1961. She served the community in several offices, most notably as Sister Secretary 1962–83 and again 1990-99. She was also at various times Librarian, and Visitors' Sister. In her seventies, she learnt Braille, transcribing books for the Guild of church Braillists, and becoming Treasurer of the Guild for many years.

From the 1990s, her health deteriorated gradually, but her intelligence remained undimmed. She had a wonderful memory for poetry and did the *Times* crossword every day until her final months. She continued to oversee the postage and mailing list, and write up the Community Annals until about a year before her death. She was brave in the face of the continuing and accelerating indignities of old age and prepared, even down to planning her funeral, which included the O'Brien family's hymn 'Be thou my vision' (and the two composers who had taught her at school, Holst and Vaughan Williams).

Sheila was a wonderful 'character' in CSJB and is much missed.

Alexander Macdonald Allchin (1930–2010)

Donald Allchin, priest and theologian, and friend to Anglican Religious communities was born on 20 April 1930 and died on 23 December 2010. Among many ministries during his life, he served as warden of the Sisters of the Love of God in Oxford and the Society of the Sacred Cross, Tymawr. He was the author of The Silent Rebellion *(1958), a study of the revival of Religious life among Anglicans. His other books attested to his wide ecumenical and spiritual interests: on the Virgin Mary, Celtic spirituality and Welsh tradition, the Danish theologian Grundtvig. He was particularly interested in the Orthodox tradition and was at one time editor of* Sobornost.

Here, Sister Christine SLG remembers his influence:

Sometime in 1966, when I was seriously wondering how to go about entering the Religious life, I found two books in my college library which influenced the quest. The first was Peter Anson's *The Call of the Cloister*, the second A. M. Allchin's *The Silent Rebellion: Anglican Religious Communities, 1845–1900.* There was not much else about the Religious life on the shelves, let alone the Anglican Religious life, but the latter book did persuade me that I did not have to leave the Anglican Church to become a nun. It was, however, some years after I entered Fairacres that I realised that the dynamic Warden, 'Father Donald', was the author. I did not know then, either, how influential he would be both in my life and in the Anglican Religious life in the last half of the twentieth century.

When I joined the Sisters of the Love of God in 1968 Donald Allchin was Librarian at Pusey House and had been Warden of the community for a year. He was at the beginning of his close association with us which lasted until his death. The previous Warden, Father Gilbert Shaw, had been preparing him as his successor, and Donald took on what was at that time a clearly-defined authoritarian role within the community's hierarchy. We were just beginning to appropriate some of the changes to the Religious life and monastic liturgy recommended by Vatican II, and Donald was in a position to give us assistance and teaching both to encourage and enable us. For the twenty-eight years of his time as Warden he endeavoured to widen our horizons, and deepen our theological understanding of the Religious life. His emphasis on use of the mind to understand the things of God and to deepen one's prayer led to several sisters pursuing serious study, and to SLG Press adding a wide range of theological subjects to its lists. Reflecting on the prolific number of papers, sermons and books he wrote, I can see how much of my own theology is based in his teaching.

He would not subscribe to the authoritarian father-image of previous Wardens – indeed he once said that the one thing he was careful to do was never to tell nuns how to live their community lives! However, he had many theological convictions about the Religious life, and a vision for the unity of the Church which he was always eager to share with us and convince us to share in. His *Theology of the Religious Life: an Anglican Approach* (Fairacres Publication 21, 1971) remains one of the best essays on the subject, despite being written for its time and for a particular audience.

His wide interests in all aspects of Church unity led to a succession of visits over the years from noteworthy theologians from the Reformed Churches, the Roman Catholic Church, and, especially, the Orthodox Churches. He was a staunch member of the Fellowship of St Alban and St Sergius, and the first Warden of St Theosevia House in Oxford, which encourages dialogue between Orthodoxy and other denominations. While he was a residentiary Canon of Canterbury, and before, he had served for many years on ARCIC in its original form, and in the 1990s was instrumental in the foundation of the Thomas Merton Society in the UK. His last substantial book was a study of the Danish Lutheran theologian, N. F. S. Grundtvig.

No tribute to Donald would be complete without mentioning his love of Wales, which included learning to speak Welsh fluently and to retire to Bangor. It was a city within reach of both the Llyn Peninsula, where several solitaries from our community and elsewhere had settled, and of the Society of the Sacred Cross at Tymawr, where he was Warden for a time.

Donald was born on Easter Day. Perhaps the date influenced his whole life and spirituality more than we know. His message was always one of hope, of believing in the inexpressible change to the whole of creation effected by the resurrection, which overcomes all the darkness and division of Church and society. Those of us who heard it and try to live by it remember him with great thanksgiving and affection.

Sister Denzil CSA (1919–2011)

Sister Denzil was born in 1919 in rural Shropshire and, as the eighth child, was given the middle name of Octavia. After attending the CSMV Wantage school, she did the Froebel training for primary school teaching. In 1945–47 she did relief work in Germany with the St John's Ambulance Corps. After training at the Institute of

Medical Social work she worked as an Assistant Almoner at St Thomas alongside Cicely Saunders.

Denzil came to the Deaconess Community of St Andrew in 1956. Her novitiate included experience in orphanage work and after her first annual vow she was sent to St Michael's Convalescent Home, Westgate-on-Sea. Some years after ordination as a Deaconess and life profession (11 June 1961), she became Sister-in-Charge at St Michael's where her training as an almoner and her gifts for hospitality and friendship began to blossom.

Later came parish and chaplaincy work: 1969–73 at St John's, Notting Hill; then at the Royal Foundation of St Katharine and Queen Mary College; in the 1980s, she was back in Notting Hill at St Peter's, helping when that church was united in a single benefice with St John's. In 1987, she was made deacon and in 1994 ordained a priest. Alongside these ministries, she served the community as Novice Guardian from 1969–73 and again 1990-94. She was also Guest Mistress at the Mother House for some years (especially for the resident students) and secretary for the Associates.

Prayer and spiritual direction were also prominent among her ministries. She became involved in the early stages of the diocesan Re-evaluation Co-counselling programme (for clergy and church workers) and soon was teaching it. She also led weekends on prayer and meditation to ordinands. From the late 1970s, Sister Denzil had found people coming to her for spiritual direction and so in 1984 she entered the two-year training course in spiritual direction at Heythrop College. She also served on committees dealing with ministerial selection and formation.

She retired from parish work in 2001, but continued to minister to many. However, in 2008 increasing infirmity took her to St Mary's, Chiswick, SSM's nursing home. Sister Denzil died on 24 April 2011, aged 91, in the 49th year of her diaconate and profession, and the 17th of her priesthood.

Mother Susila CSS (1924–2011)

Susila Sitther CSS, the Mother Foundress and first Reverend Mother of the Christa Sevika Sangha was born on 27 December 1924 and died on 16 May 2011, having been professed for 56 years. Her vows were taken in 1955 in the Sisterhood of the Epiphany but in January 1970 she was released from that community to found CSS. This fulfilled her long-held dream of an indigenous Anglican Religious Community.

The realisation had not been without considerable difficulties, including the long process of changing nationality from (Southern) Indian to East Pakistani, and again to Bangladeshi. The late 1960s and early 1970s saw considerable unrest and fighting around both Jobarpar and Barisal and there were times when the small community was in great danger. Mother Susila's resourcefulness and cunning, along with her belief that God would not let them perish, kept her, the first three Sisters and the children in their care safe. Eventually on 16 December 1971 the independent State of Bangladesh was born and relative safety ensued, although unrest was never very far away.

Sister Anne CSJB writes:.

My first meeting with Mother Susila was when she came to stay at Clewer in 1995/6 for a few days with a number of her Sisters. I remember her asking if it would be possible to have a bowl and a jug put in the two bathrooms they were using, because that was how the Sisters preferred to 'bath'. Also, the hour long conversation we had when she told me her story. Her love of her Lord, and her huge commitment to what she had chosen to do with her life, clearly gave her great joy.

She also told me a lot about Bangladesh, the way of life of the Christa Sevika Sangha, the children they cared for and of the people in the villages around and she ended our time together by saying "You'll have to come and see for yourself". Those words became a reality when in December 1998 Sister Edna Frances and I were able to do so. The things that stood out on that visit were:

– Seeing her welcoming wave beyond the mesh barrier at Dhaka Airport when we got through the check out and were heading towards the exits.

– Being driven immediately after we were united outside the terminal through Dhaka (at about 10 o'clock at night and feeling exhausted) to find sandals that we could just push our feet in and out of for when we went to chapel.

– Going with her to a meeting of the Deanery at which the Bishop was to be present and where there was a lunch after the meeting – and one vehicle after another broke down and it got later and later, but Mother Susila was not to be deterred; we would keep going. (We arrived for about the last 10 minutes of the meeting but in time for the lunch before setting off back home.) I decided not many people of Mother's age would keep going so determinedly because she did not want the Bishop to think we hadn't bothered to go.

I returned for a second visit to Bangladesh in March 2009 and to my great joy Mother Susila was well enough to be sitting in her wheelchair at the head of the table to welcome us when we arrived at Barisal. It was wonderful to meet with her again and we were able to have some time talking together in her room. Her joy, enthusiasm and commitment had not lessened, in spite of her frailness and her mind was still very active – she was still very much the Mother Superior. She certainly supervised all the arrangements for my return journey by coach to Dhaka, insisting that *'the boy'* would accompany me because I could not travel on my own.

Susila Sitther leaves behind a considerable legacy – the Sisters of the Christa Sevika Sangha, a truly indigenous Anglican Community, deep tube wells in a large area around Jobarpar, and many, many people grateful for the opportunities they have had because of her vision and hard work, and above all the legacy of her deep faith and prayerfulness. May she rest in peace and rise with Christ in glory.

Abbess Gloria Mary Goller, PCLS (1915–2012)

Gloria Gayle Lutz Goller was born in Mandan, North Dakota on August 17, 1915. From a very young age Gloria showed musical talent and became well known for her beautiful soprano voice. After hearing her sing in his church Louis Goller introduced himself and they married in 1940. They had three sons and 60 years together.

For many years Gloria was a devoted member of St Barnabas Episcopal Church, Bainbridge Island, Washington State and an active member of The Third Order SSF. Gloria, along with five other women, entered into Franciscan Religious life in 1982 under an Episcopal Visitor who did not believe in the ordination of women. When St Barnabas called a woman associate rector, there was a roadblock to be overcome. With the assistance of Bishop Sanford Hampton of the Diocese of Olympia, Gloria and the Sisters overcame that obstacle successfully. In 2002, a new community The Little Sisters of St. Clare was recognized by the Committee for Religious Life, House of Bishops of the Episcopal Church. Gloria said that her mission was to bring the contemplative spirituality of St Clare out of the cloister and into our churches.

As the primary founder of the community her title became Abbess. Abbess Gloria-Mary died on January 18, 2012. With all of her experience in the church and from a full and successful life, in her eighties she had a broad, courageous and determined vision to establish an Episcopal women's order in the Northwest. Her talents as a spiritual director were put to use as she worked with many diverse women, both the curious and those sincerely testing a Religious vocation. Our gratitude and memories will unfold in the years to come for Abbess Gloria, a woman of vision, energy and love for her spiritual daughters.

Photograph on page 156

Brother Michael BSG (1938–2012)

Brother Michael Elliott BSG died on 8 February 8, 2012, three weeks before his 74th birthday. Born and raised in New Zealand, Michael lived an extremely full life, ministering and working around the world. After ordination and curacy, he took a further degree in the USA, before working in several countries in positions that reflected his interest and commitment to social justice and working for the poor. Later, he went to Oxford, UK, as a Tutor for Applied and Community Theology at Westminster College and was involved in curriculum development and teaching in several contexts. In 2002, Michael was appointed as the Director of Ministry and a residentiary Canon in the Diocese of Swansea and Brecon in Wales, which he recounted as his happiest period in ministry. He continued to teach and supervise at the University of Lampeter until 2009. Amongst his many books and articles, his most widely acclaimed is *Freedom, Justice and Christian Counter-culture* published in 1990 by SCM Press, London, in which he set out his manifesto for Christian anarchism.

He leaves behind him a global network of friends and students and the lasting legacy of his contribution to the development of reflective practice and situation analysis pedagogy in applied theological education. He instilled in all who met him his deep commitment for social justice, political and theological integration, the power of the Gospel to transform the situations of the poor and marginalized and the renewal of the Anglican Catholic tradition.

Having long felt a deep call to some form of the Religious life, Michael entered the postulancy of the Brotherhood of Saint Gregory in 2005 and made his first profession of vows on July 26, 2008 as a Gregorian Friar.

Sister Edna Frances CSJB (1918–2012)

Edna May Wilson entered the noviciate of the community of St John Baptist in October 1959, taking the name Sister Edna Frances at her clothing. Professed in First Vows in 1962, she took her Life Vows in 1965.

During her time in community, her wide experience with a farming family gave her the ability to hold various positions; cook, Retreat Wing Sister, Bursar, Novice Guardian, Assistant Superior. She was elected Mother Superior in 1978 and held that position until 1992 when it began to take its toll, but during which the links with the Sisters in the USA continued to increase. In 1993 she was asked to become the Novice Guardian which she did until 1996. From then, and after our move to The Priory at Begbroke, her greatest joy was working in the garden, an enjoyment she continued after going into nursing care at St Mary's Convent and Home in Chiswick. We are most grateful to the Sisters and staff at the Home for the loving and understanding care they gave her.

Eventually Sister Edna Frances suffered a series of minor strokes, which made speech and movement very difficult; but she remained her cheerful self, retaining her contact with her large family and her Sisters until shortly before her death on 22 May 2012.

Sister Lydia CSC (1919–2012)

Sister Lydia CSC was born on 22 May 1919 and died on 29 September 2012. Here, Sister Hilda Mary CSC reflects on Lydia's long and eventful life.

"Well get on with it then": familiar words to us all from our dear Sister Lydia. Not a woman to hang around, she was a woman of action. Yet, it was the still place, where she learned simply to breathe and be, that her energy for life came from. Even as a young child, she loved to be alone and in silence. As she grew older her prayer very much simplified. Prayer became more and more about being with God in silence and less and less about words.

Lydia was born in London. She grew up near the first CSC Convent in Kilburn and went to one of CSC's schools from the age of five until fourteen. She then trained in embroidery and was given a job in the Convent embroidery room. Lydia got involved with the Sisters' work with poor families, the severe poverty they encountered making a deep impression on her and influencing the rest of her life.

She was noviced in CSC on 19 February 1938 and began a life of extraordinary activity and variety: a world traveller, a home maker, spiritual guide and mentor, a teacher and a gardener. Anything she planted flourished – would it dare not to! I think of all the lives she touched that flourished too. She looked after so many children: at Kilburn, the Ormcrod, at St Anne's, St Mary's Broadstairs and St Edith's, Clevedon.

She had trained in child care at Preston and at Bristol University and Lydia never ceased to learn: she also studied clinical theology, Ignatian spirituality, did a counselling course at Westminster Pastoral Foundation, went to the Tantur Ecumenical Research Institute in Bethlehem, and in her eighties did a diploma in psychosynthesis – among other things! Her pioneering work included chaplaincy with male prisoners in Liverpool, work as an inspector of residential homes for children and the elderly in the same city, ending up with running a girls' remand and assessment centre. She 'retired' to Clevedon where she accompanied many people in their journey of prayer and helped run a spirituality course in Wells for the diocese, as well as parish ministry. She learned to listen not only to God and her inner world but to the many people who came to her. And I believe her ability to listen enabled her to be such an effective carer and leader and friend.

In her nineties, she was gradually moving from us, getting more and more confused but she still continued to make friends and keep in touch with all people she loved and cared for. After a splendid celebration of our community festival, Michaelmas, in which she had taken a full part, she held her head, said "I don't know what is happening" and ten minutes or so later was with the very Angels we were celebrating.

Sister Angela WSHS (1940–2012)

Sister Angela Blackburn, WSHS, died at the age of 72 years on October 14, 2012 at Crossville, Tennessee. She was the Founder of the Worker Sisters and Brothers of the Holy Spirit more than forty years ago, which is a contemporary Religious community based in the Episcopal Church of the United States and the Anglican Church of Canada. Her dedication to helping people to develop their own spiritual lives through concentration on a Benedictine-based rule of life, and living and developing the nine qualities of the Fruit of the Spirit, has brought about strong bonds of friendship, love and deep inward growth.

Organizations

CSPH convent at Horbury, UK

AUSTRALIA

Advisory Council for Anglican Religious Life in Australia

The Council consists of:

Rt Revd Godfrey Fryar, Bishop of North Queensland *(chair)*
Ms Ann Skamp, Diocese of Grafton, *(Secretary)* Email: annskamp@aapt.net.au
Rt Revd Keith Slater, Bishop of Grafton
Revd Michael Jobling, Diocese of Melbourne

The Brother Robin BSB
Mother Rita Mary CCK
Sister Sue Nirta CSBC
Sister Linda Mary CSC
Sr Carol Francis CHN
Brother Wayne LBF
Fr Keith Dean-Jones OGS
Abbot Michael King OSB
Sister Juliana SI
Sister Eunice SSA
Br Christopher John SSF
Father Christopher SSM

Members from New Zealand:
Mother Keleni CSN
to be announced *(liaison bishop)*
Observers:
Sister Jill Harding fcs *(for Catholic Religious Australia)*
Revd Dr Helen Granowski TSSF *(Third Order Society of St Francis)*

EUROPE

Advisory Council on the Relations of Bishops & Religious Communities (commonly called 'The Advisory Council')

Rt Revd David Walker, Bishop of Dudley (*Chair)*
Rt Revd John Pritchard, Bishop of Oxford
Rt Revd Humphrey Southern, Bishop of Repton
Rt Revd Anthony Robinson, Bishop of Pontefract
Rt Revd Dominic Walker OGS, Bishop of Monmouth *(co-opted)*

Communities' elected representatives (elected December 2010 for five-year term):

Sister Anita Cook CSC
Father Colin Griffiths SSM
Brother Damian SSF
Sister Elizabeth Pio SSB
Sister Joyce Yarrow CSF
Sister Mary Julian CHC
Sister Mary Stephen Packwood OSB
Sister Rosemary Howarth CHN
Abbot Stuart Burns OSB

Co-opted: Father Peter Allan CR
Revd Canon Chris Neal
Revd Ian Mobsby *(Moot Community and representing new and emerging communities)*
ARC representative: Dom Simon Jarrett OSB
Conference of Religious Observer: Sister Kate McGovern OSF
Hon. Secretary: Father Colin CSWG Email: father.colin@cswg.org.uk

Conference of the Leaders of Anglican Religious Communities (CLARC)

The Conference meets in full once a year.
Hon. Secretary: Father Colin CSWG Email: father.colin@cswg.org.uk

General Synod of the Church of England

Representatives of Lay Religious

Sister Anita OHP (Elected 2006, re-elected 2010)
Brother Thomas Quin OSB (Elected 2010)

Representatives of Ordained Religious

Revd Sister Rosemary CHN (Elected 2002, re-elected 2005 & 2010)
Revd Thomas Seville CR (Elected 2005, re-elected 2010)

Anglican Religious Communities in England (ARC)

ARC supports members of Religious communities of the Church of England. Its membership is the entire body of professed members of communities recognised by the Advisory Council *(see above)*. ARC holds an occasional conferences when members can come together both to hear speakers on topics relevant to their way of life and to meet and share experiences together. A news sheet is regularly circulated to all houses and ARC represents Anglican Religious life on various bodies, including the Vocations Forum of the Ministry Division of the C of E, The Advisory Council and the *Year Book* editorial committee. Some limited support is also given to groups of common interest within ARC who may wish to meet. Its activities are coordinated by a committee with members elected from Leaders, Novice Guardians, General Synod representatives and the professed membership. The committee normally meets three times a year.

Prior Simon OSB & Sister Sue CSF *(representing Leaders)*
Father Thomas Seville CR *(representing General Synod Representatives)*
Sister Beverley CSF *(representing Novice Guardians)*
Sister Hilda Mary CSC *(Chair)*, Sister Anne CSJB *(Vice-Chair)*,
Sister Pam OHP, Brother Vaughan SSF
& Sister Mary John OSB *(representing professed members)*
Sister Chris James CSF *(Administrative Secretary)*

More information about Anglican Religious Life (in England) or about ARC itself, may be obtained from:

The Anglican Religious Communities, c/o The Secretary to the House of Bishops, Church House, Great Smith Street, London SW1P 3AZ

Email: info@arcie.org.uk Website: www.arcie.org.uk

Conference of Anglican Religious Orders in the Americas (CAROA)

The purpose of CAROA is to provide opportunities for mutual support and sharing among its member communities and co-ordinate their common interests and activities, to engage in dialogue with other groups, to present a coherent understanding of the Religious Life to the Church and to speak as an advocate for the Religious Orders to the Church. CAROA is incorporated as a non-profit organization in both Canada and the USA.

Brother Jude Hill SSF (*President*)
Father David Bryan Hoopes OHC (*Vice-President*)
Sister Elizabeth Ann Eckert SSJD (*Secretary-Treasurer*)
The Revd Dr Donald Anderson (*General Secretary*)
PO Box 99, Little Britain, Ontario K0M 2C0, CANADA
Tel: 705 786 3330 *Email: dwa@nexicom.net*

House of Bishops Standing Committee on Religious Orders in the Anglican Church of Canada

The Committee usually meets twice a year, during the House of Bishops' meeting. Its rôle is consultative and supportive.

Rt Revd Linda Nicholls, Suffragan Bishop of Trent-Durham, Diocese of Toronto *(chair)*
Most Revd Fred J Hiltz, Archbishop & Primate of Canada
2 further positions for Bishops to be filled in autumn 2013
The Superiors of CSC, OHC, SSJD & SSJE
Revd Dr Donald W Anderson, General Secretary of CAROA
The Ven Paul Feheley, Principal Secretary to the Primate (*Secretary*)

General Synod of the Anglican Church of Canada

Religious Synod members:

Sister Elizabeth Ann Eckert SSJD
Brother Reginald-Martin Crenshaw OHC

National Association for Episcopal Christian Communities (NAECC)

The NAECC is an inclusive association that shares and communicates the fruits of the Gospel, realized in community, with the church and the world. It is primarily a forum for those who are living or exploring new or continuing models of religious commitment within the context of community.

Brother Bill Farra SCC *(Convenor)*
Masud Ibn Syedullah TSSF *(Recorder)*
Brother James Mahoney BSG *(Treasurer)*

Website: home.earthlink.net/~naecc/index.htm

Glossary and Indices

Harriet Monsell House, Cuddesdon, UK,
the new home of the Community of St John the Baptist.

Glossary

Aspirant
A person who hopes to become a Religious and has been in touch with a particular community, but has not yet begun to live with them.

Celibacy
The commitment to remain unmarried and to refrain from sexual relationships. It is part of the vow of chastity traditionally taken by Religious. Chastity is a commitment to sexual integrity, a term applicable to fidelity in marriage as well as to celibacy in Religious Life.

Chapter
The council or meeting of Religious to deliberate and make decisions about the community. In some orders, this may consist of all the professed members of the community; in others, the Chapter is a group of members elected by the community as a whole to be their representatives.

Clothing
The ceremony in which a postulant of a community formally becomes a novice, and begins the period of formation in the mind, work and spirit of the community. It follows the initial stage of being a postulant when the prospective member first lives alongside the community. The clothing or novicing ceremony is characterised by the Religious 'receiving' the habit, or common attire, of the community.

Contemplative
A Religious whose life is concentrated on prayer inside the monastery or convent rather than on social work or ministry outside the house. Some communities were founded with the specific intention of leading a contemplative lifestyle together. Others may have a single member or small group living such a vocation within a larger community oriented to outside work.

Enclosed
This term is applied to Religious who stay within a particular convent or monastery – the 'enclosure' – to pursue more effectively a life of prayer. They would usually only leave the enclosure for medical treatment or other exceptional reasons. This rule is intended to help the enclosed Religious be more easily protected from the distractions and attentions of the outside world.

Eremitic
The eremitic Religious is one who lives the life of a hermit, that is, largely on his or her own. Hermits usually live singly, but may live in an eremitic community, where they meet together for prayer on some occasions during each day.

Evangelical Counsels
A collective name for the three vows of poverty, chastity and obedience.

Habit
The distinctive clothing of a community. In some communities, the habit is worn at all times, in others only at certain times or for certain activities. In some communities, the habit is rarely worn, except perhaps for formal occasions.

Novice
A member of a community who is in the formation stage of the Religious Life, when she or he learns the mind, work and spirit of the particular community whilst living among its members.

Oblate

Someone associated closely with a community, but who will be living a modified form of the Rule, which allows him or her to live outside the Religious house. Oblates are so-called because they make an oblation (or offering) of obedience to the community instead of taking the profession vows. In some communities, oblates remain celibate, in others they are allowed to be married. A few oblates live within a community house and then they are usually termed intern(al) oblates. The term oblate is more usually associated with Benedictine communities.

Office/Daily Office/Divine Office

The round of liturgical services of prayer and worship, which mark the rhythm of the daily routine in Religious Life. Religious communities may use the services laid down by the Church or may have their own particular Office book. The Offices may be called Morning, Midday, Evening and Night Prayer, or may be referred to by traditional names, such as Mattins, Lauds, Terce, Sext, None, Vespers and Compline.

Postulant

Someone who is in the first stage of living the Religious life. The postulancy usually begins when the aspirant begins to live in community and ends when he or she becomes a novice and 'receives the habit'. Postulants sometimes wear a distinctive dress or else may wear secular clothes.

Profession

The ceremony at which a Religious makes promises (or vows) to live the Religious Life with integrity and fidelity to the Rule. The profession of these vows may be for a limited period or for life. The usual pattern is to make a 'first' or simple profession in which the vows are made to the community. After three or more years a Life Profession may be made, which is to the Church and so the vows are usually received by a bishop. In the Anglican Communion, Life Professed Religious can usually be secularized only by the Archbishop or Presiding Bishop of a Province.

Religious (as in 'a Religious')

The general term for a person living the Religious life.

Rule

The written text containing the principles and values by which the members of a community try to live. The Rule is not simply a set of regulations, although it may contain such, but is an attempt to capture the spirit and charism of a community in written form. Some communities follow traditional Rules, such as those of St Benedict or St Augustine, others have written their own.

Tertiary/Third Order

This term is usually associated with Franciscan communities, but is used by others too. A Third Order is made up of tertiaries, people who take vows, but modified so that they are able to live in their own homes and have their own jobs. They may also marry and have children. They have a Rule of Life and are linked to other tertiaries through regular meetings. In the Franciscan family, the Third Order complements both the First Order of celibate friars and sisters and the Second Order of contemplative Religious.

Vows

The promises made by a Religious at profession. They may be poverty, chastity and obedience. In some communities, they are obedience, stability and conversion of life.

Index of Communities by Dedication or Patron Saint

Index by location

USA

Index of Community Wares & Services for Sale

CANDLES

CHURCH LINEN & NEEDLEWORK, EMBROIDERY & VESTMENTS

CRAFTS & RELIGIOUS ARTEFACTS

Index of Communities by Initials

Worship and Ordination

... at the ordination of Sister Veronica CSC in the UK

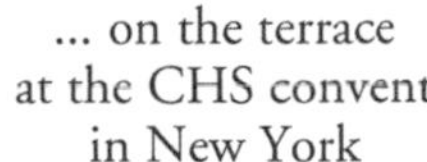

... on the terrace at the CHS convent in New York

... at the first Mass of Brother Nathan James SSF in Australia

Making Music

... on the harp in Australia (Brother Bart SSF).

... on guitars at the Sisters of Jesus' Way, UK

... on wind instruments in Korea, (Sisters of the Society of the Holy Cross).

Cooking

... in the Solomon Islands (CSC Sisters).

... bread-making at SSJD in Canada.

... jam-making at Malling Abbey, UK *[thanks to Thomas Paley]*

Study

... some of the novices attending the Inter-Novitiate course in Oxford, UK, in January 2013.

... in Seoul, Korea, SHC Sisters role-play Bible stories.

...in Toronto, Canada, SSJD Sisters engage in a Bible study.

Notes and Amendments

Notes and Amendments

Notes and Amendments